# Women and Work in Africa

## Also of Interest

Scientific-Technological Change and the Role of Women in Development, edited by Pamela M. D'Onofrio-Flores and Sheila M. Pfafflin

Women and Technological Change in Developing Countries, edited by Roslyn Dauber and Melinda L. Cain

*The Women of Rural Asia, Robert Orr Whyte and Pauline Whyte

*The Underside of History: A View of Women Through Time, Elise Boulding

Women in Changing Japan, edited by Joyce Lebra, Joy Paulson, and Elizabeth Powers

*New Space for Women, edited by Gerda R. Wekerle, Rebecca Peterson, and David Morley

*Alternative Futures for Africa, edited by Timothy M. Shaw

*Africa's International Relations: The Diplomacy of Dependency and Change, Ali A. Mazrui

Tanzania: An African Experiment, Rodger Yeager

Senegal, Sheldon Gellar

Migration and the Labor Market in Developing Countries, edited by R. H. Sabot

*From Dependency to Development: Strategies to Overcome Underdevelopment and Inequality, edited by Heraldo Muñoz

Planning African Development: The Kenya Experience, edited by Glen Norcliffe and Tom Pinfold

Women and the Social Costs of Economic Development: Two Colorado Case Studies, Elizabeth Moen, Elise Boulding, Jane Lillydahl, and Risa Palm


*Available in hardcover and paperback.

# Westview Special Studies on Africa

## *Women and Work in Africa*
### edited by Edna G. Bay

The emphasis on economic development in Third World countries has raised questions about how women share in that development and what exactly is the nature of women's contribution to the economic activity of their countries. This book--an outgrowth of the 1979 Annual Spring Symposium of the African Studies program at the University of Illinois at Urbana-Champaign entitled "Women and Work in Africa"--focuses on the livelihood of women in Africa, tracing the decline in female productivity that occurred in many countries as the colonial system disrupted traditional patterns, outlining the continuing economic and ideological handicaps women have faced in the years since independence, and suggesting alternatives available to women in coping with these handicaps. The authors return frequently to the policy implications of their research, and some point to the growing expression by African women of dissatisfaction with oppressive social, political, and economic systems. Assessing current trends, they see the possibility that African women's developing awareness of their plight, combined with outside pressures that affect economic policies, may begin to reverse the processes that have for so long negatively affected the masses of women in Africa.

Dr. Edna G. Bay is assistant director of the Graduate Institute of the Liberal Arts at Emory University. She has been assistant professor in African Studies, University of Illinois at Urbana-Champaign; done research on women in Dahomey; and been a participant in and consultant to USAID for several conferences and seminars on women and development. Dr. Bay is coeditor of Women in Africa: Studies in Social and Economic Change (1976) and of a special edition on women of African Studies Review XVII, 3 (1975), among other publications.

# Women and Work in Africa

## edited by Edna G. Bay

Westview Press / Boulder, Colorado

Westview Special Studies on Africa

Published in 1982 in the United States of America by
    Westview Press, Inc.
    5500 Central Avenue
    Boulder, Colorado  80301
    Frederick A. Praeger, President and Publisher


Library of Congress Catalogue Card Number:  82-70243
ISBN:  0-86531-312-1


Composition for this book was provided by the editor
Printed and bound in the United States of America

# Contents

# Tables and Figures

Figure

# Preface

   This collection of articles grows out of a symposium
on the subject of women and work in Africa held on the
Urbana-Champaign campus of the University of Illinois in
the spring of 1979.  The organizing committee for that
program sought first, to update the field of economic
studies of women in Africa and second, to provide a forum
for the exchange and stimulation of ideas among scholars
and professionals concerned for women in Africa.  The
publication here of the majority of the symposium papers
represents a logical final step in the fulfillment of the
objectives of the symposium program committee.

   As a selection of case studies, the collection does
not pretend to cover comprehensively the economic activities of women in all parts of the African continent. Although one article explores women's economic life in an
Islamic setting, for example, none deals specifically with
women in North Africa.  Similarly, no articles treat women's economic roles within the complexity of male migra-
tory labor patterns in the geographical area of contemporary white South African economic domination.  Nevertheless, the articles as a whole highlight many broad issues
of women's work in Africa and illustrate recent trends and
directions in the field of women's studies in Africa. They
explore generally women's means of livelihood and how they
have been affected by and have reacted to colonial and
national government policies.  And the papers describe
specific patterns of women's social behavior and economic
strategy as they attempt to come to terms with contemporary society.

   Many individuals and organizations are to be thanked
for their support for the symposium and for the publication
of these papers.  The African Studies Program of the University of Illinois provided the initial impetus by naming
a women's topic the subject for its sixth annual symposium.
The African Studies Program provided both staff and financial support for the symposium and the publication efforts.

Seven additional units on the Illinois campus plus the United States International Communication Agency and the Office of Women in Development, USAID, generously supported the symposium program.  The Program Committee members worked for more than a year to prepare the symposium and to plan for the dissemination of its results.  Its members included Evelyne Accad, Donald Crummey, Doris Derby, Jean Due, Corinne Glesne, Jane Mohraz, Ehimwema Omo-Osagie, Sabine Orsot-Dessi, Yvette Scheven, Mary Ellen Seaver, Cindy Smith, Elizabeth Stewart, Becky Summary, Marti Thomson, and Barbara Yates.  Appreciation needs to be expressed, too, to the Emory University Graduate Institute of the Liberal Arts which supported the camera-ready preparation of this publication.  Three individuals were central to that effort:  our editor Barbara Reitt, typist June Mann, and proof-reader Julie Sabin.
The "Introduction", though built upon the discussion at the University of Illinois symposium and the data from the articles included here, does not necessarily reflect in its entirety the opinions of all the authors.  I wish to thank Kristin Mann and Irène d'Almeida for their valuable critical readings of the "Introduction". Finally, Raymond Ganga contributed ideas, encouragement, and assistance at every stage from the planning of the symposium to the completion of the book.

E. G. B.

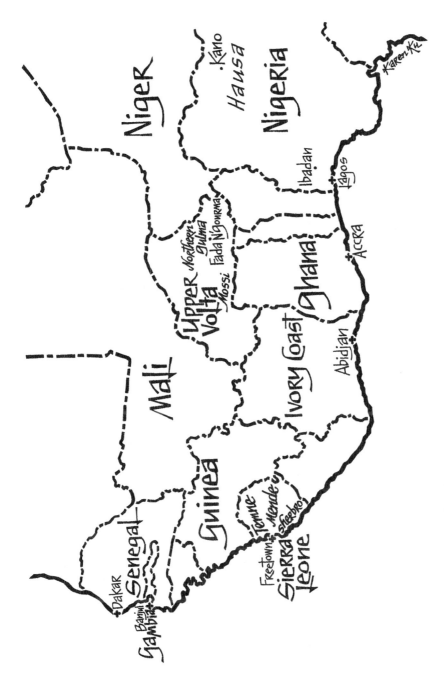

WEST AFRICA IN 1980 (including selected sites mentioned in the text)

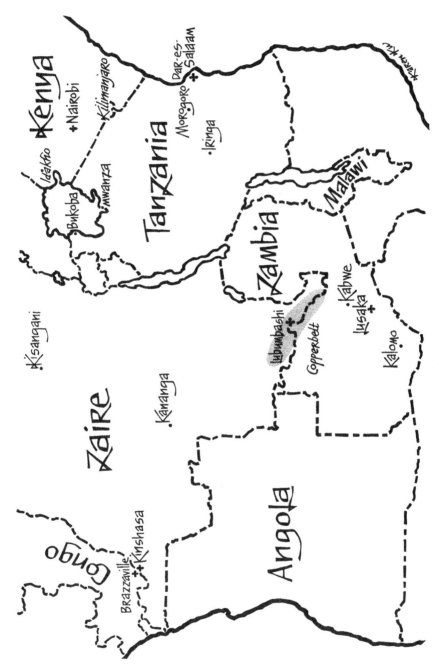

CENTRAL AFRICA IN 1980 (including selected sites mentioned in the text)

# Introduction

*Edna G. Bay*

The field of women's studies in Africa has expanded
with remarkable rapidity over the past decade. The number of researchers from both sides of the Atlantic and
the quantities of field data amassed have increased dramatically. In the United States, for example, only thirteen doctoral dissertations and master's theses on women
in Africa were produced in the 1960s, in contrast to the
same number completed for all the years between 1917 and
1959. But in the 1970s the figure from the previous decade more than tripled, with forty doctoral dissertations
completed between 1970 and 1979. Nonspecialists, too,
have become increasingly sensitive to women's issues.
Authors of introductory texts, scholarly studies, and
monographs of various kinds have begun to incorporate
results of research on women in their writing (e.g.,
Turnbull, 1977; Julien, 1977-78; Mojekwu, Uchendu, and
Van Hoey, 1977). The analysis of this rapid accumulation
of fresh data has provided the basis for constantly
changing theoretical perspectives. Women and Work in
Africa, a product of this heightened interest, represents
and illustrates a new direction in the development of
the literature on women in Africa. The book is composed
of fourteen articles based on field research and/or
statistical analysis; all but three were presented at a
symposium of the same name held at the University of
Illinois in the spring of 1979. The articles focus on
the economic activities of African women. They trace a
decline in female productivity as the colonial system
disrupted older patterns of production; they outline
continuing economic and ideological handicaps for women
in the years since independence; and they suggest possible alternatives for women and predict changes for
the future.

Earlier studies and collections concentrated on a
documentation of women's historic prerogatives and accomplishments, analyzing threats to their well-being as a

1

result of colonial policies. Beginning in the early
1970s, a number of researchers explored on a micro level
the patterns outlined by Ester Boserup in Woman's Role
in Economic Development (1970). Again and again, field
studies confirmed that colonial policies and so-called
development had lowered women's productivity relative to
that of men. At the same time, women's physical work
load had been increased in an absolute sense. The phrase
"the negative impact of development on women" became
commonly accepted as evidence mounted that for Africa
Boserup's analysis had been substantially correct. Thus,
African women were admired for their resourcefulness and
initiative in trying to adapt to diminishing resources.
But in the long run, small gains and greater efforts
had proved insufficient to meet the challenges of an
economic system that seemed bent on excluding them at
every turn. The twentieth-century African woman, it
seemed, lived on an economic treadmill that moved at
ever-accelerating speeds; she was forced to work harder
and harder simply to keep even. In contrast, the precolonial past appeared a period of relative prosperity
when women enjoyed control over economic resources and
exercised a degree of political power.

Studies from the late 1970s have not revised these
findings but rather have amplified them through two new
developments that are reflected in Women and Work in
Africa. First, the focus of recent research has turned
to contemporary African women and to the specific constraints under which they work; implications for development policy are frequently made explicit. A related but
much more significant phenomenon in the long run is the
growing expression by African women themselves of dissatisfaction with social, political, and economic systems
that they define as oppressive.

The growth of concern for contemporary African
women can be traced to other trends of the 1970s. Obviously, the feminist movement in the West initially encouraged certain European and American scholars to raise
or rephrase questions about women in a cross-cultural
perspective. Some feminist scholars sought evidence in
non-Western cultures of alternatives to Western sex-role
stereotypes. African women's economic independence of
their husbands, for example, presented an intriguing
contrast for American middle-class women reared in a tradition of female financial dependency. Though women's
political activities were sometimes romanticized and
their powers exaggerated, the average African woman's
political and civil status in their own political systems
in the late nineteenth century was undeniably higher
than that of most European women in the same era. Many
Western researchers, however, gradually became sensitized
to contemporary African women's problems by their own

female informants, who would comment on women's lot in
far from positive terms. By the late 1970s, researchers
and developers had begun to study the past in order to
understand the present and to study traditional culture
in order to analyze the pressures of modernization.

In the early seventies, too, drought, famine, and
the recognition that world food shortages had reached
crisis proportions turned the attention of the development community to food producers, processors, and distributors. Not only do women make basic decisions about
the quantities and types of food to be consumed in the
family, developers discovered, but they typically play
a large part in its production and processing. A United
Nations study, for example, estimated that women in Africa
supply 70 percent of the work in food production, 50 percent in domestic food storage, 100 percent in food processing, 50 percent in animal husbandry, and 60 percent
in marketing (UNECA/FAO, 1975). In 1973, an interest in
women was mandated for United States development agencies
by the Percy Amendment to the Foreign Assistance Act,
requiring that certain areas of aid "be administered so
as to give particular attention to those programs . . .
which tend to integrate women into the national economies
of foreign countries" (United States, 1973). International
organizations have been especially active in encouraging
the study of women and the adoption of policy changes
on their behalf. Though the International Women's Year
conference in Mexico City (1975) and the World Conference
of the United Nations Decade for Women in Copenhagen
(1980) were the largest and best publicized, literally
dozens of conferences on topics of concern to women have
taken place since 1975, in large part under the impetus
of the United Nations' Decade for Women programs.

Of late, African women in various occupations have
become more openly critical of the policies of governments and international organizations that are detrimental to their well-being. Paralleling the sentiments
shared with researchers by other African women, many
writers, academic, and professional women are increasingly
expressing bitterness and anger at the failures of their
own governments and their own men to be concerned for
their problems. Many feel that, in return for their
work in the nationalist struggle and for their sacrifices
in the name of the nation, they have received nothing
but criticism and an increased burden of work. A common
theme, discussed in detail below, argues that contemporary
men define as traditional only those practices of benefit
to them. In the words of one Sudanese woman:

The African woman is unrecognized and oppressed
by society--both traditional and modern. She is
misunderstood and misinterpreted by and large. It

> is common, especially among our men, to excuse
> injustice for women with phrases like "It is Afri-
> can." Well, let me tell you there is certainly
> nothing "African" about injustice--whether it
> takes the form of mistreated wives and mothers,
> unemployment and so on. And often these very men
> who so condemn women to lives of servitude in the
> name of African culture are wearing three-piece
> suits and shiny shoes! (Chernush, 1979, p. 4)

Women and Work in Africa addresses several metho-
dological problems pertinent to women's studies in cross-
cultural perspective. First, basic interpretation of
data about African women in the 1970s continued to pro-
voke controversy. Value judgments are inevitable and
necessary when scholars evaluate societies that are
deliberately attempting to alter economic and political
institutions toward specific ends. Yet, conclusions
drawn about women seem particularly plagued by ideological postures and culturally biased assumptions. In a
period when little consensus exists either in the West
or in Africa on what women's roles should be in contemporary society, scholars have been left to evaluate
change with little more than their own personal visions
of women's proper place. The result is that the same or
similar data may be given quite different interpreta-
tions and readers are left with their proverbial glass
half filled or half empty. A 15 percent primary school
enrollment rate for girls, for example, will be considered
an encouraging sign of progress by one author and evidence by another of the exclusion of girls from opportunities to enter the modern sector. A rural sociologist
may lament women's exclusion from cash crop production,
while a development agency specialist speaks proudly
of releasing women from the burdens of field labor. Men
and women alike debate whether increased economic dependence on a man is a good or a bad thing for a woman.
After all, the question taunts, who would not give up a
life of hard labor for relative luxury and leisure?

The definition of work itself has produced metho-
dological problems. Until recently, most economists
counted only paid labor as "work" and national statistics
as a result tended to show only a tiny proportion of
women in the labor force. Micro studies of African women's
daily activities which have documented average female
working days up to 16 to 18 hours long have begun to
alter scholars' perceptions of the meaning of work. Of
late, they have been stressing the need to record statistically the unpaid labor of women on farms and in households. At the same time, what had been researchers'
and administrators' oversights are being recognized as
developing social problems. The evidence increasingly

suggests that Africans themselves have begun to devalue household work generally and unpaid labor on family farms because it is not salaried (Hill, 1978; Nantogmah, 1979). Economists have erred, too, in assuming that people turn to alternative economic activities in situations of declining return for their labor. The returns on petty trading, for example, have been exaggerated by scholars who have assumed that large numbers of West African women were attracted to commerce by relatively large profits. In fact, it appears that a lack of alternatives coupled with a pressing need for income have pushed more and more women into an already overcrowded field.

An even more serious problem has been the application to African data of Western notions of incompatibility among the female roles of mother, wife, and worker. The interdependence of multiple female roles was one of the strongest themes of discussion at the symposium on women and work in Africa and is the focus of Barbara Lewis's paper on women in the Ivory Coast. The African women present stressed that motherhood is all-important and that traditionally a mother gives all and invests all in her children. But at the same time they noted that work in the sense of income-generating activity is very much an essential and expected part of life. African women typically do not choose one or the other, to work or to have children. In practice, they work because they have children. Women become then reproducers and producers. Their economic decisions must be seen in the context of multiple and inseparable roles, ambitions, and desires, just as women as a whole must be understood in the context of a broader society.

The understanding of women's economic activity in Africa has been hampered, too, by an assumed dichotomy between the "traditional" and the "modern" economic spheres. Economic development theory in particular tends to perceive women as part of a "traditional sector" that is removed from and effectively unrelated to the so-called modern sector (Tinker, n.d., p. 3). Only recently have theorists begun to explore the complex interlocking, on individual and institutional levels, of elements of African and Western economic systems. Finally, "traditional" itself is a term laden with misleading connotations. As used by the authors of Women and Work in Africa, "traditional" is simply a convenient catchword that refers to values and structures perceived by contemporary peoples as relatively unchanged by Westernization. That which is traditional is not necessarily linked to a particular period of time or style of living. Nor does the term refer to practices or attitudes that remained unchanged over long periods of time. Rather, "traditional" is used to distinguish African ideas, beliefs,

technologies and social structures at a given moment
from comparable institutions and values that have been
recently imported, mainly from the West.

The authors of Women and Work in Africa do not share
a unified analysis of women's state or the means to improve it.  Yet, a general agreement among the authors,
apparent here in these papers, was evident at the original symposium.  The authors concur, first, that women in
Africa, past and present, have economic obligations as
well as social responsibilities.  During the twentieth
century, women have suffered a decline in their ability
to fulfill these expected responsibilities.  For the
authors of Women and Work in Africa, the solution to
African  women's decreasing productivity is not to take
responsibility and obligation from them, but to restore
to them the ability to function as economically productive members of their societies.

The articles in this collection are grouped into
four sections.  Like all categorization, their placement
is to a degree arbitrary; certain themes from section I
reappear in later discussion and likewise some of the
major ideas of later sections are foreshadowed by phenomena noted early in the book.  Moreover, the grouping
of the articles is deliberately ahistorical.  The patterns
of economic and social change that the book explores
occur at widely varying moments and move at differing
rates of speed.  What is remarkable are the parallels
that emerge despite variations not only in historical
moment but in ethnic, religious, and geographical factors
as well.


I.   WOMEN'S PRODUCTION OUTSIDE THE DEVELOPMENT PROCESS

The articles by E. Frances White, Carol P. Mac-
Cormack, and Enid Schildkrout illustrate three major
variables related to patterns of production in African
women's lives.  White and MacCormack's papers describe
respectively women's involvement in the two most widely
prevalent female occupations in Africa, trading and
farming.  Schildkrout, in contrast, studies women's
production within the context of the social ideology of
Islam.  The historical and geographical settings of the
three papers differ, but all three are concerned with
women's productive prerogatives and possibilities in
situations initially not strongly affected by Western
capitalist development.  All three authors, however,
describe or predict changes associated with increasing
Westernization.  As such, they foreshadow patterns that
are described more fully later in the collection.

There is a tendency to idealize both African
women's traditional lifestyles and their precolonial

past, particularly in light of the troublesome twentieth
century. Yet life, in the past as in the present, was
hardly idyllic for either women or men. In agricultural
societies, the predominant pattern in sub-Saharan Africa,
farm labor was and continues to be long and hard. Natural disasters could and did bring hardship, hunger and
death from time to time, and political security fluctu-
ated according to the era. Men played dominant roles,
by and large, in precolonial political life and an ideology of male superiority appears to have been pervasive,
even in matrilineal societies. Still, the evidence suggests a balance, albeit subject to change, between male
and female obligations and privileges. Patterns instituted and maintained first by the colonial powers and
later by independent governments gradually destroyed the
potential for this balance by eroding women's protections
and prerogatives, first in the name of a "civilizing mission" and later for the sake of "development" or "modernization."

Division between the sexes is a key to understanding African women in settings relatively unaffected by
the forces of colonization and Westernization: division
of labor, division of family responsibilities, division
of social life, and division of political activities.
For the most part, adults of each sex have relatively
clearly defined rights and obligations in relation to
their patrilineage, their matrilineage, their spouse and
the spouse's kin. Women's working world--their casual
social contacts, their religious practices, even their
access to the decision-making process on the village or
regional level--is generally within a female sphere.
Separateness of the sexes carries over into status considerations, too. Women can seek and achieve high status
as women, while men strive for status through male channels. As one study suggests: "no comparison is made
between the status of men and women. They are incompar-
able entities."("Women in Kenya and Tanzania,"1972, p.35)
Thus the Western-oriented question of women's status vis-
à-vis men's is, in the African tradition, largely irrelevant. Women's achievements are effectively measured by
separate scales that differ somewhat among individual
ethnic groups. Standards of fertility, cooperative
spirit, or economic enterprise, for example, may determine a woman's rank among her kind. Similarly, men may
be compared according to standards of aggressiveness,
verbal skill, or physical prowess.

Within the limits of their sphere, women enjoy
relatively great potential for individual enterprise,
particularly since economic productivity in women is
usually highly valued. In patrilineal settings especially,
women often are able to operate as culture-brokers, persons who might mediate between differing and sometimes

competing segments of society. Because physical characteristics set them apart from the controlling (male) centers of power, women can sometimes cross boundaries closed to men. As wives in a husband's patrilineage, as strangers in the country of another ethnic group, as traders in a new town, women may benefit from a relative flexibility toward them as women in order to make economic gains. White, in her article on women traders of nineteenth-century Sierra Leone, provides an example of women's working effectively at the interface of British contact with African societies. White's women clearly understood the workings of both cultures and used their knowledge of economic opportunities in each system to maximum effect. Upcountry, they identified with indigenous peoples and enjoyed commercial advantages offered through their membership in the Bundu women's secret society. At the same time, their association with the Colony enabled them to claim British protection and to have access to the European import trade through the port of Freetown.

MacCormack's study of a rural area of Sierra Leone outlines the dynamics of women's independent economic existence which is currently being altered through the effects of capitalist development. Heirs of a tradition of political prominence for women, Sherbro women nevertheless typify general patterns of women's economic participation in African societies relatively unmodified by Westernization. Access to land and control over the product of their labor are guaranteed women through their kin relationships. All production is based on interdependence among members of the extended family. The division of agricultural labor, for example, is such that the input of both sexes is essential and irreplaceable. Cooperative economic ventures between spouses or among co-wives are common. Wives, for example, may process and sell fish caught by husbands, or co-wives resident in different areas can supply each other with commodities to trade. Wives share child care and the household and farm work load. In brief, the interdependence and mutual support provided through the lineage structure and marriage assure women access to the means of production (land in particular) and protect them against the appropriation by men of the product of their labor.

Examples like the women studied by White and Mac-Cormack, whether taken from the past or from contemporary settings, underline African women's relatively greater economic potential and independence in a nonindustrialized and non-Westernized world. Women's contributions to the economic well-being of family and community are recognized and respected. Paradoxically, though, at the same time that women may be admired for accomplishments within their realm of expectation, women as a sex may be

subject to derision and contempt. Male-determined socie-
tal values argue women's inferiority and insure the ideological preeminence of men's sphere of activity. The
balance between the sexes, then, is not a balance of
equals, but one in which men claim greater importance.
This ideology of male superiority has generally resulted
in very real economic advantages for men in traditional
systems (Van Allen, 1976, pp. 67-68). To the extent that
men control the allocation of the lineage's land or own
the more lucrative crops, for example, the male sphere
of activity is bound as a whole to remain more prestigious. Tension is constant between men's and women's
spheres; the balance between them appears to undergo
constant readjustment.

Ideology is directly related to women's productive potential. The theme of ideology and women's place
is one that appears repeatedly in this volume--in
Christian and Islamic religious traditions, in Western
political and economic institutions, and in contemporary
responses to the failures of development policies. In
this sense, Schildkrout introduces a topic that in its
various manifestations proves a key element in African
women's economic lives. Schildkrout deals with women in
Islamic northern Nigeria, describing a situation in which
religious values have been superimposed on a traditional
African women's work ethic. Islam prescribes that women
be wholly dependent on their husbands. Yet married women
subvert the ideal by generating income that they use, in
turn, both to support the marriage system and, paradoxically, to amass enough resources to renegotiate their
position within it. Physically restricted in their homes
by purdah (seclusion), they are able to be economically
active through their control over the free movement of
children, who market their wares and acquire their supplies.

White, MacCormack, and Schildkrout all note changes
outside their women's economic lives that threaten the
continuation of their productivity. Thus the authors
introduce another theme that is prominent in this collection of studies: economic and political change, even
when it is instituted to improve women's state, has multiple and complex effects, some of which may be detrimental to women's economic potential. Moreover, change
may well affect men and women differentially. In White's
case, international political factors associated with the
beginning of the colonial era circumscribe Krio women's
trade. MacCormack observes that technological change in
capitalized farming schemes compensates male but not
female labor, thus increasing women's work load. The
proposed move to privatize land in Sierra Leone, she
predicts, would set off a chain reaction resulting in
greater social stratification and increased female de-

pendence on male wage-earners. Schildkrout notes that
the introduction of universal primary education in northern Nigeria, by removing from women the children who act
as links between households, threatens women's ability
to continue their income-generating activities.

## II. ECONOMIC CHANGE AND IDEOLOGICAL CONFLICT

Colonial governments in Africa developed policies
toward their subject peoples that were based on conceptions of male-female power relations as they existed in
Europe. Thus the colonizers' central concern was to
affect and transform the lives of men. Assuming that
women were not or should not be involved in political or
economic life, the male-staffed colonial administrations
sought first to insure their political control over men
and second, to compel men's cooperation and collaboration
in the exploitation of resources. Though women were involved with men in resistance to the colonizers' efforts, the deliberate and constant exclusion of women
from the political and economic activities thrust upon
African men gradually began to make the colonizers' assumptions about women a self-fulfilling prophecy.
Obviously, African men suffered from colonization.
Forced labor, personal taxation, and conscription into
armies were early examples of much-despised policies
instituted in various colonial situations. Men, too,
were more often subjected to the less physically demand-
ing but equally destructive efforts to educate them into
contempt for their own cultural heritage. In short, it
was mainly men who were forced into direct confrontation
with the European colonizers and the institutions they
established in Africa. Yet this very confrontation led
men to a greater familiarity with Western ways and to a
facility for dealing with the changing international
order. Because colonial institutions over time became
the basis for Westernized independent societies, men
ultimately were better prepared to understand and manipulate the modern African state systems that emerged in
the second half of the twentieth century.
The colonial system thus upset the delicate power
balance between men and women in African societies.
African women became victims of double discrimination
through policies developed to promote first, the interests of the colonial powers and second, the interests
of African men. And by developing men's capabilities for
work in altered economic and social institutions, colonialism advanced African men at the expense of their own
women. Moreover, African ideologies of male superiority
were reinforced by Western and Christian patriarchal
conceptions of women's place.

In her study of the railway region of Zambia, Maud
Shimwaayi Muntemba traces the impact of more than seventy
years of colonial and independent government policies on
women's economic life. The precolonial system of agricultural production as it existed in the late nineteenth
century was transformed by a series of innovations directed
toward men and designed to effect objectives related to
a white settler population, the mining industry, and the
needs of the British economy. Men were trained in the
use of modern agricultural implements, schooled in Western agricultural techniques, encouraged to produce crops
for sale, offered credit and extension services, and provided opportunities to amass capital through wage labor.
Despite efforts to retain their tradition of independent
agricultural production, rural women in the railway region
by 1970 were a deprived group often distinguishable from
their own husbands by their relative poverty, their lack
of knowledge of improved methods of production, and their
inability to obtain agricultural inputs.

Barbara Yates's study of a comparable period in
colonial Zaire (Belgian Congo) explores another facet
of women's experience with colonialism--Western education
as it was adapted for African women. With ideological
objectives more strongly articulated than those of the
British in Zambia, Belgian government and church representatives worked to inculcate notions of Christian patriarchy and white supremacy directly into their system of
education. Belgian administrators, like their colonial
counterparts elsewhere in Africa, considered female farming an aberration. Thus women's training was directed
to the creation of Christian wives and mothers on an
idealized European model. Closing all but a few "female" occupations to women, Belgian colonial officials
fostered Zairian women's economic marginality, leaving
the few women who were educated in the system without
language and other skills necessary for participation
in the modern economy.

The studies of Ilsa Schuster and Francille Rusan
Wilson move from a concentration on colonial patterns of
economic and educational exclusion of women to women's
work and social image in contemporary Zambia and Zaire.
In both settings, the mass of women appear to have found
few alternatives in their search for economic security.
Schuster provides a kind of urban epilogue to the story
of rural Zambia as told by Muntemba, who notes in closing
a dramatic rise in female migration to urban areas.
Schuster describes the literal struggle for survival in
a city with few employment opportunities for women who
have little or no Western schooling. Though central
Africa has no deep-rooted female commercial tradition
comparable to that of many areas of West Africa, women in
Lusaka have responded to economic need by going into

trade, and particularly the marketing of produce. Wilson, in her discussion of Zaire in the 1970s, highlights the dearth of economic possibilities for women of similar backgrounds and notes that, given the alternatives, prostitution became one of the more viable routes to a modicum of economic security.

Both Schuster and Wilson explore the complex and contradictory contemporary social and governmental attitudes toward women. Highly visible in urban settings in their economically marginal roles, women have at times tended to become scapegoats for the frustrations of development efforts. For example, the anti-corruption actions of the Rawlings military regime in Ghana in the summer of 1979 included the demolition of Makola Market in Accra. Witness to the loss of capital goods by the market women, a journalist commented:

> The political tactics of punishing scapegoats is a classic method of averting more serious damage to the existing order. The action at Makola was full of myths and scapegoats. There was the old one of the omnipotent Market Queens who it is true have at various times sold or hoarded anything from sugar and air mail letters to soap and engine oil--but more as the retail end of the distribution chain and therefore not the largest speculators. There was the even older scapegoat of women as the oppressors of men--Makola on that Monday was rank with mysogyny; 'all women are evil,' said a corporal with conviction and another affirmed that destroying Makola would teach Ghanaian women to stop being wicked. (Bentsi-Enchill, 1979, pp. 1591-2)

As outsiders to the controlling centers of policy, women are easy targets for governments bent on demonstrating visible action to alleviate economic ills. Moreover, women are often also victims of a double bind in popular thought that condemns them both for not preserving traditional life and for not promoting modern development. Women may be charged, on the one hand, with the maintenance of traditional values, particularly those related to the family, yet be despised on the other as backward and illiterate brakes on progress toward economic development. Urged to work harder to promote development, women who are perceived as Westernized may be condemned as morally suspect.

Though this ambivalence toward women is most dramatically illustrated in Schuster's and Wilson's articles on central Africa, it emerges in other studies in this collection and is directly related to another theme seen frequently in <u>Women and Work in Africa</u>, the growing

crisis of marriage relationships in many contemporary
settings. Although heightened tensions in marriage
systems have been evident from as early as the nineteenth
century among Africans who adopted Western lifestyles
(e.g. Mann, in press), the recent rush to modernize on
a large scale has accelerated processes of change. Evidence from these articles suggests that, at least from
the perspective of many African women, contemporary marriage offers few of the protections of former times yet
requires undiminished, even increased, energies from
women. Several authors note that a growing minority of
women have opted out of marriage altogether.

In rural areas, the movement from kin-centered
systems of agricultural production to capitalist indi-
vidual- and commodity-centered systems has reduced the
symbiotic productive relationships of spouses and left
legal control over labor, land, and profits mainly in
the hands of individual men, rather than under the control of the former male (or female) heads of households
who exercised responsibilities for an entire extended
family. As technological innovation has reduced men's
work load, an unchanging division of labor has required
women to work harder, often in absolute as well as relative terms. Muntemba describes, for example, the pressure on rural women in Zambia whose husbands demand increasing labor from their wives in their own fields but
who refuse to divide cash profits equitably or to support
women's traditional rights to cultivate their own fields.
Two authors (Wilson, Muntemba) cite the impoverishment
of widows who lose through customary law the farm implements and other material possessions said to be owned by
the husband and therefore the property of his family.
Others (Louise Fortmann, White) observe that men see innovations in women's activities as threatening to themselves. Indeed, William F. Steel and Claudia Campbell
argue that men have real incentives to maintain the subordination of women and their exclusion from full participation in the wage economy.

Often, the result of Westernization and economic
development is increased dependency by women on men. And,
in the evolving system, men have little reason to be concerned for women's plight. Western models promote increased dependency as an ideal, and several authors
(Barbara Lewis, Schildkrout) note that nonworking wives
are a male status symbol. At the same time, men naturally
resent urban wives who do not, as women do in traditional
agricultural life, contribute directly to the economic
well-being of the family. As Schuster points out, mutual
role expectations of men and women in marriage are in
tremendous flux. At worst, men and women may, as in
Lusaka, support incompatible ideals of appropriate
marital behavior. In town, "outside wives" and mistresses

may be tolerated as expressions of African traditional values even though the women in such liaisons no longer have rights at the death of the "husband." It is little wonder that some women charge that "tradition" has become defined as those African values and customs that benefit men.

## III.  DIFFERENTIAL EFFECTS OF DEVELOPMENT POLICIES

The articles by Grace A. Hemmings-Gapihan, Fortmann, Kathleen A. Staudt, and Steel and Campbell focus on the effects of policies devised and instituted to improve the economic well-being of African peoples in four different countries. All are set in the recent past; three describe rural agricultural economies and one a wage-based urban economy. All describe policies adhered to by independent governments whose ideological stances range from capitalist to socialist. And all suggest that activities designed to promote the "common good" may well have unanticipated negative effects on the economic well-being of women.

Hemmings-Gapihan's study of a rural area of Upper Volta in the 1970s telescopes the lengthy process experienced elsewhere in Africa that has led to women's underdevelopment. A village economy relatively unchanged by colonial policies was dramatically transformed by international intervention to relieve the drought of the early 1970s. From traditional methods of interdependent farming and manufacturing, the area moved into a cash economy with classic relations of exchange of male labor for manufactured goods. Hemmings-Gapihan notes that women early in the process were able to maximize trade opportunities with their own agricultural surplus and invest in their sons' activities. However, as "development" occured, individualization of units of production ultimately led to women's working harder. Competition with imported manufactured goods destroyed the local market for home-produced products, and women in the end found themselves more economically dependent on men.

Much contemporary literature on economic development stresses the need to integrate women into development. Yet Hemmings-Gapihan makes the crucial point implicit in other articles in this collection, that women are already active participants in bringing about change. Women, by filling labor gaps left by men departed from the agricultural economy, by working harder to assist in the production of cash crops, by providing capital for men's enterprises, and by donating labor to self-help projects, make development possible, even though they may ultimately be damaged by the economic transformations that result.

Communal agricultural production through Tanzanian
ujamaa villages appears in theory an attractive alternative to the capitalist production so often disadvan-
tageous to women's interests.  However, Fortmann found
that, in general, ujamaa production was inadequate to
meet even the subsistence needs of participants.  Moreover, women in ujamaa villages did not participate fully
in community decision making and tended to carry a heavier
share than men of the burden of labor.

Staudt studied the agricultural extension services
in western Kenya to determine if and why discrimination
against women existed in the delivery of services.  She
discovered that women farm managers were not equally
served by visits of extension field staff, by farmer
training centers, or by government agricultural loan programs.  Moreover, discrimination was evident against even
the relatively wealthy land-owning women who were recognized as innovative farmers.

Both Fortmann and Staudt noted that certain cultural impediments reinforced the tendency for differential treatment of women in these government-sponsored
activities.  Fortmann, for example, observed that women
who spoke publicly in village meetings might be criticized for their boldness by both women and men.  Staudt
noted that male extension agents could not be seen talking with a married woman if her husband was not at home.
Similar cultural constraints are frequently cited by development literature and indeed appear on occasion to
be used by planners to justify continued discrimination
against women.  Yet, as is clear from the cases here described, relatively simple changes in administration--an
altered structure for ujamaa decision making or the
addition of female agents for farming instruction, for
example--might help alleviate inequities in the implementation of development policy.

Steel and Campbell explore the implications of a
statistically dramatic increase in female labor force
participation in Ghana between 1960 and 1970.  After developing a conceptual framework for analyzing factors
associated with women's employment, the authors conclude
that women's increased participation represents a change
in labor supply only, and is the reflection of women's
efforts to maintain real family income in a period of
economic stagnation.


IV.  WOMEN AND WORK IN AFRICA:  PRESENT AND FUTURE

Lewis and Eleanor R. Fapohunda, by focusing on
Western-educated contemporary urban women, depart from
the emphasis of the majority of the contributors on rural
or non-professional women.  Nevertheless, both explore

phenomena that illustrate, again, that so-called modernization may have unanticipated effects on women's ability
to maintain their economic independence.

Lewis's study of fertility behavior in Abidjan,
Ivory Coast, underscores the positive and direct interaction between the productive and reproductive roles of
women. Testing the assumption of a basic incompatibility
between motherhood and labor force participation, Lewis
found instead that educational level and not employment
status had an impact on desired family size. Lewis notes
that salaried urban women at the time of her study were
able to acquire child care relatively readily. She warns
that tensions are beginning to arise, however, as young
relatives, who traditionally filled child-care needs,
continue in school and seek salaried employment themselves.

Fapohunda effectively takes Lewis's study a step
further as she discusses the problem of and emerging solutions for the child-care needs of salaried women in Lagos,
Nigeria. There, as in many contemporary cities, modern
urban lifestyles dictate smaller household units and the
ideal of marital monogamy means that the possibilities
in polygyny of sharing child-care responsibilities are
lost. Finally, the institution of universal primary
education and possibilities of wage employment mean that
fewer persons are available for household child care.
Thus women, no longer able to depend on child care
through the support system of the extended family, have
begun to utilize the commercial day-care businesses
springing up around the city. Ironically, Fapohunda's
findings of unanticipated difficulties for Western-educated women parallel those of Schildkrout, whose Islamic
northern Nigerian women similarly are adversely affected
by universal primary education. Yet because girls are
included in the educational effort, another generation of
women will benefit in the long run by acquiring tools to
cope with the emerging social order.

Coumba Ceesay-Marenah describes changing patterns
of women's responses to development in urban and rural
Gambia. Sensitive to the differential impact of development policies on women, the Gambian government, like
numerous other African states, has recently authorized
the creation of a series of government-supported units
charged with assisting women at work. Particularly significant in the Gambian scheme are the women's cooperatives, which support agricultural production and marketing and the programs for the training of women in new
income-generating skills.

These final articles all touch indirectly on the
central dilemma facing African women today, the need to
embrace the realities of the modern world despite the
evidence that processes of development have proved harm-

ful in the past to their well-being. Lewis, Fapohunda, and Ceesay-Marenah all show women attempting to maintain work values related to their African heritage at the same time that they come to grips with the continuing changes fostered by modernization. For Lewis's and Fapohunda's women, the central importance of motherhood and women's financial responsibility to self and children will be upheld despite the constraints of the Western work model. The women that Ceesay-Marenah discusses seek to apply new technologies to their traditional occupations of agriculture and trade.

Nigerian novelist Buchi Emecheta, in remarks addressed to the symposium, spoke of the electric lights that have replaced moonlight in the villages of Africa and lamented the fact that people no longer gather together beneath the moon to listen to village storytellers. But she added that no one would dream of taking away those electric lights. There can indeed be no return to the past, and African women, too, must look forward. Yet in embracing the present and future they will not blindly imitate Western women. Indeed, many African women explicitly reject feminist ideology as inappropriate to their lives. Their position is well expressed by Marie Sivomey, who urges African women, as guardians of tradition, to save something of the past but to move forward into the future (1975, p. 501).

African women are becoming more visible and forceful in their nations' affairs, and national governments and development agencies are aware that women's needs should be addressed. Reports such as that by Ceesay-Marenah on projects designed by and involving women are becoming increasingly common. Yet African women need to be wary of typical training for rural women that "confines them . . . to what is claimed to be their 'natural aptitudes'" (Famille et Développement, 1980, p. 34). The negative impact of development has affected African women of all socioeconomic levels, rural and urban. The imbalance between the sexes that resulted from the colonial experience must be redressed by women's gaining a balanced share of control over the means of production. Well-meaning individuals and institutions may well develop projects to assist African women. However, in the final analysis, the problems of work and womanhood in Africa, as they have been in the past, will be defined and solved by African women themselves, and that process is underway.

Edna G. Bay

REFERENCES

Bentsi-Enchill, Nii. 1979. "Losing Illusions at Makola
    Market." West Africa, no. 3242 (3 Sept.): Pp.
    1589-92.
Boserup, Ester. 1970. Woman's Role in Economic Develop-
    ment. New York.
Chernush, Kay. 1979. "Straight Talk in Sudan." Agenda,
    (June): Pp. 2-4.
Hill, Polly. 1978. "Food-Farming and Migration from
    Fante Villages." Africa 48, no. 3: Pp. 220-30.
Julien, C.-A. 1977-78. Les Africains [biographies of
    important historical figures]. 10 vols. Paris.
Mann, Kristin. In press. "Women's Rights in Law and
    Practice: Marriage and Dispute Settlement in
    Colonial Lagos." In Marcia Wright and Margaret
    Jean Hay, eds., African Women Under the Law. Boston.
Mojekwu, C.C., V.C. Uchendu, and L.F. Van Hoey. 1977.
    African Society, Culture and Politics: An Intro-
    duction to African Studies. Washington.
Nantogmah, Matilda. 1979. "The Images of Ghanaian
    Women Workers." Paper presented at symposium on
    Women and Work in Africa, University of Illinois
    at Urbana-Champaign.
Senghor, Diana. 1970. "La fabrication des femmes."
    Famille et Développement. No. 23 (July-Aug.-Sept.):
    Pp. 29-42.
Sivomey, Marie. 1972. "Vers la Révolution Culturelle
    de la Femme Noire." In La Civilisation de la
    femme dans la tradition africaine. Présence
    Africaine (Paris, 1975). Pp. 493-502.
Tinker, Irene. n.d. "New Technologies for Food Chain
    Activities: The Imperative of Equity for Women."
    Unpublished paper, Women in Development Resource
    Center, U.S. Agency for International Development.
Turnbull, C. 1977. Man in Africa. New York.
UNECA/FAO. 1975. Women, Population and Rural Develop-
    ment--Africa. New York.
United States. 1973. Public Law 93-189. 93rd Cong, S.
    1443. 17 Dec.
Van Allen, Judith. 1976. "'Aba Riots' or Igbo 'Women's
    War'? Ideology, Stratification, and the Invisi-
    bility of Women." In N.J. Hafkin and E.G. Bay,
    eds., Women in Africa. Stanford. Pp. 59-85.
"Women in the Rural Areas of Kenya and Tanzania." 1972.
    Women in Developing Countries. Stockholm: Swedish
    International Development Authority. Pp. 23-37.

# 1. Women, Work, and Ethnicity:
# The Sierra Leone Case

*E. Frances White*


On his way to the Congo in search of gorillas, Winwood Reade met a Mandingo woman who asked him to take
her to Sierra Leone "because Sierra Leone was <u>free</u>. If a
women did not like her husband she could leave him and
marry another, and there was no palaver. So it seems
that Freetown is free in a sense which was not contemplated by its philanthropic founders" (Reade, 1873,
pp. 398-99).[1] Indeed, for women, nineteenth-century
Sierra Leone was probably one of the freest places in the
world. In Sierra Leone, a woman could move about with
remarkably little restraint imposed by the male world.
Staying for months or even years at a time (and presumably
forming other alliances), women could decide to embark
on trading or missionary ventures unilaterally. Surely,
few eighteenth- or nineteenth-century philanthropists
would have contemplated such freedom for women. Ample
evidence exists that demonstrates their horror at this
turn of events (for example, see Ingham, 1895, pp. 316-
17; British Parliamentary Papers, 1844, p. 322; Church
Missionary Society Papers, G3. Al/L14, 1881).

Clearly, this way of life appealed to many nineteenth-century women; Reade's Mandingo acquaintance was
but one. She understood that to participate in this exciting new way of life, she merely had to cross over into
Sierra Leone, her Mandingo heritage notwithstanding. If
this woman ever made it to Freetown and learned the
Colony's ways, she could have returned to the hinterland

---

I am indebted to the African American Scholars Council
and the Danforth Foundation for financing my research in
Sierra Leone and to the Archives and Institute of African Studies at Fourah Bay College for assisting me during
my research in Sierra Leone from 1975 to 1977. I would
also like to thank Steve Baier, Sara Berry, and Jean
Hay for helping me to formulate the ideas found in this
paper and Emma Lapsansky for commenting on the final
draft.

as a Sierra Leonean and continued her liberated life-
style.
        This paper chronicles the development of this lib-
erated lifestyle while focusing on the economic determinants of ethnic identity.  During the nineteenth century, ethnicity was not a limiting factor; instead,
occupation became the important issue in determining
ethnic identity.  A hinterland woman who traded independently became Sierra Leonean while a Sierra Leonean
woman who settled up-country and farmed became Mende or
Temne.  As this paper demonstrates, during the twentieth
century, Krio women were forced to turn away from trading to the professions (i.e., teaching, nursing).  These
new occupations isolated Krio women from other African
groups and, for those Provincial women interested in
trading, Krio identity grew less appealing.  Thus, the
boundary between Krio and Provincial became more rigid.
        By the mid-twentieth century, Krios had evolved
into a distinct ethnic group that jealously guarded its
distinctiveness from other groups.  But it would be a
mistake to read the present-day gulf between Krio and
other ethnic groups into the past (Skinner and Harrell-
Bond, 1977; White, 1978).  In the nineteenth century,
Sierra Leoneans were a diverse group whose individual
members defined their ethnic backgrounds as Yoruba, Ibo,
Mandingo, Temne, and the like, rather than as Krio.
During the nineteenth century, this diversity aided
Sierra Leoneans in fulfilling their primary function--
that of intermediaries in Afro-European contact.  Learning the British economic system, religions, and life-
style, their diversity set them enough apart from the
other Africans to free them to associate closely with
Europeans.  Sharing a common West African background,
the Sierra Leoneans remained close enough to the indigenous Africans to learn their languages, philoso-
phies, and economic systems.
        Although few reached the economic heights of the
most successful men, women traders (and missionaries)
were as important in this Afro-European contact as men
were.  Not surprisingly, the British, coming from a
culture where men dominated trade, were astonished at
the way Sierra Leonean women adapted to commerce.  In
the first place, the British had never intended that
trade be the economic mainstay of their experimental
colony.  Instead, farming was to provide the basis of
a new, agricultural society, exporting raw materials
to their industrializing society.  From the Nova
Scotians to the Liberated Africans, however, the Sierra
Leoneans quickly realized that the British notion of
farming was ill conceived for Sierra Leone's rocky and
heavily leached soil (Blair, 1968; also, Church, 1957)
and that only commerce would provide a suitable economic
basis for the fledgling colony.

Many Sierra Leonean women brought with them cultural backgrounds that helped them adapt to Sierra Leone's economic opportunities.  Nova Scotian women, for example, came with a tradition of independence gained in the New World, a tradition that fit conveniently with the life-style required of women who traded up-country.  Many Liberated Africans brought with them trading  traditions with roots centuries old.  Most important of these were the Yoruba, perhaps the premier women traders of West Africa (Hodder and Ukwu, 1969; Sudarkasa, 1973).

Once in Sierra Leone, women traded at every level. Many women sold produce in their local village or Freetown markets.  Others traveled up-country to barter European goods for rice that they in turn sold in Freetown.  Many based on Sherbro Island became wealthy on the kola trade--a trade that women dominated in the late nineteenth century.

While in the interior, these women took a flexible attitude toward their ethnic identity, often changing from a special ethnic group of the Colony to a member of the indigenous culture.  Some of the women were closely associated with the Africans of the interior, a result partly of the number of Recaptives who were indigenous to the area and partly of the inherent strength of the local culture.

The growth of the women's secret society Bundu in the Colony demonstrates the appeal of the local culture to the immigrant Africans.  Bundu had much to offer the Colony's women.  First, in Bundu, these uprooted women found solidarity among themselves and the indigenous women.  Second, membership in Bundu helped establish moral standards by which Sierra Leonean women felt constrained to lead their lives.  Through a shared religious and cultural experience, women traders established a foundation on which to base trust.  And in an economy in which contractual relations had to be based on personal knowledge of the people involved, establishing the basis for trust was essential.  Third, membership in Bundu helped provide a basis for authority.  By establishing a hierarchy of women, traders were obligated to adhere to the decisions made by women in the upper reaches of the society.  Thus, women's activities were effectively regulated and monitored.  Finally, Bundu offered much that Colony women found lacking in missionary schools.  In the Bundu bush, young girls could gain an education based on West African realities; there, girls learned how to survive in West Africa. For example, many women were attracted to Bundu during a smallpox epidemic in the 1830s (Peterson, 1969, p. 268). The women in the upper levels of the Bundu hierarchy were among the best medical practitioners of the day and the Sierra Leonean women recognized this fact.

Resistance to women's participation in Bundu, especially among Christian missionaries and Colony men, grew as Bundu spread (Hotobah-During, 1976). For example, in February 1887, Henry Willock accused Sarah Williams of beating a Bundu drum all night without a license just outside the village of Goderich in the Colony. During the trial, it was found that the defendant was trying to introduce Bundu into the village. She was found guilty and sentenced to jail with one week of hard labor (Sierra Leone Weekly News, 19 Feb. 1887; cited hereafter SLWN). But this did not deter Sarah Williams because, soon after her release, she was accused with nine other old women of forcibly initiating a little girl, Jane Davies, into the society. The women were found guilty of assaulting and wounding young Davies and were committed to prison (SLWN, 26 Feb. 1887).

The Krio paper, the Sierra Leone Weekly News, had the following to say about this incident:

> A nest of Bundooism has been broken up at Goderich, and its inmates brought to account, but unfortunately not before they had succeeded in carrying off Jane Davies, a little girl, living in the village making her another victim to their nefarious and heathenish rites. . . .
>
> The crime of these women is tenfold the more worthy of condemnation, in as much as in a country like this where Christianity is so wide-spread, one cannot but surmise that the perpetrators of such act have had at sometime or another, the benefit of Christian teaching. It is to be hoped that the punishment will be meted out to them in full measure, thereby making them an example for others. (SLWN, 26 Feb. 1887)

It would seem that, for some women at least, Christianity left a void that Bundu filled.

This attraction to Bundu for Colony women demonstrates the fluidity of cultural boundaries. Indeed, the attraction of the indigenous culture was often so great that Colony women completely assimilated, leaving behind their Colony identity. For those women who married indigenous men and settled permanently in the hinterland, assimilation proved easy.[2] Akintola Wyse has described his own Krio family, which included a paternal grandmother who traded up-country where she learned Temne, joined a secret society, and appeared fully assimilated into Temne culture (Wyse, 1977, pp. 238-39).

Similarly, Colony culture attracted indigenous women. Women easily crossed ethnic boundaries to take on Sierra Leonean identity through marriage; others simply claimed Colony identity. By moving to Freetown, learning Krio and the ways of trade, a woman could return

up-country to begin trading as a Krio, while utilizing
the contacts made in Freetown. The ambiguity surrounding Sierra Leonean identity in the nineteenth century
helped interior women claim Colony connections. In an
1895 case, a certain Sabadu (alias Sarian Smith),having
annoyed the Alikali of Kambia, turned to Freetown for
protection. Secretary for Native Affairs J.C.E. Parkes
sided with the Alikali and eventually determined that
Sabadu was not really from the Colony and thus out of
British jurisdiction (Native Affairs Letterbook, 1894,
1895). Obviously Sabadu, whom the interior people had
easily accepted as Sierra Leonean, viewed a Colony-based
identity as an asset in her trading ventures in Kambia.
       There were several advantages that an interior woman
could receive from this identity. For example, she could
appeal to Freetown for protection from looters and
debtors, as Sabadu attempted to do. In addition, a
trader could become a part of the loose-knit trading
diaspora that the Colony had developed. This diaspora
had important connections in the port towns, connections
that extended across the ocean to the very heart of the
industrialized world. Wearing distinctive print dresses
with Madras headscarves, the diaspora's female members
were identified by their Krio uniform (Alldridge, 1901,
p. 41). In addition, Sierra Leonean women were either
Christian or Muslim. All these were attributes that other
women could take on if they wanted to claim to be Sierra
Leonean. As proselytizing religions, Christianity and
Islam welcomed all. Moreover, Sierra Leoneans possessed
neither identifying facial marks nor an exclusive language, for facial marks stemmed from a variety of ethnic
groups found throughout West Africa and Krio developed
as a trading language that many understood. In the nineteenth century, to be Sierra Leonean meant to be a
trader and/or a member of a universalistic religion,
Christianity or Islam, who looked to Freetown as a
source of political authority.
       Writing of the Hausa merchant community, Paul Love-
joy has noted the incorporation of non-Hausa, such as
Nupe, Bornu, and Fulani, into Hausa diaspora settlements. As stranger-traders, Hausa and non-Hausa shared
experiences that bound them together as a community.
These included Islam, the use of Hausa as a lingua
franca, intermarriage, and common residence (Lovejoy,
1973, pp. 27-28; cf. Haaland, 1969, and Baier and Lovejoy, 1975). Lovejoy's conclusion is apt: "People vary
their identification with the situation, and a wide
variety of factors influence a person in determining his
group loyalty" (1973, p. 71).
       Similarly, given the fluidity of Sierra Leonean
identity in the nineteenth century, interior women found
it easy to claim Colony connections when it aided their

trading ventures. As Lovejoy asserts, "ethnicity was a
product of participation in a dynamic economy" (1973,
p. 239). But it would be an error to suppose that the
interior women who opted for Sierra Leonean identity completely relinquished their hinterland identities.
Rather, they sometimes brought their cultural backgrounds
with them, supplementing their former identity with their
new Sierra Leonean outlook. As illustrated by the spread
of Bundu among Colony women, this dynamic process aided
in the diffusion of hinterland culture within the Colony
and further demonstrates the fluidity of culture in
nineteenth-century Sierra Leone and its hinterland.

   Although Colony connections aided women in their
trading, these connections could not solve all of their
problems. With protection based in distant Freetown,
women often suffered from looting and even enslavement.
As cosmopolitan strangers, they were irritants particularly in many hinterland villages. But in addition to
the economic challenges posed by all Sierra Leoneans,
the women presented a special challenge. Traditional
authorities must have been threatened by Sierra Leonean
women who combined the authority and power based on Bundu
connections with the independence of stranger-traders.
From the time of the Colony's foundation, chiefs complained of slaves' seeking refuge within the British
sphere. So, too, they must have resented women who,
attracted by the independence of the Colony women, left
their homes to become traders. If they claimed to be
Sierra Leonean, renegade women could escape a chief's
rule. Sabadu, for instance, sought British protection so
that she could ignore the established authority in Kambia. Given the value of women in these agricultural
societies, any loss of women's labor was resented. More
importantly, independent and wealthy women represented
a threat to female subordination in general and thus a
potential decline in men's control over the labor of all
women.

   In 1898, Sierra Leonean traders found themselves
caught between British and Provincial hostility. Responding in general to the 1895 British-declared protectorate over the hinterland and specifically to the 1898
British-imposed house tax, the Protectorate peoples
struck out. Although many of the Colony traders supported the revolt and thus indicated their sympathy with
the hinterland people,[3] many found themselves the target
of the rebellion's fury, particularly in the south. The
official inquiry into this so-called hut tax war noted
that several Sierra Leonean women complained of looting
and the loss of family members (British Parliamentary
Papers, 1899). Seeking a convenient scapegoat, the
British blamed the Sierra Leoneans for the revolt. Thus,
the stage was set for economic decline and ethnic isolation.

The 1898 war's end ushered in a new era of challenges for women traders from the Colony. Banks and a
cash economy were introduced and transportation was
gradually improved. Unfortunately, Krios faced these
challenges without allies. During the war, the British
had crystallized a policy of excluding Sierra Leoneans
from top civil service jobs and from participation in
trade. Whereas the British had once turned to the Colony
traders as a bridge in their trade, they now began to
treat their former allies with hostility.

The Krios' decline in the twentieth century was
among the most spectacular falls of nineteenth-century
African intermediaries. Several authors have attempted
to explain the change. Cox-George emphasizes the advantages that European traders had over Krios (Cox-
George, 1961, pp. 162-63, 299; see also Howard, 1966,
pp. 48-51), while Spitzer focuses on the political and cultural side of the British-Krio relationship. He argues
that the British, with their increasing ethnocentrism,
betrayed the Krios in their joint venture to "civilize"
Africa; while withdrawing their support, they restricted
the Krios' upward mobility (Spitzer, 1974, pp. 151-79,
passim).

Although both Cox-George and Spitzer discuss the
displacement of Krio intermediaries by Lebanese traders,
Leighton offers the most coherent discussion of this
competition and brings into focus the trilateral relations among the Krios, the Lebanese, and the British
(1971). During the period between 1898 and 1910, European traders, taking advantage of the new railway line,
began to move Krio traders out of the retail produce
trade. But even the Europeans proved ineffective
against the new Lebanese competition.

Lebanese immigrants had begun arriving in West
Africa in the late nineteenth century. The early immigrants had not set out for West Africa but for the New
World, where they hoped to escape poverty. Because of
strict immigration laws in the United States and Brazil,
however, many were redirected en route to Dakar, Senegal.
From there, they began spreading out across West Africa
(Winder, 1962). Once in Sierra Leone, the Lebanese had
certain advantages over the Europeans. First, having
left a poverty-stricken land, they were willing to
economize. They lived cheaply, saved scrupulously, and
reinvested most of their profits. Europeans, on the
other hand, built expensive homes, sent money home to
Europe, and went on costly leaves (Crowder, 1968, p.
291). Second, the Lebanese were better prepared to do
business in the interior than the Europeans. The
Lebanese accepted lower profit margins and understood
how to bargain shrewdly with African producers. Third,
they changed the nature of the trade by offering producers cash for goods instead of bartering. This tactic

forced many Europeans out of business (Hopkins, 1973,
p. 291). In Barbey, Senegal, for example, the ratio of
European to Lebanese traders virtually reversed itself
between 1919 and 1935. While there were 47 Europeans
and 4 Lebanese in 1919, by 1935 there were 20 Europeans
and 105 Lebanese (Winder, 1962, p. 309).

Similarly, in Sierra Leone, European traders lost
out to the Lebanese in the interior trade because
European firms were too large and cumbersome to handle
effectively the numerous small producers in the hinterland.[4] With little overhead, the Lebanese easily captured this end of the trade, and the Europeans came to
depend on them. Krios could have continued to play this
intermediary role, but as potential nationalist leaders,
they threatened colonial rule in a way that the nonindi-
genous Lebanese did not. While today the gulf between
Krios and Provincials seems particularly glaring, in the
early part of this century, it was their similarity and
their closeness that threatened the British. And it was
to the colonial government's advantage to play down
these similarities and to isolate potential bourgeois
national sentiment from a mass following.

The close ties between Krio and Provincial women,
their joint membership in secret societies, and the
easily crossed cultural boundary have already been
pointed out. Recognizing such connections, the British
sought to sever Krio-Provincial ties by fanning ethnic
animosities and thus breaking the Krios' power base.
Moreover, as Leighton proposes, once the British
recognized that they still needed intermediaries, they
found the Lebanese traders suitable substitutes for the
Krios.

> The Lebanese as non-indigenous middlemen were
> visible, culturally identifiable, and did not
> have access to either the prerequisites of power
> under Imperial Rule or ascribed positions of in-
> fluence within the traditional social structure.
> Lastly, they had little opportunity to acquire the
> necessary skills to challenge the Europeans and as
> time was to show, no opportunity to enter the Civil
> Service where considerable influence could be
> brought to bear in policy implementation. . . .
> Thus the firms in league with the government were
> the cause of the displacement of the Creoles, a
> necessary step in not only establishing the economic
> hegemony of the firms, but solidifying the extention
> of Colonial Rule throughout the entire territory of
> Sierra Leone. (Leighton, 1971, pp. 192-93)

Although trading remained the preferred occupation
for most Krio women, many found that they had to turn
elsewhere to supplement their declining incomes.[5]

Since they had been trained as seamstresses in school, many women took up sewing as an alternative to full-time trading. An example is Miranda Coker, granddaughter of Simeon George, a wealthy Krio  trader, who in the 1930s inherited part of her grandfather's business.  At the turn of the century, Simeon George had owned three shops in Freetown's main business district.  Every other year, he and his sister, Christiana Thomas, a kola trader, traveled to Britain to purchase goods (Miranda Coker, 1976; Hotobah-During, 1976).  Miranda Coker's mother, Gertrude Judge-Coker, managed George's business while he was away and inherited the best of his shops when he died.  By the time Miranda Coker inherited Simeon George's business through her mother, the nature of the shop had changed.  George had imported dresses from London for Freetown's elite, but Miranda Coker ordered cloth through the European firm Patterson Zochonis and sewed the dresses herself (Miranda Coker, 1976).  Many of the shop's dresses still went to Freetown's Krio elite, but they lacked the prestige of being imports from the metropole.  Clearly, the general trend for Krio women was one of economic decline.

As part of their response to their declining economic fortunes, Krio men and women searched for political solutions to their problems.  Their move into the political arena was part of a larger movement throughout British West Africa, for the decline of the Christianized, educated elite drew similar reactions in Bathurst (Banjul), Lagos, and Accra.  In the past, the Europeans had used these Africans as a link to African markets and producers.  But after the establishment of colonial rule, traditional African leaders became more important to the Europeans because they could help maintain order.  In addition, because the educated elite claimed equality with the Europeans, they threatened the hegemony of the colonial overlords.  Thus the Europeans increasingly turned to British civil servants for upper-level positions where in the past they had used the Western-educated African elite to run their offices (Webster, 1974, p. 570).

Meeting in Accra in 1920, the aggrieved Africans banded together to form the National Congress of British West Africa.[6]  Still loyal to Britain, the National Congress asked not for independence but for more representation in the running of the colonies.  Essentially a male-conceived and -dominated movement, the congress nevertheless had a place for women.  Soon after the Sierra Leone delegates returned to Freetown, a women's branch was formed "under the distinguished Presidencies of Madam E.J. Scotland and Mrs. Rose Palmer and a strong Committee."  The newspaper added, "This section is now engaged in a vigorous financial work and has already assisted the Congress financially" (SLWN, 31 July 1920).

The role for women, then, was to be a subordinate one,
assisting the main branch.

Indeed, the congress had already run into conflicts
with women in another Freetown organization.  The women's
section of the Universal Negro Improvement Association
(UNIA), the Freetown branch of Marcus Garvey's movement,
created consternation among the congress delegates.
Ironically, the women were led by Agatha Casely Hayford,
the wife of a key founder of the National Congress.  The
delegates objected to her proposed trip down the coast
in search of money to support a proposed technical and
industrial school for girls (SLWN, 12 June 1920).  "Ma
Mashado," the author of a critical article in the Sierra
Leone Weekly News, claimed that "any attempt to collect
money for the U.N.I.A. would divert the pecuniary resources of Sierra Leoneans from the Congress" (SLWN, 12
June 1920).  In the same issue, a leading barrister and
member of the congress criticized the very nature of the
proposed school.  Moreover, he intimated that Hayford's
intentions were not entirely honorable, for if they were,
she would turn her attention to the neglected "native"
women in the Protectorate (SLWN, 12 June 1920).  As a
result of such criticisms, Hayford severed relations with
the UNIA and decided to turn instead to the United States
for funds.  The Weekly News, in the following issue,
apologized to Hayford for any unintended aspersions on
her character and declared her proposal a worthwhile
project (SLWN, 19 June 1920).  Clearly, political activity by women in these early years was to take place
within the framework of male-controlled politics.

Conflict between male and female Krios, however,
was minor compared to the developing gulf between Krios
and Provincials.  The roots of this gulf lay in the
establishment of the Protectorate.  As Porter declares,
"It is one of the paradoxes of history that this declaration of the Sierra Leone Protectorate, while uniting the
country politically, divided it culturally and ethnically" (1963, p. 61).  The British, by creating competing political units within the larger polity of Sierra
Leone, created a rivalry between the Krios and a Mende/
Temne-dominated alliance.  For example, by legitimizing
tribal headmen in Freetown in 1905, when Krios had no
such institution, they built into the administrative
system structural inhibitions to the integration of
various ethnic groups (Porter, 1963, p. 62).

It was during this era, then, that the ethnic
rivalry which other historians have read into the nineteenth century emerged as the overriding feature of Krio-
Protectorate relations.[7]  If the nineteenth century was
an era of fluidity with regard to ethnic boundaries, the
twentieth century was one of boundary crystallization, as
ethnicity became an increasingly important factor in

Sierra Leonean politics.  One sign of this crystallization in the social realm was a decrease in marriages
between Krios and Provincials, symbolizing the increased attention paid to maintaining the ethnic and
cultural integrity of the Krio world.[8]  Several others
have reported the developing tribalism during the
colonial era (cf. Arens, 1976; Fried, 1967).  Abner
Cohen called the process retribalization, a response to
a struggle for power and privilege in which people
"manipulate customs, values, myths, symbols and cere-
monials from their cultural traditions in order to arti-
culate an <u>informal</u> [Cohen's emphasis] political organization which is used as a weapon in the struggle" (1969,
p. 2).

Responding to new cleavages and power alignments
created by the extension of colonialism to the Protectorate, Krios became more conscious of their "Krioness."
No longer did women claim to be Temne when up-country and
Krio in Freetown.  More important, no longer were women
traders by definition Krio.  Women still crossed ethnic
boundaries, but they did so less obviously, and the
attraction of becoming Krio lessened for women primarily
interested in trade.  Taking advantage of their closer
contacts to the interior producers, Temne and Mandingo
women gained control of the petty trade in produce (Jones,
1976).  Finally, the nature of the relationship between
Krios and Provincials changed as Krios abandoned trading.
While traders are usually viewed as outsiders and
strangers (see, e.g., Dorjahn and Fyfe, 1962), trade
necessitates contact and understanding between people and
thus brings them closer together.  As Krios moved out of
trade into the civil service and the professions, they
had less contact with Provincials.  Krio and Provincial
women, then, were less likely to meet and exchange cultural ideas than they were in the nineteenth century.

Krios have been criticized for forsaking commerce
for the professions and thus losing their economic
position in Sierra Leone (Cox-George, 1960; Porter, 1963,
pp. 113-14).  Yet this view ignores the restricted
opportunities in commerce after 1898.  Many turned to the
professions only after their businesses failed or after
it became clear that economic opportunities were severely
limited.  Bure Palmer represents such a businessperson.
From 1917 to 1935, while stationed in Bathurst, the Gambia, with her civil service husband, Palmer established
a thriving business with her Freetown-based mother.  Ruth
George, the mother, would send kola nuts to Palmer, who
in return would send her groundnuts.  After Palmer's
return to Freetown in 1935, she and her mother were unable to maintain their import/export business; they soon
found themselves selling their kola to Lebanese intermediaries.  As profits from the trading declined, Palmer

turned to teaching and sewing, professions she had
learned as a girl attending Buxton Memorial School
(Palmer, 28, 29 Dec. 1976; 2 Jan. 1977).

Palmer's early Western-style education gave her an
alternative to attempting to eke out a living as a poor
trader.  In addition, as insurance for the future, Palmer had invested in her children's education.  In 1977,
she lived with the most successful of her three children.
Her daughter, Ruth Luke, was a schoolteacher and substantial property holder.  More importantly, Luke was
influential in Freetown and Sierra Leone politics.  Having decided to ally herself closely to the ruling party,
the All-Peoples' Congress (APC), Luke had access to
Sierra Leone's President Stevens.  And as vice-president
of the APC Women's Movement, she worked actively for the
government.  Luke stands as an example of the power that
Western education has given Krios.  By continuing to
dominate the civil service and professions, they have
influence in Sierra Leone beyond their numerical strength
of less than 2 percent of the population (Cohen, 1971,
p. 429).

Yet, this change from traders to professionals and
politicians affected the ethnic identity of Krio women.
First, it created greater ethnic cohesion, as Krios felt
themselves attacked by the British, indigenous groups,
and newly arrived Lebanese.  Second, this cohesion
created a more closed group, which neither assimilated
new members easily nor allowed women the freedom to claim
ethnicity other than Krio.  These changes occurred in
part because of the political evolution of Sierra Leone
but also because of the changing nature of the women's
work.  No longer intermediary traders who developed
necessary links with both the British and the indigenous
people, the Krio women became an isolated group in their
professional role, relating to others as distant civil
servants.  Thus, they joined with their men in the
crystallization of the Krio world.


NOTES

1.  In 1791, after some false starts, a group of
British businessmen and philanthropists formed the
Sierra Leone Company to establish in the Sierra Leone
estuary a plantation which would be based on the free
labor of Africans returning from the West.  The first
settlers to Sierra Leone came from London's unwanted
black population.  The Black Poor, as they were known,
were followed the next year by black Nova Scotians, in
1800 by Jamaican Maroons, and after 1807 by Liberated
Africans who had been recaptured from the slave trade by
the British.   In the twentieth century, these settlers

became known collectively as Krios or Creoles.

2. The literature on domestic slavery in Africa demonstrates the ease with which outsiders, especially women and children, were incorporated into the family (Grace, 1975; Meiers and Kopytoff, 1977).

3. The Sierra Leoneans in Port Loko initially refused to pay the tax; the women actually jeered the District Commissioner (Colonial Office, 1898).

4. As Hopkins affirmed, this was a reality that Europeans had to face throughout West Africa. "The idea of direct trade with the producers, though appealing at a time when expatriate firms were trying to cut their costs, was an economic fantasy. In a situation where producers and consumers were both numerous and scattered, abolishing the middlemen would have meant reducing the size of the market" (1973, p. 206).

5. Cf. the biography of Bure Palmer in Chap. 5 of White (1978).

6. On the National Congress of British West Africa, see Webster (1974, pp. 575-80), Crowder (1968, pp. 405-71), Spitzer (1974, pp. 171-79). Many of the founders had come to know each other during their days in Freetown, the "Athens of West Africa," while they attended Fourah Bay College (Webster, 1974, p. 593).

7. See Chaps. 1 and 2 of White (1978) for criticisms of other historical views of Krio history.

8. Although statistical data have not been compiled on the frequency of Krio-Provincial marriages, the opinion of several observers supports this contention (Hotobah-During, 21 Sept. 1976; Palmer, 5 Dec. 1976; Smith, 1976; Fariana Coker, 1976). After World War II and especially after independence, this situation may have changed. Because of the growing status of Provincial men, low-status Krio women began to marry professional non-Krios (Harrell-Bond, 1975, p. 38).

REFERENCES

Alldridge, Thomas Joshua. 1901. The Sherbro and Its Hinterland. London.
Arens, W. 1976. "Changing Patterns of Ethnic Identity and Prestige in East Africa." In W. Arens, A Century of Change in Eastern Africa. The Hague.
Baier, Stephen, and Paul Lovejoy. 1975. "The Desert-Side Economy of the Central Sudan." The International Journal of African Historical Studies, 7:551-81.
Blair, James A. 1968. "York Settlement After One and a Half Centuries." Sierra Leone Geographical Journal 12:27-44.
British Parliamentary Papers, Vol. 52. 1844.

British Parliamentary Papers, Vol. 60. 1899.   Chalmers
     Report.
Church, R.J. Harrison. 1957. West Africa: A Study of
     the Environment and of Man's Use of It. London.
Church Missionary Society Papers. 1880-1885. G3.Al/Ll4.
     London.
Cohen, Abner. 1969. Custom and Politics in Urban Africa:
     A Study of Hausa Migrants in Yoruba Towns. Berkeley.
     _____. 1971. "The Politics of Ritual Secrecy." Man
     6: 427-448.
Coker, Fariana. 1976. Interview of 3 March.
Coker, Miranda. 1976. Interview of 17 Sept.
Colonial Office. 1898. 267/437, Conf. 10, No. 2. Col.
     Cardew, 3-9 Feb. 1898.
Cox-George, N.A. 1961. Finance and Development in West
     Africa: The Sierra Leone Experience. London.
     _____. 1960. "Report on African Participation in the
     Commerce of Sierra Leone and the Government State-
     ment Thereon." Freetown.
Crowder, Michael.  1968. West Africa Under Colonial Rule.
     London.
Dorjahn, V.R., and Christopher Fyfe.  "Landlord and
     Stranger: Change in Tenancy Relations in Sierra
     Leone." 1962. Journal of African History 3:391-97.
Fried, Morton H. 1967. "On the Concepts of 'Tribe' and
     Tribal Society." In J. Helm, Essays on the Problem
     of Tribe, Proceedings of the American Ethnological
     Society.
Grace, John. 1975. Domestic Slavery in West Africa with
     Particular Reference to the Sierra Leone Protec-
     torate, 1896-1927. New York.
Haaland, Gunnar. 1969. "Economic Determinants in Ethnic
     Processes." In F. Barth, Ethnic Groups and Boun-
     daries: The Social Organization of Culture Dif-
     ference. Boston.
Harrell-Bond, Barbara. 1975. Modern Marriage in Sierra
     Leone: A Study of the Professional Group. The Hague.
Hodder,  B.W., and U.J. Ukwu. 1969. Markets in West
     Africa. Ibadan.
Hopkins, Anthony G. 1973. An Economic History of West
     Africa. New York.
Hotobah-During, I.C. 1976. Interviews of 25 May, 21 Sept.
Howard, Allen. 1966. "The Role of Freetown in the Com-
     mercial Life of Sierra Leone." In C. Fyfe and E.
     Jones, eds., Freetown: A Symposium. Freetown.
Ingham, E.G. 1895. Sierra Leone After a Hundred Years.
     London.
Jones, Theodore. 1976. Interview of 21 Dec.
Leighton, Neil O. 1971. "Lebanese Middlemen in Sierra
     Leone:The Case of a Non-indigenous Trading
     Minority and Their Role in Political Development."
     Ph.D. dissertation, Indiana University.

Lovejoy, Paul Ellsworth. 1973. "The Hausa Kola Trade
    (1700-1900): A Commercial System in the Continental
    Exchange of West Africa." Ph.D. dissertation,
    University of Wisconsin.
Meiers, Suzanne, and Igor Kopytoff. 1977. "African
    'Slavery' As an Institution of Marginality." In
    Slavery in Africa: Historical and Anthropological
    Perspectives, ed. Meiers and Kopytoff. Madison, Wis.
Native Affairs Letterbook. 1894-1895. No. 115: Parkes to
    Alikali Bubu, 10 Dec. 1894; Parkes to Alimani Bubu,
    11 June 1894; No. 119: Parkes to Smith, 25 Nov.
    1895.
Palmer, Bure. 1976,1977. Interviews of 5, 28, 29 Dec.,
    2 Jan.
Peterson, John. 1969. Province of Freedom: A History of
    Sierra Leone, 1787-1870. London.
Porter, Arthur T. 1963. Creoledom: A Study of the
    Development of Freetown Society. Oxford.
Reade, Winwood. 1873. The African Sketch-Book. London.
Sierra Leone Weekly News. 1887, 1920.
Skinner, David, and Barbara E. Harrell-Bond. 1977.
    "Misunderstandings Arising From the Use of the
    Term 'Creole' in the Literature on Sierra Leone."
    Africa 47:305-20.
Smith, George. 1976. Interview of 22 Dec.
Spitzer, Leo. 1974. The Creoles of Sierra Leone: Re-
    sponses to Colonialism, 1870-1949. Madison.
Sudarkasa, Niara. 1973. Where Women Work: A Study of
    Women in the Marketplace and in the Home. Ann Arbor,
    Mich.
Webster, J.B. 1974. "Political Activity in British West
    Africa." In J. Ajayi and M. Crowder, History of West
    Africa 1:568-95. London.
White, E. Frances. 1978. "Creole Women Traders in Sierra
    Leone: An Economic and Social History, 1792-1945."
    Ph.D. dissertation, Boston University.
Winder, R. Bayly. 1962. "The Lebanese in West Africa."
    Comparative Studies in Sociology and History 4:
    296-333.
Wyse, Akintola J.G. 1977. "Sierra Leone Creoles, Their
    History and Historians." Journal of African Studies
    4:228-39.

## 2. Control of Land, Labor, and Capital in Rural Southern Sierra Leone

*Carol P. MacCormack*

INTRODUCTION

Compared with women in other areas of the world, women in the coastal Sherbro area of Sierra Leone have overt political power and relatively high social status. Today women are paramount chiefs, section chiefs, town chiefs, heads of cognate descent groups, heads of sodalities, and up to 59 percent of residential compounds in villages are headed by women (MacCormack, 1976).
There is no single cause for their high status, but a set of variables work in their favor. In previous publications I have explored political, social structural, and religious variables (1972, 1974, 1975, 1976, 1977, 1978, 1979, 1981). This paper explores the economic variable, concentrating on control and utilization of the basic factors of production: land, labor, and capital. Because of the structure of Sherbro society, some high-status women are able to transact in all the things human societies value most: rights over land, labor, and capital; and rights over people in marriage, clientage, and, in the past, slavery.
The economy is not fully monetized, although there is a range of capital assets that are not consumed immediately but are used to achieve enhanced production in the future. Land is the corporate estate of cognatic descent groups and individuals have usufructry right to it but cannot buy and sell it. Labor is a social obligation regulated by one's social status in the community. For these reasons, this discussion of economics must necessarily be largely about the nature of kin groups, rural-to-rural migration, and the way clients and their descendents obtain rights to the basic factors of production.
Data for the paper are from ten years' intermittent field work in this area, and especially from recent field work in a sample of six villages chosen because

they engage primarily in (1) land-extensive upland rice
cultivation, (2) labor-intensive swamp rice cultivation,
and (3) relatively capital-intensive coastal fishing.
Social and economic information was collected on 1,500
people, the sample deliberately including men and women,
high-status "aristocrats" who control land, low-status
"strangers," the young, and the elderly.

The physical environment is low lying and swampy,
well within the tsetse fly belt, where cattle are of
little economic and social importance.  One hundred
eighty inches of rain fall in the May-to-October wet
season, and tropical diseases take their toll.  Population density is now 91 per square mile and was considerably less in the past.  Post-menopausal women on average
have given birth to 8.5 children, with 3.9 surviving
(Dow, 1972; MacCormack, 1982).  Although women are losing
more than half the children they bear, the population is
nevertheless increasing, putting pressure on land resources.  The response is that which Boserup (1965) has
suggested.  People are beginning to use the land more
intensively, and less extensively.


SHERBRO WOMEN AND THE DIVISION OF LABOR

In every one of the 191 residential compounds surveyed, the adult women were economically active.  Their
role in production, physical reproduction, and maintenance of the society was publicly acknowledged by men
and women.  Beyond the domestic services women provide,
all contributed to farming, fish processing, or trading.
They worked within the joint residential compound, which
is the basic unit of production.  Men's and women's work
is categorized by culturally defined division of labor.
Men's work and women's work is not entirely arbitrary,
nor a pure cultural relative.  Men tend to do dangerous
tasks, such as cutting and burning the forest, climbing
palm trees, or fishing in deep water. Women take physical
risks in childbearing.  Because women's fertility is
highly valued in this area of tropical disease and high
infant mortality, and only women can give birth, work-
related dangers are spared them, but work itself is not.
They plant, weed, harvest, store and process food.  They
also dry fish, make salt and process vegetable oils,
and market a wide variety of products.

Women "cook," which for Sherbros is a richly poly-
semic term.  For example, women cook salt by evaporating
sea brine.  One stage in making palm oil is the boiling
of palm fruits to break down the fibers of the pericarp
in order to squeeze the oil free.  Coconuts are grated,
then parched in early stages of coconut oil making.  Dis-

tilling palm wine into concentrated spirits is "cooking" it.  Rice must be parboiled to split the husk, then pounded to remove the husks before it is ready to be marketed.  Fish are smoked and dried over a fire to pre- serve them for marketing.  By cultural definition, only women, not men, cook, thus insuring women's domain over a wide range of productive activities and marketable goods.  Indeed, they dominate the local markets.

Although women have a clear domain of vital produc- tive activities and opportunities to market surpluses, they are no more economically autonomous than men.  Men rely on women to finish off the process of food produc- tion by "cooking," and women rely on men to initiate the productive process.  Men do the heavy, dangerous work of cutting and burning before the soil is ready to plant. They climb palm trees to cut the fruit before women can begin to process the oil.  They go into the sea to catch the fish women will preserve and market.  In the total productive process, from raw materials to marketable product, women are usually dependent upon men for initi- ating the process, somewhat compromising their economic autonomy.  But even if men initiate the labor process, they are as utterly dependent upon women to do female tasks as women are dependent upon men.  This culturally created interdependence accounts in part for men and wo- men's desire to marry in order to be fully adult and fully social, even though the pull to remain within the emo- tional security of their natal household group is great for both males and females.


RESIDENTIAL COMPOUNDS AND THEIR HEADS:  BASIC UNITS OF PRODUCTION

The residential compound, the basic unit of produc- tion, averages eleven people.  Although most compounds contain some non-kin who are clients or wards, the core residents are related by cognatic descent or mar- riage.  The head of the compound is the eldest member of the core group (unless ill or senile), who may be a man or a woman.  If husband and wife are residing together, the husband will usually be the head, but there are rare cases where a wife of strong character and ability, liv- ing in her natal village, will be acknowledged as head even though her husband also resides  in the compound.

With polygynous marriages, the question of who heads the compound is a bit clouded.  Some men have all wives residing with them in the same compound.  In this kind of household, a senior wife might set her junior wives up in their own businesses.  Some men, however, have wives in different villages.  A wife in a fishing village,

for example, might supply dried fish to a co-wife in a
farming village.  The wife in the farming area would
reciprocate by supplying rice and other foods to her
co-wife to market in the fishing village.  If the husband
regularly resides in both households on an alternating
basis, I have counted him as head of both households.
But in households where the husband resides at some distance, has not visited for years, and does not send
wealth into the household, I have counted the resident
wife, who manages the household, as its head.  In the
gray area are wives whose husbands live in another area
but who send occasional wealth to be used for hiring
male labor, or send one or more male client "strangers"
to live in the compound to provide labor for masculine
productive tasks.  I have tended to count these as women-
headed compounds because the wife has day-to-day responsibility for managing land, labor, and capital.
     By these definitions, 18 percent of residential
compounds in fishing villages were headed by women, 23
percent of compounds in farming villages were headed by
women, and 59 percent of Sherbro compounds in the chiefdom capital were headed by women. The latter statistic
is explained by the presence of aristocratic elderly
women who have either never left their natal village or
have returned there in old age, a point I will elaborate
later in the paper.


FISHING VILLAGES AND RURAL-TO-RURAL MIGRATION

     The task of writing about productive and distribu-
tive activities of men and women is easier in communities
where the process is partially monetized, and money
serves to some extent as a measure of value for goods and
for alternative uses of labor time.  The coastal fishing
village of Katta, which mushroomed to over 1,000 inhabitants in the 1960s, the largest town in Kagboro Chiefdom,
is very much within the cash nexus.
     In 1976, I surveyed one-half of the village, a sam-
ple of 44 residential compounds with a total population
of 530 people.  The smallest compound contained a soli-
tary male shop trader, the largest contained 38 people,
the average was 12 people.  Eight of the 44 compounds
(18 percent) were headed by women, all primarily traders
in fish and other foods.  Of the male heads of compounds,
there was only one farmer, and the rest were fishermen
or traders.  Only 4 (9 percent) of the compounds were
headed by Sherbros; the rest were founded by first-
generation migrants of other, mostly northern, ethnicity.
     Immigration continues as individuals, in the social
category of "strangers", attach themselves as clients to

a household head.  Of the 44 households, 35 (80 percent)
had resident adult non-kin "strangers".  Households had
as few as 1, as many as 30, but on average 6.5 resident
clients.  Of a total of 156 codable clients 14 (9 percent)
were women, all without resident husbands, all engaging
in buying or selling a product, usually fish. The male
clients totaled 142, but only 27 (19 percent) of them had
a wife.  These mobile men were mostly young and unmarried.
The bulk of male clients gave labor, especially in fishing crews, to their patron, rather than trading autonomously, as women did.  Some married clients hoped in time
to establish their own residential compound.

Two kinds of fishing boat were used, the dugout
canoe and locally made planked boats.  The former will
accommodate only the owner and a helper, but the larger
boats require a crew of from six to ten men.  Only men
fish, turning the catch over to women in a formal financial transaction.  Only women smoke-dry fish and sell it
to long-distance traders.  One or two women can dry, pack,
and sell all the fish a crew of six to ten men catch.
It is not surprising, then, that there is a surplus of
adult men over adult women.  In all fishing communities
surveyed, on average there are 1.56 adult men to every
one woman.  The ratio is reversed in farming villages
where there are, on average, 1.49 adult women for every
one adult man.  Female labor encompasses more tasks and
constitutes a larger proportion of labor time in farming
households.

The ratio of dependants, being too young or too old
to work, to able bodied workers, is low in fishing villages.  Only 24 percent of the residents were dependent,
compared to an average of 42 percent in the farming
villages surveyed.  This difference can be explained by
(1) the number of unmarried young adult male migrants in
fishing villages, (2) the nature of fishing work where
child labor is not useful, and (3) the fact that some
wives of polygynous male compound heads were literally
farmed out to inland villages, residing there with their
young children.  In calculating polygyny ratios, I
counted only resident co-wives, since men tend to boast
about the number of wives they have, perhaps inflating
the number by reference to putative absent wives.  In
farming villages, male compound heads had, on average,
1.56 resident wives; in fishing villages they had, on
average, 1.26 resident wives.

As interesting as this synchronic statistical picture is, we need models to explain the dynamics of rural-
to-rural migration and the absorption of immigrants.  At
one level, people come to the coast to maximize profit,
to get as great a return on their labor as possible.  If
they prosper, they augment human labor power with capital

TABLE 2.1
Comparison of Fishing and Farming Villages

| | Ratio, Adult men: women | Percentage dependents | Polygyny ratio, male heads:wives | Percentage women heads |
|---|---|---|---|---|
| Fishing | 1.56 : 1 | 24 | 1 : 1.26 | 18 |
| Farming | 1 : 1.26 | 42 | 1 : 1.49 | 23 |

goods, such as petrol engines for their boats or lorry
transport, and hope for a good return on their capital
investment.  But this Weberian model of rational economic
activity does not tell us enough.

In fishing, as in farming, there is a strict division
of labor based upon gender.  Men fish, women smoke-dry
and sell the fish.  Men cut and burn the bush, women
plant and weed.  Women are married  at about age seventeen, after puberty and initiation into the Sande (Bondo)
society (MacCormack, 1979).  Men are sexually mature by
about age seventeen but marry at about age twenty-nine
or thirty, when they have accumulated bridewealth.  As
soon as women can do adult labor, they are taken up in
marriage to older men, where they begin to work within
the division of labor in their residential compound, or
trade.  Female wage labor is not marketed.  The only way
a man can have a viable household is to marry female
labor, but first he must accumulate a brideprice of from
Ь25 to Ь60 sterling.  As these young men begin to accumulate wealth, it is drained away from them in a male per
capita tax of Ь2 per annum.  They also tend to incur
court fines for crimes against property and for sexual
misconduct, some becoming indentured servants for as
long as seven years in order to pay off court fines.
Not all young men wander about looking for a shortcut to
bridewealth.  Some remain in their parents' compound, do
not receive wages, but receive the gift of bridewealth
in time.  Many hope to shorten that waiting period by
going to Freetown, the mines, the swamp rice farming
areas, or fishing areas to accumulate wealth quickly.
Some begin to drift about to evade the tax collector;
others, after drifting, begin to look for someone to
feed them, especially in the preharvest rainy season,
the hungry season.

Heads of compounds take these drifting men in, in a
formalized patron-client relationship.  The patron must
feed them, give them a place in his house to sleep, pay
their head tax, and pay their court fines if they are in
trouble.  He/she sees that they are taught to fish or do
swamp rice farming or learn other skills. Clients are
usually not paid a wage.  In fishing villages, they may
only be maintained, or they may be "dashed" some pocket
money if there has been an especially lucky catch.  Or
a group of six to ten men, constituting a boat crew,
may be allowed by their patron to divide the catch on
one day a week among themselves.  If the patron judges
some of the male clients to be "serious" and mature, he/
she may pay their bridewealth in order to encourage them
to settle down.  Commonly, the marriage will be to a
junior kinswoman of the patron; the husband resides uxori-
locally, continuing to give his labor to the joint household of his parent-in-law (former patron).  Thus, some

worthy young men who begin to drift first become client
"strangers", then are absorbed by marriage, becoming
affinal kin.  Since the Sherbro have a cognatic descent
system, the children of the young couple, by taking
descent group identity through their mother, become sem
tha che, "heads of the place" or "owners of the land."
This is especially important where the use of communal
corporate farm land, or the right to high office, is at
stake.


ANALYSIS OF FISHING VILLAGE COMPOUNDS

    All of the 8 women who were heads of residential
compounds in Katta were traders.  Two smoke-dried fish
and sold it to dealers.  One was a long-range trader,
taking fish to inland markets.  Two traded in dried fish
and foods.  The other 3 traded in foods and petty commodities, one specializing in locally distilled palm
wine spirits.
    Of the 37 male heads of residential compounds, 20
(54 percent) were primarily fishermen, 13 (35 percent)
were primarily traders, 3 (8 percent) were tailors, and
1 (3 percent) was a farmer.
    The poorest woman compound head was an elderly
woman, originally from Freetown.  For years she had been
trading fish from Katta to Freetown, a distance of about
200 miles by road.  She had become too old and ill to
take the rigors of long-range trading and had settled in
Katta.  Although she had kin in Freetown, inflation had
made the cost of living too high for her to settle
there.  She had made an arrangement to live in a house
she did not own.  A man and his wife and daughter also
lived in the house, farmed, and were financially autonomous.  Two fishermen also lodged in the house.  The
woman did not feed them, but they sold their catches of
fish to her.  She dried it and sold it.  She also made
rice cakes that she sold in the village.
    The wealthiest woman head of a compound was a
widow, with resident adult daughter, adult son, daughter-
in-law, their 2 children, and 5 fishermen lodgers.  Of
a total of 11 residents, 9 were able-bodied workers.
The household head owned the house, a fish-drying house
(banda), boat, petrol engine, nets, and other equipment.
Her son and the lodgers constituted the fishing crew.
Her son paid his mother for use of the boat and sold all
his catch to her. The catch was smoke-dried by the
daughter and daughter-in-law and was sold to dealers by
the household head.
    The poorest man to head a residence was a solitary
migrant trader in petty commodities. The wealthiest

man to head a compound was barely middle-aged, with 3
rather young wives and only 3 dependent children.  His
brother's wife and her 2 dependent children also lived
in the household.  There were 20 fishermen, 4 wives of
fishermen, and 4 other adult laborers in the compound,
making a total of 38 people, 33 of whom were able-bodied
workers.

The head owned two planked boats, two engines, nets,
and two houses.  The 20 fishermen constituted two crews,
and all the catch was dried and sold by the head's wives,
with assistance from the sister-in-law, under the direction of the head wife.

This fisherman was heavily capitalized and was having
a third boat built at a cost of Ł1,565 sterling.  The
fisherman spoke at some length of his risks.  Submerged
rocks snapped propeller shafts on his engines.  Sharks
tore the nets.  His operating costs ran to Ł50 per day,
but some days he had bad luck and caught little.  In the
rainy season the catch was generally poor, and in the
transitional seasons (March and September) there could be
sudden  storms, high winds, or fog.

In 1970, two other men were the most wealthy in
Katta.  In 1976 they spoke of many nonproductive dependents, capital losses, and inflation.  In two and a half
years' time the cost of petrol, oil, engines, nets, and
other equipment had roughly trebled, but the selling
price for fish had barely doubled.  They could not simply
pass on additional costs to the consumer because inland
households which bought fish had not increased their
purchasing power by the same increment.  Both men had
returned to their natal village to farm swamp rice.
There they enjoyed the prestige of elders and felt that
the return on household labor was much more certain than
it was in fishing.  Because of world marketing agreements,
especially for petroleum products, which they could not
control, they had been forced back toward a type of production based upon human energy power alone.


HUSBAND-WIFE ACCOUNTS

For most households, the level of capital accumulation was quite low.  A fisherman with a canoe and nets
had an average daily catch worth Ł1 to Ł3.  On only four
days in a month in the dry season, the best fishing time
of the year, was a fisherman's catch worth Ł10 or more.
For a fisherman with planked boat and engine, who could
go out as far as 10 miles, a very good catch was worth
Ł100 to Ł120, but of course his expenses and risks were
greater.

A wife had first claim on the fish her husband

caught.  She would either pay him cash on the beach for
his fish, or, more commonly, they would count the catch,
she would dry it, sell it, and return a portion of the
profit to her husband.  A quantity of wet fish worth
Ь100 was worth about Ь140 when it was dried and packed.
If the woman could not obtain that margin of profit from
the dealers who came to her, she might transport the fish
by lorry to an inland market and attempt to market it
herself, thus protecting herself from possible exploitation by middlemen/women.  Some wives also sought to buy
the catch of other fishermen and augment their business.
The more fishermen lodgers in the household, the better
her potential supply of fish.  A woman without a husband
would attempt to attract as many fishermen clients into
her house as possible.  Even when the fisherman was not
a woman's husband, brother, son, or client lodger, the
trading relationship between her and her supplier tended
to be personalized and multiplex. After the bargain had
been struck on the beach, the woman would send down
cigarettes, palm wine, or cooked food, "encouraging" a
regular supplier.

     In the majority of cases, husband and wife kept
their capital funds independently.  In some cases, however, when husband and wife had joint goals, such as an
improved boat, they pooled their earnings.  Both would
benefit from the larger catches.  More commonly, the
husband would meet expenses for equipment replacement,
petrol, labor, and capital investment from his fund, and
the wife would meet expenses for firewood, haulage, and
perhaps investment in a new fish-drying house from her
fund of profit.  In some cases, the wife loaned money to
her husband for capital investment in improved fishing
equipment.


CO-WIVES

     Cooperation among co-wives, rather than rivalry and
destructive jealousy, is a moral value explicitly taught
to each woman during her puberty initiation into Sande,
the pervasive women's secret society (MacCormack, 1979).
Wives are precisely ranked, the head wife being the first
wife married.  In a polygynous household, the husband
is obliged to sell his fish to his head wife if she
wishes to deal in fish.  If the catches are large, from
a planked boat, there may be enough work for all wives
to have a role in drying, transporting, and marketing
fish.  Usually, however, junior wives do complementary
work.  In some households a junior wife (wives) resided
in a farming village, sending grain, fruit, and vegetable
goods to Katta.  The wife in Katta reciprocated with
dried fish and sometimes petty trade goods, such as soap,

kerosene, and matches.  If both wives resided in Katta,
a head wife might give seed capital to her junior wife,
to enable her to trade in goods from the veranda of the
house, or to work as an itinerate trader.  Or, the
junior wife might be helped to begin a business of providing cooked food for unmarried migrant fishermen, or
distilled spirits (omoli).

Head wives who had assisted their junior wives in
this manner were careful to explain that the initial
capital was a gift, not a managed investment.  They did
not inquire about the fledgling business, and if the
younger woman squandered the wealth on clothing, the
older woman should not be angry.  If, however, the wealth
were wisely managed and it began to produce greater
wealth in the future, the junior wife should give gifts
from the profits to her benefactor.  An ideal gift was
tins of tomato paste or other imported foods, which could
be used in the communal cooking pot, giving pleasure to
the entire compound.  Some young wives, of course, fell
short of the ideal and were spoken of as lazy and will-
ful, gossip being a device for social control.  The extreme individualism of the Western entrepreneur, as an
ideal type, is not encouraged in this society, which is
organized on the principle of corporate descent groups
and corporate responsibility.

Because women marry at about age seventeen and men
marry at about age thirty, the chance of a woman's becoming widowed and gaining control of an established compound is great.  Not all older women are financially
successful, though.  The poorest households in my combined sample were those headed by an old woman and a
single female companion or lodger.  Those were widows
who had no surviving children to feed them, who had lost
the strength to farm and supported themselves by making
baskets and accepting food from neighbors or perhaps
an  adult they once fostered as a child.

In farming villages, some widows well into their
sixties  continued to farm without male labor, if necessary.  They lacked the strength to hoe up the heavy mud
for planting padi rice, nor could they cut and burn
heavy bush fallow to prepare ground for upland rice, but
they did plant cassava and groundnuts in partially exhausted land that was easy to clear.  They then bartered
surplus cassava and groundnuts for rice, vegetable oils,
and other needs.  They were surprisingly cheerful and
dignified, notwithstanding their relative poverty.

Nor were all men secure in old age.  Ideally, a man
would like enough wealth to marry a second, young, strong
wife who would provision the household when he weakened.
But some men had never been able to acquire enough wealth
for even a single wife and had no legal rights over

children to sustain them in old age. The best hope for
these men was to be attached to a household in a clientage
relationship, with the moral connotation of quasi-kin-
ship, and to be as useful to their patrons as possible.

FARMING VILLAGES AND RURAL-TO-RURAL MIGRATION

Farmers in the Sherbro country cannot produce without use rights to land, the corporate estate of cognatic
descent groups. All immigrants must become clients to
land-controlling aristocrats. Of the farming villages
surveyed, Marthyn had the greatest in-migration. The
village is sited on a ridge of dry land between a vast
saline mangrove swamp along one of the tributaries of
the Kagboro River on one side, and a vast fresh-water
swamp on the other. Salt-resistant strains of rice
allow both saline and fresh-water swamps to be cultivated
for padi. The black organic mud can be kept under con-
tinuous cultivation, and yields per acre were often more
than twice the yield from upland rice farms. The price
for rice being offered by the Sierra Leone Rice Corporation was perceived as an opportunity for cash income
beyond household subsistence.

Seventeen (35 percent) of the 49 residential compounds had at least one non-kin male client in residence
at the time of survey. Some hard-working migrant men acquired bridewealth in as little as three years. Some
married a woman and set up their own "stranger" compound,
continuing to pay tribute (mata) to their patron in return for the use of land. If a man was fortunate enough
to marry a woman from the land-controlling descent group,
the migrant passed from the social and statistical category of "stranger" to "affinal kinsman." Twenty-seven
(55 percent) of the 49 households in Marthyn were headed
by "owners of the land" (sem tha che). That is, the members of the compound were using ancestral land of the
dominant descent group by genealogical right. The other
22 households (45 percent) were clients who gave tribute
(mata) in return for a client's right to use the land.
However, among the 55 percent of compounds that were in
the category of "owners of the land," I counted compounds
headed by former "stranger" men, but the household was
using land by genealogical right through the head's wife,
mother, father's mother, or some matrilateral kinship
link. Many of those compounds were headed by men in the
early stages of absorption into the dominant cognatic
descent group.

Another indicator of the extent of rural-to-rural
migration into this swamp rice growing area is the percentage of household heads who identified themselves as

being of Sherbro ethnicity.  Thirty-one (63 percent) of
the 49 compound heads were Sherbro by self-definition.
That included Sherbros who had recently arrived from
other parts of the Sherbro ethnic area, or people who had
a foreign patronymic but spoke the Sherbro language
and had a Sherbro mother.  Others, especially some Muslims
from the north, wished to maintain their distinctiveness
and self-defined themselves as non-Sherbro even though
they were born in Marthyn and spoke the Sherbro language.

DIVISION OF LABOR IN FARMING

     In farming villages there is an explicit division of
labor based upon gender and age.  Girls below the age of
twelve or thirteen, and boys below the age of sixteen or
seventeen were not considered to be strong enough, nor
to have enough experience and good judgment to do the
full range of adult farming activities (MacCormack, 1981).
Elderly people were not expected to work hard, but to be
cared for by their children.
     Table 2.2 indicates the division of labor in farming
tasks based upon gender.  This table is abstracted from
the responses of 50 secondary school pupils, aged seventeen to twenty-five.  When asked which parent gave them
tasks to do, they named their mother or other senior
woman of the compound as the person who gave them domestic work and field work such as weeding, and their
father or other senior man of the compound as the person
who gave them tasks which are men's work.
     All able-bodied men and women worked to provision
the granary of their residential compound.  Resident
married sons and daughters of the head might make their
own farms and keep their own granary within a parent's
compound, but they also contributed heavily to the central storehouse if the parent was old or ill.  Decisions
to sell rice  from the granary for bridewealth, secret
society initiations, school fees, mortuary ceremonies,
court fines, and gifts to kin were the most emotional
decisions taken.  Ideally, a husband and his head wife
consulted together and reached a consensus decision on
such matters, but only one person actually keeps the
key to the granary.  In an attempt to quantify economic
decision making, I asked, in all farming compounds, who
kept the key.  In 51 percent of the households it was the
husband, in 49 percent it was the wife.  People explained
that if a wife had the personal qualities of restraint
and good judgment and was respected by her junior wives,
she would have it.  If there was rivalry or dissension
between co-wives, the husband would keep the key, unless
he was judged to be a wastrel.  Since unfortunate com-

TABLE 2.2
Men's and Women's Work

| Men | Women | Both |
|-----|-------|------|
| Cut, burn bush | Plant cassava and | Scare birds |
| Hoe swamp for | sweep potatoes* | Harvest rice |
| planting | Transplant rice | Build houses |
| Hoe mounds for | seedlings* | Make fish nets |
| cassava and sweet | Weed upland farm | Distill spirits |
| potatoes* | Harvest vegetables | Market |
| Broadcast seed* | Plant kitchen garden | Make medicine |
| Hoe seeds into | Thresh rice | |
| land* | Parboil rice | |
| Plant rice nursery | Husk rice | |
| Fence farm | Dry and preserve crops | |
| Set traps in fences | Make dry season garden | |
| Make farm shelter | in swamp | |
| Cut palm fruits | Farm groundnuts* | |
| Build boats | Collect wild food and | |
| Fish at sea | medicine* | |
| Tap palm wine | Make vegetable oil | |
| Tailoring | Care for young and old | |
| Blacksmithing | Keep compound clean | |
| | Make mats and baskets | |
| | Fish in rivers | |
| | Dry fish | |
| | Make salt | |
| | Cook | |

*Other gender may do this.

pounds were carried by the village at large, there was
often subtle extra-domestic pressure brought to bear on
the decision about who was to keep the key to the food
store.
    Women not only produced for the joint granary but
might make a supplemental farm, or dry season garden
in swampy land. All wealth from those extra farms was
theirs for consumption or investment. Along tidal rivers
women distilled salt and made coconut oil. Women also
made palm oil and a number of other products, which they
marketed. Some upland rice farming communities in the
survey were not self-sufficient in grain production, and
men as well as women readily explained that women's
extra labor in salt or vegetable oil making allowed the

village to meet its subsistence needs.  Women produced
and sold salt or edible oil for cash, and used the cash
to buy rice, cassava, and other foods to make up the
margin of subsistence.

Cash crops such as coffee and cocoa did not grow
well in this swampy area, but where they were grown,
men could not take the crop to market without some female
labor, especially in drying and cleaning the fruits.  The
husband might give his wife or wives part of the crop or
part of the cash sale, but if he did not, women commonly
stole some of the crop they were drying.

Women also generated their own wealth by marketing
a wide range of foods and petty commodities on the veran-
das of their houses, or by walking from village to village  as itinerate traders, or by traveling by lorry to a
provincial town with a market.  One example will suffice.
In 1976, the value of a bushel of rice at harvest was
about Ƀ2, rising to Ƀ3 in the preharvest rainy season.  A
bushel contains 6 dozen "cups" (small Blue Band margarine
tins) of rice.  The price per "cup" ranged from 5 pence
sterling at harvest to 7 or 9 pence in the preharvest
scarce period.  Selling rice at 5 pence per "cup," the
trader received Ƀ3.60, a profit of Ƀ1.60 per bushel.  If
she had enough capital to buy a year's supply at harvest,
her profits in the rainy season would be much greater.


DESCENT GROUP HEAD:   RIGHTS OVER LAND AND PEOPLE

In every Sherbro village there is a dominant descent
group.  It originated with a conqueror, or a first
settler of the area.  Historically, the first settlers
have been women as well as men (MacCormack, 1976).  The
descendents, who are resident on descent group land,
constitute the effective membership of each cognatic
group.  Each localized descent group has a head, a notable
elder, often its eldest living member.  That head may be
a man or a woman.  In two of the five farming villages
surveyed, the head of the dominant descent group was a
woman.

In this organization of cognatic descent, both men
and women are named and revered ancestors.  Where there
is considerable in-migration by "stranger" men, the women
they marry, if they are aristocratic "owners of the
land," will become focal ancestresses to all the descendents from such marriages.  By virtue of descent from
that woman, the descendents will claim rights to land,
chiefship, and other restricted resources.  She becomes
a focal ancestress for her descendents, specifically
named in ancestral ceremonies.  If women, as well as
men, are respected ancestors, it follows that they will

also be respected elders, enjoying some political power
and control of resources.

The head of a descent group, in consultation with
other elders, allocates use rights to corporate farm
land.  Members of the descent group have a birth right
to use the land.  "Strangers" give a client's gift to
the head of the descent group to beseech patronage and
every year give a bushel or two of rice as tribute
(mata) to the head of the descent group.  It is disposable
wealth and potential investment capital for the head.

All the women descent group heads I know of had
once married and moved away from their natal village for
a time.  But they returned in old age with the status
of an elder.  When they were chosen by their descent
group to be its head, they became "principal persons,"
and as such they were always officials in the local chapter of Sande (Bondo), the women's secret society.  Some
girls were wards in the elder's compound before and
after initiation; she controls the product of their labor
during that period.  The woman was not sole marriage
guardian over them but usually consulted with their parents before a marriage was made.  Even so, she had considerable prerogative in making marriages that would
link the elder, through the girls, to other politically
powerful families.  Or she might reward loyal, hard-
working client men with such wives (MacCormack [Hoffer]
1974, 1979).  Those elite rural women, in their multiple
capacities of compound head, descent group head, and
Sande chapter official, control access to land, organize
labor, receive tribute, and make marriage alliances.


HISTORICAL DIALECTIC

Women in this structure of cognatic descent and age
status can command the basic means of production, especially farming land, and can even invest in such things as
fishing boats.  Because they have clearly defined
spheres of economic activity, especially those in the conceptual category of "cooking," they have potential investment assets.  They have markets in which to realize
these assets.  In addition to incipient capital, they
also have rights to land and control some labor.  Therefore, it is difficult for men, as a social category, to
appropriate the product of women's labor.

The most common investment women made was in school
fees for their children.  In 1976, the cost of tuition,
uniforms, and supplies in the small Kagboro Chiefdom
secondary school was about ₤40 per year.  Women invested
in their children in other ways as well.  One woman made
coconut oil, saved, and invested in a canoe for her son.
He had become a fisherman with a crew of three.  By in-

vesting in their children, women invest in their own
security in old age.

In 1976, some women, as well as some men, invested
in a relatively heavily capitalized farming venture.  The
local member of parliament arranged, through the district
agricultural agent, for a tractor to be brought into a
grassland area of the chiefdom.  A deposit of ₤500 was
raised by people buying into the scheme.  They paid ₤5
per plowed acre, one-half in advance and the remainder
after harvest.  Use of land was free; the people made
a public decision to set aside the distinction between
"strangers" and "owners of the land" for this venture.
About thirty people bought in, and a total of 134 conti-
guous acres were cultivated and planted.  The smallest
plot was 1 acre, the largest was 16 acres, the mode was
3 acres.

Fertilizer cost ₤2.50 per bag, and one bag per acre
should have been applied.  Some labor was hired at 20
pence a day plus food, but most was supplied by members,
clients, and wards in each residential compound.  The
cost of seed rice was ₤1.50 per acre, plus 25 pence
for transport.  Total cash expenses, excluding labor,
was ₤9.25 per acre.  The yield was about 15 bushels per
acre.


TABLE 2.3
Yield on Capital Investment, per Acre

| Market price per bushel | | Gross | Net* | % Profit |
|---|---|---|---|---|
| At harvest | ₤1.25 x 15 bu. per acre = | ₤18.75 | ₤9.50 | 103 |
| Late dry season | ₤2.00 x 15 bu. per acre = | ₤30.00 | 20.75 | 224 |
| Rainy season | ₤3.00 x 15 bu. per acre = | ₤45.00 | 35.75 | 386 |

*Minus ₤9.25 expenses per acre.


Those with enough cash to buy into the venture and
to withhold rice sales until the hungry season made
about 386 percent profit on their investment.  In terms
of social class formation, with the use of capital tools

such as a tractor, those with some wealth become very
much wealthier, and those who cannot buy in become
relatively poorer. In regard to gender, about a third
of those who bought into this scheme were women, who
have traditionally had their own small capital fund.

Another socioeconomic conclusion is that capital
goods available for purchase compensate for male labor
but not for female labor. Tractors do the equivalent of
cutting, burning, and hoeing the land. Petrol engines
do the equivalent of paddling a boat. When a productive
process is partially mechanized, labor bottlenecks will
result. In the tractor cultivation scheme, vast additional acreage was planted, but women then had to work
very, very long hours to weed, harvest, thresh, and mill
the rice. Women were able to tell me clearly the kinds
of machines they wanted, especially rice mills and oil
crushers, but they were either not available in the
country or were too expensive. Women told me that they
had priced rice-milling machines in Freetown. The
cheapest cost ₤3,000. Since the cost of bridewealth was
between ₤25 and ₤60, a woman's best strategy was to produce a surplus that she and her husband jointly might use
to acquire another co-wife. Additional wives have the
advantage of not only producing, but reproducing the work
force and assuring continuity to descent groups.

With the current price for rice being offered by
the government's Rice Corporation, urban elites had
perceived that considerable profits might be made from
farming. They were strongly advocating a national legislative act that would privatize all farming land. Where
now all men and women in the Sherbro country have a
birth right to use land that is the corporate estate of
their descent group, with such legislation a class of
the dispossessed, a landless proletariat, would be
created. There is not an adequate industrial sector to
offer wage employment to that proletariat. For women,
the process would be that so ably described by Boserup
(1970). Specifically, all Sherbro women who want to farm
now have the use of land. They work where they live, or,
if they trade, they take the baby with them on their
back. They may also leave children in the care of co-
wives or other women in large residential compounds.
Proletarianized, they would have to seek wage work away
from living space, and small urban households do not
facilitate cooperative child care arrangements. Few
rural women have formal educational qualifications.
Because of the traditional early age of marriage, they
often become pregnant before sitting their qualifying
examinations. In Sierra Leone schools, conception dis-
qualifies the mother, but not the father, from remaining
in school. With few formal qualifications for wage in-

come, women will become increasingly dependent upon
men who may be employed.

REFERENCES

Boserup, E. 1965. The Conditions of Agricultural Growth.
    London: George Allen and Unwin.
    _____. 1970. Woman's Role in Economic Development.
    London: George Allen and Unwin.
Dow, T.E. 1972. "Fertility and Family Planning in Sierra
    Leone." Studies in Family Planning (The Population
    Council) 2:153-65.
MacCormack, C.P. (C.P. Hoffer). 1972. "Mende and Sherbro
    Women in High Office." Canadian Journal of African
    Studies 6:151-64.
    _____. 1974. "Madam Yoko: Ruler of the Kpa Mende Con-
    federacy." In Woman, Culture and Society, ed. M.Z.
    Rosaldo and L. Lamphere. Stanford: Stanford Univer-
    sity Press.
    _____. 1975. "Sande Women and Political Power in Sierra
    Leone." West African Journal of Sociology and
    Political Science 1:42-50.
    _____. 1976. "The Compound Head: Structures and Strat-
    egies." Africana Research Bulletin 6:44-64.
    _____. 1977. "Wono: Institutionalized Dependency in
    Sherbro Descent Groups." In Slavery in Africa:
    Historical and Anthropological Perspectives, ed. S.
    Miers and I. Kopytoff. Madison: University of
    Wisconsin Press.
    _____. 1978. "The Cultural Ecology of Production:
    Sherbro Coast and Hinterland." In Social Organiza-
    tion and Settlement, ed. D. Green, et al. Oxford:
    British Archaeological Reports.
    _____. 1979. "Sande: The Public Face of a Secret
    Society." In The New Religions of Africa, ed. B.
    Jules-Rosette. Norwood, N.J.: Ablex.
    _____. 1981. "Proto-social to Adult: A Sherbro Trans-
    formation." In Nature, Culture and Gender, ed. C.
    MacCormack and M. Strathern. Cambridge: Cambridge
    University Press.
    _____. 1982. "Health, Fertility and Childbirth in
    Southern Sierra Leone." In Ethnography of Fertility
    and Birth, ed. C. MacCormack. London: Academic
    Press.

## 3. Dependence and Autonomy: The Economic Activities of Secluded Hausa Women in Kano, Nigeria

*Enid Schildkrout*

In the literature on women in West Africa, two factors have been described in some detail; the participation of women in the market economy (for example, Bashir,
1972; Boserup, 1970; Brooks, 1976; Hill, 1969, 1971;
Hodder and Ukwu, 1969; Lawson, 1972; Lewis, 1976, 1977;
McCall, 1961; Mullings, 1976; Oppong, 1974, 1975; Peil,
1975; Robertson, 1974, 1976; Sanjek and Sanjek, 1976;
Schildkrout, 1973; Sudarkasa, 1973) and, in Islamic
areas, the institution of purdah, that is, the seclusion
of married women (Barkow, 1972; Hill, 1969, 1971, 1972;
Ogunbiyi, 1969; Schildkrout, 1978, 1979; M. Smith, 1954;
M.G. Smith, 1952, 1954, 1955). Seclusion is based on
the premise that men provide for the material needs of
women and children. Islamic ideology thus gives religious sanction to the dependent status of women and children and enhances the political and social status attached
to the economic roles of men. By defining dependency relationships in terms of kinship, this ideology enhances
the importance of the family and of marriage. At the
same time, religion has thus played a part in curtailing
the economic roles of women in many parts of the Islamic
world. Since the seclusion of wives is an expression of
their husbands' economic success, it has obviously been
more prevalent among the middle and upper classes than

A version of this paper has been published in Christine
Oppong, ed., Female and Male in West Africa (London: G.
Allen and Unwin, in press). The research on which this
paper is based was conducted in Nigeria between 1976 and
1978 with support from the American Museum of Natural
History, the National Science Foundation (grant no. BNS
76-11174), the Social Science Research Council, the Wen-
ner-Gren Foundation for Anthropological Research, and the
Ford Foundation. I am grateful to Carol Gelber for her
patient assistance in analyzing the data.

among peasants and the urban poor. However, in Islamic
West Africa, there is evidence to suggest that the practice of purdah is increasing (Barkow, 1972; Hill, 1972;
M.G. Smith, 1954), in urban areas becoming more common
even in families where the economic status of the husband
does not insure the support of women and children. This
has been facilitated by the continued participation of
secluded women in the market economy.

African women have traditionally played very important economic roles in both rural and urban economies.
While purdah restricts these activities ideologically
and spatially, in practice, Muslim women in Africa continue their economic activities, albeit in modified ways.
This paper describes how secluded women in the city of
Kano, in northern Nigeria, participate in the market and
how this economic activity relates to the formal division
of labor by age and sex in Hausa society. It describes
how women are able to be economically active through the
control they exercise over children. In Hausa society,
as in other Muslim societies, the activities of adults
are strictly segregated by gender. However, until
puberty, children are not restricted by the same religious and cultural injunctions. They are therefore able
to act as intermediaries between the male and female
domains. Children mediate between the domestic domain
of the house and family, which is controlled for the
most part by women, and the public domain, which is
dominated by men. In the formal division of labor,
women are defined primarily as consumers, not as producers. However, through their control over the allocation of children's time and labor, Hausa women are able
to alter considerably the formal structure of the domestic economy. Children give women access to the market
and enable them to subvert some of the implications of
purdah. The limited economic leverage which women
thereby obtain does not give them status or power in the
public arena, but it does give them resources to renegotiate their position in a very restricted domain.

In the first section of this paper, I consider the
system of reproduction in Hausa society, focusing on
urban Kano specifically. I deal with marriage, the
institution of purdah, and the expectations of men and
women in the domestic domain, exploring the religious
ideology on which sex roles and patterns of male/female
interaction are based, and the significance of this
ideology in segregating male-dominated and female-
dominated institutional spheres. The second section of
the paper deals with the economic system, places the
domestic economy in a wider context, and examines the
sexual division of labor in urban Hausa society. The
third part of the paper concerns the roles of children

and the division of labor based on age.  Children are
the crucial links between the domestic domain, which is
the arena of reproduction and consumption, and the wider
society, including the economic institutions that control production.  Here I consider how the economic roles
of children vary according to age and sex and also
briefly discuss the impact of Western education on the
status and roles of women and children.  In northern
Nigeria, Western education has been introduced on a large
scale only recently due to a colonial policy that protected traditional Islamic education by restricting the
establishment of Christian mission schools in the colonial period (Fafunwa, 1974; Hiskett, 1975; Hubbard, 1975;
Ogunsola, 1974).  By removing children from full-time
participation in the domestic economy, Western education today is altering the division of labor in the
household.  More than any other single factor, the enrollment of children in primary school challenges the
position of secluded West African Muslim women, or,
perhaps, threatens the institution of purdah itself.


FEMALE/MALE RELATIONS IN KANO

    The ideology on which female/male relations in Hausa
society are based is similar to that of most Islamic
societies in stressing the dominance and superiority of
men and the subordination and inferiority of women.
While there are undoubtedly male and female versions of
this ideology, as have been described for parts of the
Middle East and North Africa (Dwyer, 1978; Rosen, 1978),[1]
the dominant male ideology, sanctioned by religious and
political institutions, defines women's status primarily
in relation to men.  Women are thought to be in need of
male care and protection; many passages of the Qur'an
make this point.
    Sexual activity, except in marriage, is regarded as
incompatible with social order (Mernissi, 1975).  Contact with women, especially those of reproductive age, is
always seen as in some sense sexually charged, and it is
antithetical to a state of ritual purity for men.  The
prohibition of men's touching women after performing
ablution, of women's entering the main area of the mos-
que, and  of sexual activity during fasting, are examples
of the many rules meant to protect men and women against
sexuality.  Adults can be protected from their own im-
pulses by Allah, by their willingness to follow the
teachings of the Prophet Mohammed, and by social institutions which define segregated social spheres for men
and women.  Hausa folklore (Rattray, 1913, pp. 200ff.;
Skinner, 1969, passim) and conversation are replete with

references to female sexuality and the danger it poses
to men and women and to the social order.
     The rules of purdah follow from these attitudes and
are meant to protect adults from the chaotic effects of
uncontrolled sexuality.  Neither children nor postmeno-
pausal women are seen to be threatened by sexuality and
are therefore able to move much more freely than are men
and women of reproductive age, for whom sexuality can be
channeled to the legitimate end of procreation only
within the parameters of marriage.  As in other Islamic
societies, there is a strong fear and disapproval of
sexual activity outside of marriage, although in Hausa
society it is in fact institutionalized in the role of
the courtesan, or karuwa.[2]  However, women who engage in
sexual activity outside of marriage do lose status and
damage the reputation of the men who are related to them
as guardians.  There is a strong emphasis on virginity
before first marriage but little prejudice against re-
marriage to either divorced or widowed women.  Children
born out of wedlock are castigated, and courtesans
usually marry if they become pregnant.  This is a society
in which marriage is the most important institution in
defining adult status for both men and women.  The terms
used for stages of the life cycle in Hausa culture reflect the importance of marriage and the structural dependence of women on men.  All terms for stages of the
female life cycle express sexual and/or reproductive
status and only approximately indicate age.
     Although Western education is beginning to change
traditional patterns with regard to the age of marriage,
the end of childhood for women still usually coincides
with the onset of puberty.  Girls are expected to marry
as soon as they reach puberty, often as early as age ten.
The average age of first marriage for women of all ages
in our Kano study is twelve years, and only those girls
attending Western school are marrying later.  Young girls
move from dependence on their fathers to dependence on
their husbands; men have the obligation to support and
care for their daughters and wives.  Later, when women
have passed menopause and are less likely to remarry
after divorce or widowhood, they have the right to seek
support from their sons and brothers.  The minority of
Hausa women who spend a good part of their adult lives
independently, engaging in those occupations open to
women who are not in purdah (as pounders of grain, maid
servants, traders, courtesans, and recently, in very few
cases, as teachers, nurses, and secretaries) have inevitably been married at some time, even if only in a
brief compulsory union arranged by the parents.  Marriage is an absolute prerequisite for full adult status.
     For both boys and girls, first marriage marks the

transition from childhood to adulthood, and the ceremony
of first marriage differs markedly from that of subsequent marriages.  The marriage ceremony involves two very
distinct aspects:  the union of the spouses and the
transition for each spouse to full adult status.  The
latter obviously occurs only once in a person's lifetime, so that ceremonies for second marriages are usually
far less elaborate than ceremonies for first marriages.

For boys, the transition to adulthood depends on
economic productivity as well as on reproductive capa-
city.  Even where a boy's economic activity is tied into
a family enterprise, as was the case in traditional
agriculture,[3] the boy is expected to be economically
productive before being eligible for marriage.  Young
men therefore marry in their twenties or thirties, while
the more affluent marry earlier.  Although women's
economic roles also change with marriage, the formal
definition of their social status as adults depends more
on their relation to men than on their economic activities.

The obligations of husbands and wives to each other
and to their children are clearly set out in both traditional practice and Islamic law.  Men are obliged to
provide shelter, clothing, and food for their wives and
children; women are expected to bear and raise children,
cook and care for the domestic needs of their children and
husbands, and defer to and obey their husbands.  Both
men and women can obtain divorce, but whereas men need
only denounce the marriage, women must take their case
to court.  Men have custody over all of their children
after weaning,[4] although they sometimes allow divorced
wives to keep one daughter.  Wives are expected to heed
the restrictions of purdah and thereby protect their husbands' and male relatives' reputations.  Women are not
expected to question their husbands about their activities outside the house, while men have the duty to control the very limited outside activities of their wives.
As we will see below, however, they have no control over
one crucial area:  their wives' incomes--so long as this
income is generated without violating the rules of
purdah.

When girls are first married, their lives change
abruptly, for almost all Hausa women are secluded after
marriage.  As children, girls are free to move in and
out of their own and other peoples' houses.  Married
women, regardless of how young they may be, are confined to their own houses and are further confined by
the prohibition against receiving visitors other than
children (who may indeed be older than they are), certain
categories of relatives, and other women.  Most married
women are allowed to leave their houses for ceremonial

events, for example to attend naming ceremonies, marriages, and funerals.  Most are permitted to visit relatives and to seek medical care.  The strictness with
which seclusion is enforced depends upon the husband's
wishes and the wife's willingness to comply.  There are
women who do not go out for any social occasion at all,
and there are others who simply inform their husbands
that they are going out.  Only one woman in our sample
of seventy married women was not in purdah, and the explanation for her unique position was poverty.  Most
women comply with the restrictions of purdah and go out
only at night when, in theory, they cannot be seen.  They
take children with them as escorts and cover their faces
with shawls.  They are not fully veiled, however, as are
women in parts of North Africa or the Middle East, for
their shawls often cover only their heads and do not
conceal their clothing.

In practice, male control extends primarily over
the activities of wives and daughters outside the home,
mainly by restricting women's spatial mobility.  Purdah
also restricts access to secluded women by other males.
However, because they spend very little time at home,
men have little control over the interaction of women
and children within the home.  In Kano, most men work
away from home and are involved with the running of the
household only in a perfunctory manner.  They provide
money and food, but since they are rarely present they
delegate major responsibility for domestic affairs to
women.  As in many sex-segregated societies, women expect to find most of their companionship from other
women and from children.  Thus, women have considerable
power, if not authority, within the domestic domain,
while they have very little power and no formal authority
outside this context.[5]


ECONOMY

Among the urban Hausa, the major part of family
income is ideally provided by men through their participation in mercantile activities and wage labor outside
the home.  In this sense, the urban Hausa household is
not a unit of production.  However, the domestic unit
is, in fact, often more than a unit of consumption, for
women are frequently able to subvert the idealized
structure of the domestic economy through their control
over domestic labor.

The income of Hausa men in Kano varies greatly, and
neighborhoods are not segregated according to income
level.  In general, the size of households varies with
income, more affluent men having more wives, children,

dependent relatives, and clients.  The close correlation
between household size and income reflects the obligation of the male household head to provide for dependents.

The salaried jobs of the Hausa men in our sample,
reflecting the general pattern, are mainly those which
require minimal Western education.  Because the Hausa
have only recently taken advantage of Western education,
the number of men living in the old walled city of Kano
(the birni) who have completed secondary school is very
small.  The salaried workers we studied are in the local
government administration; formerly, many of those of
Fulani ancestry were in the emirate administration and
in low-level civil service jobs in the state government.
Some work for commercial firms controlled by large companies (now Nigerian, but formerly expatriate), and
some work for wealthy Hausa merchants.  All except the
wealthiest men spend most of their salary on domestic
needs.  In fact, in attempting to obtain data on household budgets, we found that domestic expenses often
exceed wages, a situation that can be explained only by
the presence of nonwage income (many families have farms
outside of the city) and by the supplemental support provided by wives.

The merchants in Kano also are a very diverse group
in terms of income--more diverse than the salaried
workers, since their lack of literacy in English is not
a barrier in many areas of trade.  Those merchants who
are literate in English, or who are able to employ people
with Western education, are able to operate large firms
that play an important part in the national economy.
Other traders operate on a smaller, but not necessarily
local, scale.  Our sample includes wealthy merchants
who deal in cement, cattle, and textiles and others who
operate small stalls selling grain, manufactured goods,
kola nuts, and other products.  The poorest merchants
have little capital and they work for others.  The artisans in our sample are tailors and leatherworkers.
Butchers constitute another distinct category (they are
usually endogamous) and, like artisans, tend to be in
the lower income category.

The marketplace in Kano is dominated by men.  The
well-known West African market woman is virtually absent
from view in the oldest large market of Kano city,  the
Kurmi market (M.G. Smith, 1962).  Even the unmarried
Hausa women who are not in purdah rarely set up stalls
in the marketplace.  When they do trade outside their
homes, they set up stalls in residential neighborhoods.
The virtual absence of Hausa women from the marketplace
in the old walled city contrasts with the situation in
the "new" market of greater Kano, Sabon Gari market,

where Yoruba, Nupe, and other Nigerian women from
farther south have permanent stalls.

However, despite the absense of Hausa women from
the public arena, they are not an insignificant force in
commercial life.  Virtually all transactions in Kano are
on a cash basis, and women participate in the cash
economy much more than the formal division of labor
within the domestic economy indicates.  Women participate in an elaborate network of exchange and generate income for themselves, their children, and sometimes for
their husbands.  Women are able to do this because men
exercise little control over labor within the domestic
domain.

The mutual obligations of husbands and wives insure
subsistence for all members of the family, except in the
poorest families, where the ideal pattern is not realized
and where the whole family is in fact dependent on
others, or where the wife's income contributes to subsistence.  In the ideal situation, Muslim Hausa women and
children are consumers, not producers, and women's participation in economic activity consists only in preparing food, caring for the house, and bearing and raising
children.  Hausa men are expected to provide all of the
ingredients their wives need to prepare food for domestic consumption.  Women are expected to feed their
families three times a day, either by cooking or by purchasing food with the money and provisions given by the
husband.  Although Hausa women do in fact engage in productive income-generating activity, this is not part of
the formal division of labor, for purdah is based on the
premise that a wife need not work.

However, the vast majority of Hausa married women
do work for an income, albeit from within the confines
of purdah.  Husbands have no claim to their wives' incomes and in most cases do not know what it is; nor do
wives know their husbands' incomes.  Women's actual participation in the cash economy goes far beyond the purchase of cooking ingredients, although it is by investing
the cash provided by men for domestic consumption that
women generate income.  In fulfilling their obligation
to feed their families, men either provide ingredients or
cash to their wives.  Most men do both: they purchase
staples such as grain and firewood periodically and they
give their wives daily allowances to purchase perishable
ingredients.  All women see that their families eat three
meals a day, but virtually no women cook three times a
day.  In most houses, one or two meals are purchased outside the house.  Thus, instead of sending children to
buy ingredients for cooking, women send their children
to purchase cooked food from their neighbors.  Alternatively, they buy cooked food from children who come to

their house selling for other women. In our study of
sixty-nine women in purdah in two wards of Kano, twenty-
two women (32 percent) were regularly selling cooked
food. Of thirteen women not in purdah (women who were
also caretakers of children in our sample), five were
selling cooked food.[6]

The income women generate by cooking food for sale
rather than for domestic consumption, or by engaging in
other income-producing activities, is their own. The
entire activity is distinct from their obligation to prepare food for their families. The investment a woman
makes in her business, even when this business is the
preparation of cooked food, is distinct from the household budget. Although a few women do feed their families
from the food they cook for sale, the money they invest
in their business is conceptually distinct from the
money their husbands provide for domestic consumption.
In other words, some women, as wives, buy food from
themselves, as food-sellers, to feed their families.
Most women, however, purchase two out of three meals a
day from other women. The cash that wives receive from
husbands for domestic consumption is thus channeled into
a female sphere of exchange where women act not as wives
but as independent producers. In this way, men capita-
lize women's economic enterprises, even though their
manifest intention is simply to provide for the subsistence of their own families.

Women raise their initial capital, which is often
very small, from a variety of sources: change in the
household budget, their dowries, gifts from relatives
and female friends, loans from rotating credit societies,
or spending money (kudin batarwa) given by their husbands. Although Hausa men, unlike the Yoruba (Sudarkasa,
1973), have no obligation to give their wives initial
sums of capital, many give their wives regular allowances
of spending money. The amount varies, depending upon
the husband's income. Although this money is not
specifically for trading, many women invest it in business. While a few husbands are strongly opposed to
their wives' economic activity, the vast majority simply
ignore it. In addition to selling cooked food, women in
purdah earn money by trading in small commodities and
raw foods, embroidering and sewing, hair-plaiting, and
running rotating credit societies.

Since the Hausa husband has no obligation to set
his wife up as a trader, he also cannot rely on her as
a source of support. Most women do not, in fact, provide subsistence for their families, and those that do
are very reluctant to admit it. Nonsupport is grounds
for divorce and women who want to stay married to poor
men contribute quietly to their families' maintenance.

Most women spend part of their income on clothing for themselves and their children, on gifts for female friends and relatives, and occasionally on luxury items such as cosmetics and jewelry. The greatest part of women's income, however, is spent on the purchase of goods for their daughters' dowries (which consists of household furnishings) and to a lesser extent on contributions to their sons' bridewealth (cash payment, clothing, and cosmetics for the bride). The expenses entailed in marriage are said to have risen in recent years with the greater availability of consumer goods. Whether or not this is so, it is clear that the greatest part of women's income is put into the marriage system.

Although males are favored in the Islamic law of inheritance, sons inheriting twice the share of daughters, the dowry is inherited only by females. From the time they are children, girls work or save from gifts to amass dowries. Throughout their lives, women augment their own and their daughters' dowries. Dowry can be sold; it can be used to generate capital; and it can be used as a source of economic security in case of widowhood, or divorce, or in other times of need. Dowry, in the form of enamel, brass, and glass bowls and bedroom furniture, is thus a form of exclusively female property which constitutes capital, savings, and insurance for women in a male-dominated society.

These economic practices by women in purdah are significant in several respects. By taking resources which their husbands give them for consumption and diverting them into a remunerated female sphere of production, women are in effect receiving payment for their domestic labor. This is particularly obvious in the case of women who spend their time cooking food for sale rather than for their own consumption. But in any case, by not cooking for their families three times a day, all women are thereby freeing their time so that their labor can be used in income-producing activities. Whether or not this diversion of resources from domestic consumption to income-generating activities for women leads to inflation in the cost of subsistence is an intriguing question. Although we are unable to demonstrate this with quantitative data, it is logical to suggest that by adding the cost of female labor to the resources men provide for subsistence, women may inflate the price of subsistence. The cost of prepared food does include the cost of women's labor, which instead of being unpaid domestic labor is now remunerated. In a sense, then, men subsidize women's economic activities by paying a price for food which includes this labor cost. In Hausa society, where secluded women continue to work, this is one price of purdah. Although in seclusion and pre-

cluded from working outside the home, Hausa women are
able to turn their domestic labor into a productive
resource.

Independent incomes allow women to build and maintain emotionally supportive extradomestic relationships
with other women through the exchange of gifts.  Most
important, women are able to use their incomes to control the system of reproduction to their advantage.  By
diverting resources from a male-dominated productive
economy into a female sphere of exchange, women obtain
limited social mobility.  They are able to withstand the
loss of male support after widowhood or divorce and, in
some cases, their incomes enable them to instigate
divorce and manage independently outside of marriage.
In addition, they are sometimes able to use their independence to negotiate more advantageous marriages for
themselves and their daughters.  Thus, through their
control over the daily operation of the domestic economy,
women gain a measure of control over their own lives
that is denied to them in the formal definition of sex
roles in Hausa society.

Since most of women's assets are spent on marriage
expenses for themselves and their daughters, the question
arises as to what effect this has on Hausa economy and
social structure.  Men still participate more significantly in production and generate most of the income in
the community.  However, women gain greater control over
their own lives and, in a more abstract sense, over the
system of reproduction.  Their formal dependence on
men for status and support is somewhat reduced and they
are able to manage independently and renegotiate their
marriages.  The ability of Hausa women to transform the
domestic domain from an arena of unpaid domestic labor
to one of production and exchange seems to represent the
persistence of a particularly West African female behavior pattern within a family structure defined by
Islamic values regarding the sexual division of labor.


CHILDREN

Any attempt to analyze the nature of the Hausa
economic system has to consider in some detail the role
of children.  It is the labor of children that enables
secluded women to carry on their economic activities,
and it is women's ability to control this source of labor
which is the key to their limited success.

Women in purdah are extremely dependent on children
for performing their obligatory activities as wives.
Although women are expected to be able to carry on all
their domestic chores at home, in fact, many of their

tasks require communication with the world outside.
Children are the secluded women's primary and often
only means of communicating with the outside world.  They
do almost all of the shopping for cooking ingredients.
Most husbands supply their households with staples such
as grain and firewood, but children are sent daily to
buy meat, vegetables, and other perishables.  They take
grain and soup ingredients--peppers and tomatoes--for
grinding, and purchase sundries such as kerosene, mos-
quito coils, matches, medicines, and thread.  They take
refuse out of the house and sweep the external gutters.
They take clothes to the washman, the tailor, and the
seamstress.  Many women send cooked food to their husbands' relatives in neighboring houses and children
carry the empty dishes and steaming bowls of food from
house to house, often serving another crucial function
by carrying messages, news, and gossip as well.  They
also accompany women when they attend ceremonies, visit
relatives, or go out to seek medical care.

While all women rely on children (or paid servants,
in the wealthier households) for domestic help, there is
considerable variation in the extent to which secluded
women rely on children in their income-earning activities.  Some occupations require more help from children
than others: embroidery, machine sewing, and hair-
plaiting require minimal help.  These occupations are
usually pursued by women who have no children over age
five or six to help them, or by women whose children are
all enrolled in school.  Even these occupations, however,
require some assistance:  someone must collect raw
materials and deliver the finished products.  A woman may
change her occupation frequently during the course of her
lifetime, and changes in occupation are almost always
related to the availability of children under a woman's
care.  Women's incomes likewise vary in relation to the
availability of child labor.  In our study, women whose
children were engaged in full-time street trading were
earning an average of two to three times more money than
women whose children were not trading (Schildkrout,
in press).

The predicament of women without children is recognized in the willingness of men to allow their divorced
wives to keep one child, usually a daughter.  Women
without children often foster co-wives' or relatives'
children, and older women frequently foster grandchildren.  The term in Hausa for fostering is riko,
derived from rik'e (to hold or to keep).  This term is
used in reference to children whose parents are still
alive (as distinct from orphans, who are not foster
children) but whose parents have delegated parental responsibility to others.  Foster parents are known as

mariki (male) or marikiya (female). The dictionary
definition of riko is interesting in that it refers
specifically to marriage and focuses on females: riko
is defined as "keeping a child with a view to marrying
her when she is old enough" or "keeping a child for a
particular suitor until she is old enough for marriage"
(Bagery, 1934, p. 856). Fostering can in fact occur
with children of either sex, but the emphasis on females
and on marriage highlights an important aspect of the
relationship. The foster parent has the responsibility
of arranging and paying most of the expenses of the
child's marriage. Since boys are usually economically
independent and considerably older before they marry, the
link between fostering and preparing for the child's
marriage is not as evident. For boys, fostering is
often associated with apprenticeship; the foster parent
is more frequently a nonrelative and is responsible for
teaching the boy a skill or trade. In either case, the
foster parent has the right to the child's services.

Until the recent increase in primary school attendance, subsequent to the implementation of universal
primary education in northern Nigeria in 1976 (Bray,
1977, 1978; West Africa 19 Nov. 1979; 26 Nov. 1979;
3 Dec. 1979), children were available to help their
mothers or female caretakers most of the day. Formal
education is not new in northern Nigeria, for children
in the past attended Qur'anic schools from an early age.
However, since the government began a campaign to increase primary school enrollment in the north, the number
of children in Western schools has increased substantially, from 160,340 in 1975-76 to 341,800 in 1976-77
(Educational Statistics, 1975-76, p. 7). For many
children, this means that up to six hours a day are now
spent in formal education, since in addition to four
hours in primary school (and more after Class 3), many
children spend several hours a day in Qur'anic school.

There are a number of reasons for traditionally low
enrollments in primary schools in northern Nigeria, including the close association in many peoples' thinking
between Western education and Christianity. However, of
equal or greater importance is the need for children to
perform domestic tasks and the nature of the marriage
system, with its emphasis on early marriage for girls
and large initial expenditures for both brides and
grooms. The need for domestic help is clearly linked to
purdah, as we have seen, for without children or servants, purdah becomes virtually impossible, given the
division of labor between adult men and women in Hausa
society. Wealthier families can sometimes afford household help in the form of housemaids (usually poor
widowed or divorced women from rural areas), Qur'anic

students (often children), or clients of the household
head.  Among these wealthier families, the enrollment
of children in school does not cause as much disruption
as it does for poorer families.  Since purdah has become
almost ubiquitous, in families where children are the
only domestic help the children are burdened with household tasks, particuarly errands, after school.[8]
    Opposition to Western education is greater for
girls than boys for many reasons, not least of which is
the early age of marriage and the perceived need for
girls' assistance in raising their own dowries.  In
1975-76, of 160,340 children enrolled in primary school
in Kano State, 24 percent were female.  This was, in
fact, a decrease of 3 percent from 1968, when 27 percent
of the 49,580 primary school children were female
(Educational Statistics, 1975-76, p. 7; see also Trevor,
1975).  Among the reasons cited for this situation by
the Kano State Education Review Committee in 1976 were
the traditional antagonism toward Western education,
based on its association with Christianity, the very
early age of marriage for girls, the perceived moral
laxity in the schools, the lack of strong leadership by
educators, the lack of encouragement given to working
women in the society, and the negligible adult educational facilities for women.  In addition, this influential government report noted the association between
children's economic activity, particularly hawking, and
school attendance.

> It is customary in Hausa society, for a bridegroom
> to expect his bride to bring to his house, as her
> bridal gifts, an assortment of cooking utensils,
> plates, dishes for decorative purposes and loads
> of clothes.  The family of any bride who fails to
> respect this custom is often jeered at.  It is for
> this reason, that mothers, who are locked in their
> houses, use their daughters as their main contact
> with  outside world.  A girl's hawking career,
> therefore prevents her from going to school and
> unless a father is rich enough to provide for his
> daughter all her bridal requirements the mother
> will always have her way in controlling her
> daughter. (Kano State, 1976, p. 35)

    Clearly, an inverse relationship between children's
participation in economic activity and primary school
attendance affects girls even more than boys.  While
boys and girls are important in assisting their mothers
with household tasks, girls play a greater role in
income-earning activities than do boys.  By age ten they
also assume greater household responsibility.

Gender is not very relevant in defining children's roles before puberty. In fact, it is precisely the asexual way in which childhood is defined that allows children the spatial and social mobility to assist women in purdah. There are no restrictions on the movement of children inside and outside of their own and other people's houses. Before puberty, boys and girls can interact with secluded women freely. Both boys and girls assist women in minding younger children, in doing errands and carrying messages, and in shopping. Girls play a slightly greater role than boys in helping their mothers cook, but if girls are not available, boys will help with sifting flour and cutting ingredients. It is in income-earning activity that the greatest differences between boys and girls emerge. Most of children's income-earning activity is in the form of street trading, and girls are more active than boys in this regard. In a sample of one hundred and nine school-age children, 57 percent of the girls and 14 percent of the boys did not attend school and engaged in street trading most of the time (see Table 3.1). Daily diaries obtained from these children over a ten-day period showed that children who engaged in full-time street trading spent approximately six or seven hours a day in this activity. They would leave in the morning to sell one item, return with the money, and be given another tray of items to sell. This would continue throughout the day, with breaks for meals, prayers, and domestic chores, including errands. Most children traded for their own mothers or caretakers, but some traded for more distant relatives or nonrelatives on a commission basis (usually 10 percent of the value of the goods sold). The overwhelming reason girls are more active than boys in income-producing activities is the perceived need to raise dowry and the responsibility of the mother or female caretaker for raising a good part of this dowry. Girls must have this money by puberty, but boys have a longer period in which to earn the money they need for marriage.

There are two categories of children whose labor is used to contribute to subsistence before it is used to raise dowry or bridewealth. These are children who are not living with secluded women and who therefore are unable to rely on a father's support. The almajirai, or Qur'anic students, are boys who have come to the city to study the Qur'an with a particular malam. These children are expected to support themselves and sometimes reward their teachers by contributing labor or income to the teacher's household. These boys beg, do odd jobs, such as cleaning gutters or portering at railway and truck stations, or do hawking (talla) for traders for a fixed commission.[9] Of nine boys in the Kano study who

TABLE 3.1
Primary-School Attendance and Street Trading by Kano Boys and Girls in Two Wards

| | Attend school/ do not trade | | Attend school/ trade | | Do not attend school/ trade | | Do not attend school/ do not trade | | TOTAL | |
|---|---|---|---|---|---|---|---|---|---|---|
| | No. | % | No. | % | No. | % | No. | % | No. | % |
| Boys | 38 | 60 | 8 | 13 | 9 | 14 | 8 | 13 | 63 | 100 |
| Girls | 12 | 26 | 4 | 9 | 26 | 57 | 4 | 9 | 46 | 100 |
| TOTAL | 50 | 47 | 12 | 11 | 35 | 32 | 12 | 11 | 109 | 100 |

traded and did not attend primary school, three were
almajirai. These children are available to work for
people who have an insufficient number of children in
their households. Although they do attend Qur'anic
school--often for longer hours than other children--none
of them is in primary school. The other category of
children who work for subsistence and do not attend
primary school are those girls who live in female-
headed households, usually with divorced or widowed
mothers. In the Kano sample, these girls, like their
mothers, contributed to their own subsistence.

Among the children in male-headed households, there
is still an inverse relationship between certain forms
of economic activity and school attendance. While all
children engage in some form of economic activity, some
activities are more compatible with school attendance
than others. Performing domestic tasks and running
errands, providing child care, and escorting women when
they go out are chores done by all children. In the
sample of 109 school-age children, some children attended
school and sporadically did talla. A child whose
mother's primary occupation was embroidering or hair
plaiting might do talla when the mother cooked food for
sale on the weekend. Street trading, however, can only
be done as a full-time occupation by children who are
not in school. As we have seen, the incomes of the
mothers and caretakers of these children are considerably higher than the incomes of women whose children's
main economic activity is to perform domestic work and
run errands for no pay.

When children are engaged in income-producing
activities, this is usually described as a means of
earning money for marriage, except in the case of the
poorest children and the almajirai. When children earn
money, they generally give it to their mothers or
caretakers to keep for their dowry or bridewealth.
Children also occasionally engage in independent economic
enterprises, for example, cooking small pancakes for sale
to children, or renting their toys to other children, or
doing errands for strangers for money. They usually
spend their earnings on snacks; older children sometimes
save for larger purchases and marriage expenses. Since
children, like women, have considerable control over
their income, they generally feel that they are working
for themselves, not for their parents. Therefore, from
the age of five or six, girls spend most of their time
and energy on accumulating dowry. Those girls who
attend primary school increasingly rely on gifts from
suitors to buy their kayan daki (dowry).

There is a clear division of responsibility between
husbands and wives in meeting the expenses of dowry.

Fathers, or male caretakers, are expected to provide
furniture, including a bed, mattress, pillows, linens,
and a cupboard.  Mothers, or female caretakers, are expected to provide kayan daki, literally "things for the
room," in unlimited quantities.  In addition to the
traditional enamel and brass bowls, glassware and modern
appliances are increasingly becoming part of kayan daki.
It is difficult to overemphasize the importance of this
form of dowry as a status symbol and as a form of stored
female wealth.  However, it is interesting to note that
men, even prospective husbands, are only marginally concerned with their brides' kayan daki.  Because of the
rules of purdah which strongly limit adult male access to
female living space, a groom's friends and male relatives, with few exceptions, never see the bride's kayan
daki, and many profess to know little about it.  The
women who attend a marriage ceremony, however, are extremely interested in evaluating the quantity and quality
of the bride's kayan daki.[10]  The wealth stored in kayan
daki reflects the status of the bride's family generally,
but particularly that of her mother or marikiya.  Since
most women build this dowry through their independent
economic activities, this aspect of female status does
not necessarily reflect the status of the men on whom
women are otherwise dependent.  The limited interest
which men express in kayan daki may be a reflection of
their ambivalent attitude toward women's income-producing
activities.

An interesting tale quoted in Skinner (1969, pp.
357ff.), however, reveals the potential antagonism
between men and women over women's independent economic
activities.  As a form of female wealth, kayan daki can
reverse the status of the favored versus the despised
wife.  In the story a man has two wives, each with a
daughter.  He favors one wife and supports her more
generously than the other.  A friend of the poor wife
notices her plight and loans her money to trade.  The
poor wife and her daughter eventually build this into a
large sum.  The father then finds husbands for his
daughters:  a rich merchant for the daughter of the
favored wife and a poor man for the other.  After the
marriages, the husband of the favored daughter discovers
that the wife of the poor man brought many fine things to
the marriage: metal basins, fine calabashes, and imported
carpets.  After seeing this, the wealthy husband beat his
wife until she ran home to her father.  He smashed her
calabashes and pots and said, "Good-for-nothing slut--
you and your mother too, your father's favorites and you
haven't even any decent utensils.  While the daughter
he doesn't like--and her mother too--why, she's got a
hut full of things!"  Then the father beat the despised

wife, accusing her of being the cause of his favored
daughter's getting a beating.

Among that segment of the population that has
accepted Western education for women, it is expected
that the bride will contribute to her dowry from the
courting gifts of cash that she receives from men. Although courting gifts are traditional, their amount has
increased and the use to which these gifts are put has
also changed. Whereas formerly, much of this money may
have been consumed before marriage by the bride or her
family, it is now used for the purchase of kayan daki.
Formerly, these gifts were not returned if the marriage
did not take place. They consisted of small amounts of
money given when the suitor went to visit the bride.
Nowadays, the amount of money given is often larger, and
if the suitor is unsuccessful, the money is often returned. In some cases, a successful suitor will re-
imburse an unsuccessful one. There are two interesting
implications of the new pattern: first, that the
economic burden on men before marriage is increasing.
This is a matter of frequent complaint by some university
students and other men who want to marry Western-educated
women. Second, it suggests that an area of activity that
formerly represented female autonomy, that is, the
accumulation of dowry, is increasingly controlled by
men. Housewares may then become part of a conjugal fund,
rather than representing an exclusively female store of
wealth.


CONCLUSION

Despite the fact that seclusion is an ideal form of
Muslim marriage, the practicality of purdah obviously
varies with economic circumstances. The difficulty of
keeping women in purdah among rural peasants and among
the urban poor is obvious. In an economically stratified
society, women's contribution to production is essential
among the lower classes, where men simply cannot produce
enough to support numerous dependents. In comparing
female-male relationships in Kano with those in other
parts of the Islamic world, one is struck by the strength
and the particular form of the institution of purdah in
northern Nigeria. In Kano city, which by any account is
economically stratified, few married women are not in
seclusion. Even when husbands cannot fulfill all of
their wives' and childrens' material needs, as they are
enjoined to do by Islamic law, women are secluded. Out
of sixty-nine households of all income groups in this
study, in only one case was a wife not in seclusion due
to poverty. Purdah is seen as a sign of high status;

despite its restrictive character, it reflects positively
on the social status of both men and women, given the
adherence to Islamic values in the population.

In some ways, the strictness with which seclusion
is enforced in Kano (and probably elsewhere in northern
Nigeria) appears to be greater than in other parts of the
Islamic world.  In North Africa, Morocco  for example,
women use the veil to segregate themselves from men and
from public male space (Mernissi, 1975); women in Kano,
however, rarely go out at all during the day, not even
to go to market.  Their spatial seclusion is even
greater than in places where the veil enables women to
move through, if not in, male space.  The ubiquitous
adoption of purdah in Kano is possible precisely because
secluded women do continue to play economic roles and
generate income, at the same time as they participate in
the myth of being totally dependent on men.  In fact, behind the walls of individual houses, the degree of dependence varies considerably. Women in Kano seem to be
continuing the long West African tradition of female
involvement in economic life.  They are able to do this
because of the control they exercise over the activities
of children.  The availability of children and the way in
which children's roles are defined enable women to carry
on economic activities, both domestic and extradomestic,
in the manner of market women elsewhere in West Africa.

Because of purdah, northern Nigerian Muslim women
are not economically active in ways that are revealed in
labor force statistics.  They do not participate in the
formal economy, but rather in what Polly Hill has described as the "hidden trade" (1969).  While this activity gives them some mobility within the domestic domain
and enables them to improve their living conditions as
wives, it does not lead to further participation in the
male-dominated areas of economic and political life.
Women are able to move resources around within a very
limited sector of the economy, that sector which is
primarily involved in consumption.  And although they
are able to participate in selected areas of retail
trade and petty commodity production, most married
women remain basically dependent on manipulating the
limited resources that men give them for subsistence.
Moreover, the limited profit that individual women amass
is reinvested almost immediately in the very marriage
system that defines their position in the first place.
By spending most of their profit on dowry for themselves
and their daughters, women and young girls are, in a
sense, working very hard to move in a circle.  The pattern of female dependence repeats itself generation after
generation, as it should, given the Islamic value system.
Despite their prodigious economic activity, Hausa women

do little more than protect their autonomy in a sexually segregated society.

Today, however, the division of labor by sex and age in Hausa society is being severely disturbed by the introduction of universal primary education. Even in the short run, the enrollment of all children in primary school threatens the institution of purdah and the sexual division of labor. Without children available to participate in domestic work, the West African version of purdah is impossible, except in the upper classes where adults can be employed to replace the labor of children. In the long run, Western education is likely to create new expectations about marriage and about work on the part of young women and perhaps also on the part of young men. Whether these expectations will be met with new employment opportunities for secluded and nonsecluded women is a question we cannot answer. Whatever the ultimate result may be, Western education inevitably challenges the structure of all but the wealthiest families in Islamic West Africa. The positive benefits from Western education that many people--Muslim and non-Muslim alike--acknowledge can be attained only with the alteration of the traditional division of labor by sex and age and the transformation of the family structure that is based on this division of labor.

NOTES

1. Mernissi (1975) argues that Islamic attitudes toward sexuality affirm the power of the female. She therefore maintains that inequality is not a characteristic of the Islamic attitude to women.

2. As Renee Pittin (1979, p. 3) points out, there has been an overemphasis in the literature on the Hausa on the institution of karuwanci, as exemplified, she states, by M.G. Smith (1959, p. 244) and Cohen (1969, passim). Pittin argues that the status of "nonmarriage" (jawarci) is also an option for divorced or widowed women. In our Kano study, which, however, excluded prostitutes, very few women chose to remain single for long periods.

3. See Hill (1972, 1977), M.G. Smith (1955), and Wallace (1978) for varied descriptions of the way in which the traditional gandu system worked.

4. In this respect, the Hausa practice varies from that of other communities that follow Sharia law. The Qur'an stipulates that boys should remain with their mothers until puberty, after which they are given an option of which parent to live with; girls should remain with their mothers until they marry (Anderson,

1970, p. 214). There is one provision in the Qur'an,
however, which exempts Hausa practice from this rule:
that mothers retain custody "unless they marry outside
the immediate family," which indeed is the general
practice in Hausa communities.
    5. Although the public/domestic distinction seems
pertinent to a sexually segregated socity such as the
Hausa, the criticism of this dichotomy as a theoretical
construct by Schlegel (1977, pp. 17ff.) is valid.
    6. As Raynaut (1977) shows with respect to the
Hausa of rural Niger, even in agricultural communities,
women's involvement in the preparation and sale of cooked
food contributes significantly to subsistence.
    7. This is common in West Africa, where fostering
is often regarded as an obligation between kin. See
Goody (1969, 1971, 1978), Oppong (1967, 1973) and
Schildkrout (1973). The use of children as pawns for
debt does not seem to have been common among the Hausa.
    8. In a study of Yoruba schoolchildren in Lagos,
Oloko has found that there is a strong negative correlation between school achievement and trading, whereas
domestic work does not seem to affect school achievement adversely (Oloko, 1979).
    9. In a study of beggars in Zaria city, Mensah
(1977) noted that the majority (59 percent) of beggars
were male children, many of whom were Qur'anic students.
    10. Bashir (1972) reports that women will borrow
kayan daki for these occasions if they feel inadequate
about their holdings.

REFERENCES

Anderson, J.N.D. 1970. Islamic Law in Africa. London:
    Frank Cass.

Bargery, G.P. 1934. A Hausa-English Dictionary and
    English-Hausa Vocabulary. London: Oxford Univer-
    sity Press.

Barkow, J.H. 1972. "Hausa Women and Islam." Canadian
    Journal of African Studies 6 (2): 317-28.

Bashir, M.K. 1972. "The Economic Activities of Secluded
    Married Women in Kurawa and Lallokin Lemu, Kano
    City." B.Sc. thesis, Ahmadu Bello University,
    Zaria.

Boserup, E. 1970. Woman's Role in Economic Development.
    New York: St. Martin's Press.

Bray, T.M. 1977. "Universal Primary Education in Kano
State: The First Year." Savanna 6 (1):3-14.

_____. 1978. "Universal Primary Education in Kano
State: The Second Year." Savanna 7 (2):176-78.

Brooks, G.E., Jr. 1976. "The Signares of Saint-Louis and
Goree: Women  Entrepreneurs in Eighteenth-Century
Senegal." In Women in Africa, ed. N.J. Hafkin and
E.G. Bay, pp. 19-44. Stanford: Stanford University
Press.

Cohen, A. 1969. Custom and Politics in Urban Africa.
London: Routledge and Kegan Paul.

Dwyer, D.H. 1978. Images and Self-Images: Male and
Female in Morocco. New York: Columbia University
Press.

Educational Statistics for Kano State 1975-76. Kano:
Government Printer.

Fafunwa, A.B. 1974. History of Education in Nigeria.
London: George Allen and Unwin.

Goody, E.N. 1969. "Kinship Fostering in Gonja." In
Socialization: The Approach from Social Anthropol-
ogy, ed. P. Mayer, pp. 51-74. A.S.A. Monograph 8.
London: Tavistock.

_____. 1971. "Forms of Pro-Parenthood: The Sharing
and Substitution of Parental Roles." In Kinship, ed.
J.R. Goody. London: Penguin Modern Sociology
Readings.

_____. 1978. "Some Theoretical and Empirical Aspects
of Parenthood in West Africa." In Marriage, Fertility and Parenthood in West Africa, ed. C. Oppong,
G. Adaba, M. Bekombo-Priso, J. Mogey, pp. 227-73.
Canberra: Australian National University.

Hill, P. 1969. "Hidden Trade in Hausaland." Man 4 (3):
392-409.

_____. 1971. "Two Types of West African House Trade."
In The Development of Indigenous Trade and Markets
in West Africa, ed. C. Meillassoux, pp. 303-18.
London: Oxford University Press.

_____. 1972. Rural Hausa: A Village and a Setting.
Cambridge: Cambridge University Press.

_____. 1977. Population, Prosperity and Poverty:
Rural Kano 1900 and 1970. Cambridge: Cambridge
University Press.

Hiskett, M. 1975. "Islamic Education in the Traditional
and State Systems in Northern Nigeria." In Conflict
and Harmony in Education in Tropical Africa, ed.
G.N. Brown and M. Hiskett, pp. 134-51. London:
George Allen and Unwin.

Hodder, B.W., and U.I. Ukwu. 1969. Markets in West
Africa. Ibadan: Ibadan University Press.

Hubbard, J.P. 1975. "Government and Islamic Education in
Northern Nigeria (1900-1940)." In Conflict and Har-
mony in Education in Tropical Africa, ed. G.N.
Brown and M. Hiskett, pp. 152-67. London: George
Allen and Unwin.

Kano State Educational Review Committee. 1976.  Final
Report, presented to H.E. Col. Sani Bello.   Kano,
Nigeria.

Lawson, R.M. 1972.   The Changing Economy of the Lower
Volta 1954-67.  London: Oxford University Press.

Lewis, B.C. 1976. "The Limitations of Group Action: The
Abidjan Market Women." In Women in Africa, ed. N.J.
Hafkin and E.G. Bay, pp. 135-56.  Stanford: Stan-
ford University Press.

_____. 1977.  "Economic Activity and Marriage among
Ivoirian Urban Women." In Sexual Stratification: A
Cross-Cultural View, ed. A. Schlegel, pp. 161-91.
New York: Columbia University Press.

McCall, D. 1961. "Trade and the Role of Wife in a Modern
West African Town." In Social Change in Modern
Africa, ed. A. Southall, pp. 286-99.  London:
Oxford University Press.

Mensah, E. 1977.  "A Note on the Distribution of Beggars
in Zaria." Savanna 6 (1):73-76.

Mernissi, F. 1975.  Beyond the Veil: Male-Female Dynamics
in a Modern Muslim Society. Cambridge: Schenkman.

Mullings, L. 1976. "Woman and Economic Change in Africa."
In Women in Africa, ed. N.J. Hafkin and E.G. Bay,
pp. 239-64. Stanford: Stanford University Press.

Ogunbiyi, I.A. 1969. "The Position of Muslim Women as
    Stated by Uthman b. Fudi." Odu 2:43-61.

Ogunsola, A.F. 1974. Legislation and Education in
    Northern Nigeria. Ibadan: Oxford University Press.

Oloko, B.A. 1979. "Socio-Cultural Correlates of School
    Achievement in Nigeria." Ph.D. dissertation, Har-
    vard University.

Oppong, C. 1967. "The Context of Socialization in Dag-
    bon." I.A.S. Research Review 4 (1):7-18.

_____. 1973. Growing up in Dagbon. Accra: Ghana Pub-
    lishing.

_____. 1974. Marriage among a Matrilineal Elite. Cam-
    bridge Studies in Social Anthropology 8. Cambridge:
    Cambridge University Press.

_____. 1975. "A Study of Domestic Continuity and
    Change: Akan Senior Service Families in Accra."
    In Changing Social Structure in Ghana:  Essays in
    the Comparative Sociology of a New State and an
    Old Tradition, ed. J. Goody, pp. 181-200.  London:
    International African Institute.

Paden, J. 1973. Religion and Political Culture in Kano.
    Berkeley: University of California Press.

Peil, M. 1975. "Female Roles in West African Towns."
    In Changing Social Structure in Ghana: Essays in
    the Comparative Sociology of a New State and an Old
    Tradition, ed. J. Goody, pp. 73-90. London: Inter-
    national African Institute.

Pittin, R. 1979. "Hausa Woman and Islamic Law: Is Reform
    Necessary?" Paper presented to African Studies
    Association Meeting, Los Angeles.

Rattray, R.S. 1913. Hausa Folk-Lore. Vol. I. London:
    Oxford University Press.

Raynaut, C. 1977.  "Aspects Socio-économiques de la
    préparation et de la circulation de la nourriture
    dans un village hausa (Niger)." Cahiers d'Etudes
    Africaines-68 XVII (4):569-97.

Robertson, C. 1974. "Economic Women in Africa: Profit-
    Making Techniques of Accra Market Women." Journal

of Modern African Studies 12:657-664.

_____. 1976. "Ga Women and Socioeconomic Change in
Accra, Ghana." In Women in Africa, ed. N. Hafkin
and E.G. Bay, pp. 111-33. Stanford: Stanford
University Press.

Rosen, L. 1978.  "The Negotiation of Reality: Male-
Female Relations in Sefrou, Morocco." In Women in
the Muslim World, ed. L. Beck and N. Keddie, pp.
561-84.  Cambridge: Harvard University Press.

Sanjek, R. and L. Sanjek. 1976. "Notes on Women and
Work in Adabraka." African Urban Notes 2 (2):1-27.

Schildkrout, E. 1973. "The Fostering of Children in
Urban Ghana: Problems of Ethnographic Analysis in
a Multi-Cultural Context." Urban Anthropology 2 (1):
48-73.

_____. 1978. "Age and Gender in Hausa Society: Socio-
Economic Roles of Children in Urban Kano." In Sex
and Age as Principles of Social Differentiation, ed.
J.S. LaFontaine, pp. 109-37. New York: Academic
Press.

_____. 1979. "Women's Work and Children's Work:
Variations among Moslems in Kano." In Social Anthro-
pology of Work, ed. S. Wallman, pp. 69-85. A.S.A.
Monograph 19.  London: Academic Press.

_____. 1980. "The Employment of Children in Kano,
Nigeria." In Participation or Exploitation?  The
Economic Roles of Children in Low-Income Countries,
ed. G. Rodgers and G. Standing.  Geneva: International Labour Office.

Schlegel, A. 1977.  "Toward A Theory of Sexual Stratifi-
cation." In Sexual Stratification: A Cross-Cultural
View, ed. A. Schlegel, pp. 1-40. New York: Columbia
University Press.

Skinner, N. 1969. Hausa Tales and Traditions. Vol. I.
London: Frank Cass.

Smith, M. 1954. Baba of Karo: A Woman of the Muslim
Hausa.  London: Faber and Faber.

Smith, M.G. 1952. "A Study of Hausa Domestic Economy in
Northern Zaria." Africa 22:333-47.

_____. 1954. "Introduction." In Baba of Karo: A Woman of the Muslim Hausa, by M. Smith. London: Faber and Faber.

_____. 1955. The Economy of the Hausa Communities of Zaria. Colonial Research Studies No. 16. London: Her Majesty's Stationery Office.

_____. 1959. "The Hausa System of Social Status." Africa 29 (3):239-52.

_____. 1962. "Exchange and Marketing among the Hausa." In Markets in Africa, ed. P. Bohannan and G. Dalton, pp. 299-334. Evanston: Northwestern University Press.

Sudarkasa, N. 1973. Where Women Work: A Study of Yoruba Women in the Marketplace and in the Home. Anthropological Papers, Museum of Anthropology No. 53. Ann Arbor: University of Michigan.

Trevor, Jean. 1975. "Western Education and Muslim Fulani/ Hausa Women in Sokoto, Northern Nigeria." In Conflict and Harmony in Education in Tropical Africa, ed. G. Brown and M. Hiskett, pp. 247-70. London: George Allen and Unwin.

Wallace, C.C. 1978. "The Concept of Gandu: How Useful Is It in Understanding Labour Relations in Rural Hausa Society?" Savanna 7 (2): 137-50.

West Africa. 1979. "Nigeria: Blueprint for Education." Nov. 19: pp. 2127ff; Nov. 26: pp. 2178ff; Dec. 3: pp. 2234-37.

## 4. Women and Agricultural Change in the Railway Region of Zambia: Dispossession and Counterstrategies, 1930-1970

*Maud Shimwaayi Muntemba*

INTRODUCTION

This paper springs from a broad, ongoing research project on the political, social, and economic dynamics of rural Zambia (Muntemba, 1973, 1977). Some of the questions arising from this research have sharpened my interest in women. Because agriculture dominates rural socioeconomic change, the initial focus is on the position of women in agricultural change. I shall confine my discussion to the railway region of Zambia, the area from Kalomo in the Southern Province to Kabwe in the Central. I chose this region because it has become the most involved in commercial farming. It is close to urban markets and to the main lines of communication, including the railway line. The soils are favorable to most cash crops: maize (corn), cotton, tobacco, and sunflower. Because of the absence of tsetse fly, cattle can be reared. From the early 1900s, Africans have exploited these advantages. Here, between 1930 and 1964 the colonial government concentrated most of its efforts to raise agricultural productivity. From 1964 to 1970, the independent government extended help elsewhere, emphasizing agricultural productivity, but since the natural advantages persisted, the railway region continued to enjoy greater benefits.

The position of women in a period of intensive agricultural change and dislocation as that of 1930-1970 in Northern Rhodesia, later Zambia, must be seen within the framework of capitalist penetration and its operations. Before 1964, metropolitan industrial capital saw in Northern Rhodesia, as in other colonies, a source of cheap mineral and agricultural raw materials. However, because capitalist development had reached an advanced stage, capital's main interest was in minerals. Yet, at the turn of the century what later became Northern Rhodesia was dominated by precapitalist social formations,

for although commodity production had started to emerge
in the latter part of the nineteenth century, this was
in very rudimentary stages.

Capital, then, was confronted with the task of turning Africans into commodity producers. This was essential
because commodity production is a prerequisite to the
capitalist mode of production, and because of capital's
desire to accumulate. The commodities were necessary to
its productive processes. Moreover, acquired cheaply,
colonial raw materials offered a means of maintaining
the rate of profit and offsetting the tendency for that
profit to fall. The coercive power of the colonial state
was used to insure the desired production and flow of raw
materials to the metropole.

From the beginning of the century to about 1926, the
colonial state of Northern Rhodesia was concerned with
turning Africans into wage laborers for the richer mineral
centers in the Southern African economic region. This
region embraced South Africa and the countries to its
north up to and including the Congo (Zaire). Between
1926 and 1930 and after 1935, mineral production in Northern Rhodesia itself expanded and with it the labor
force that had to be fed. Then, after the 1939-1945 war,
the decimated British economy required not only mineral
but agricultural raw materials. The state had the double
task of insuring both the flow of labor to the mining
centers and increased agricultural production to feed the
workers and for export. Settler farmers could not meet
this latter responsibility alone. Therefore, it became
necessary to encourage peasant production, albeit in a
checked manner. But the newly created commodity producers, like their settler counterparts, could not produce the desired quantities unaided primarily because of
their low or nonexistent capital. It became encumbent
upon the state to see to the distribution of the resources with which to raise productivity. It offered loans
and other incentives, disseminated more efficient methods of production and technology, and organized marketing facilities.

When independence came in 1964, the importance of
mineral extraction persisted, as did the need for food
supplies for the labor force and exportable cash crops.
In addition, the new government was initially fired with
the zeal to improve the material quality of life of the
rural population. However, the desire of both the colonial and independent state to increase peasant production
met with constraints. First, there was a need to insure
the flow of labor to the capitalist sectors. Second,
there was the settler group in the period before 1964.
After 1964 some settlers left, but their ranks were
augmented by the emerging local rural bourgeoisie:

politicians, top civil servants, and professional people.
Both settlers and the local rural bourgeoisie competed
for the same scarce technical, financial, and marketing
resources as the peasants.  Because of their access to
state power, they scored over the peasants.  For these
reasons, resources were given to peasants more
selectively.

The colonial and independent governments favored male
producers.  The colonial government did so because of
Western concepts equating man with the breadwinner, in
this case the farmer; the independent government, because
its rulers had come from the emergent middle class, which
was steeped in Western value systems and concepts, thus per-
petuating the colonial attitudes toward peasant producers.
Consequently, in the scramble for resources, women ranked
the lowest.  Moreover, just as the state wished to intensify and increase productivity, so did peasants.  Male
household heads mobilized the labor of their women so
that women's productivity did in fact increase.  However,
reinforced by government attitudes toward female producers, precapitalist systems of control persisted and intensified.  Men controlled the technology, new knowledge,
and produce.  They felt justified in controlling the distribution of agricultural income.

By 1970, a differentiated peasantry had emerged in
which women were a distinguishable deprived group.  The
greater percentage of them became identifiable by a lack
of advanced implements and modern technical knowledge,
by dependence on men for technical information, and by
a lower standard of living.  A few had lost or were in the
process of losing their land claims.  There was a high
rate of female migration to urban centers despite women's
continued major role in agriculture and a lack of urban
employment opportunities.

There were several factors that influenced a social
differentiation in which women became so distinct.  However, government social and economic policies played a
very significant and decisive role.  I shall therefore
confine my discussion to these, the changes they initiated,
and the effects of these on women.


PRE-1930 BACKGROUND

I shall begin by considering precolonial and early
colonial processes of production and job distribution.
During the precolonial period, female participation and
productivity in agriculture were higher than that of men.
The means of production, land tenure, and the social
structure allowed women some measure of economic independence.  Under early colonial rule from 1899 to 1929 this
state persisted, but other economic activities were being

curtailed and wage labor was introduced.  In the 1920s,
the plow and some modern technical knowledge started to
appear.  These heralded the changing roles of the two
sexes in agriculture.

Economic change had been taking place in the centu--
ries  before the inception of colonial rule.  By the
nineteenth century, the following processes of production
dominated:  agriculture, iron smelting and smithing, salt
making, hunting, fishing, gathering, herding, cloth making,
and basket weaving.  Of these, agriculture was central,
for grain provided the staple food.  Except for the fishermen known as the Twa, who lived in the swamps and Kafue
flats, everyone, including specialists in other activities,
cultivated.  The hoe and axe were the main tools of production.  Cultivation began with the felling of trees,
which were later used to provide fertilizer.  This is why
the axe was important.  The hoe was used to turn the
soils, to make beds for crops like potatoes, yams, or
cassava, and to weed.  The household formed the main production unit; in addition, some producers utilized slave
labor, and chiefs exploited that of producers under
their control.  However, the latter relations of production will not be considered in this paper.

The distribution of jobs among and within the various branches of production was based on physiological and
age differences.  In agriculture, men felled the trees
and chopped the branches and bushes; they turned the vir-
gin soils; they burned the dry brush, helped scare away
birds, harvested, and built barns.  Women helped turn
the soils and burn the branches and bushes.  They cleared
old fields, planted, weeded where necessary, and, together with children of both sexes and older people,
played a major role in scaring birds.  They harvested
and transported the grain home for storage.  With the
help of female and male children, women prepared seed
beds.  They were responsible for planting cucurbits and
nuts.

Men alone smelted iron during the dry months and
were responsible for smithing.  Men herded cattle with
the help of boys.  Generally, women made salt.  However,
where this involved traveling long distances to salt
basins, men undertook the task.  Both sexes and all ages
participated in hunting, depending upon the method followed.  There were three main methods:  grass burning,
trapping, and shooting.  The first did not call for any
specialized techniques.  During the dry season in September and October, producers from neighboring villages
set a portion of land on fire.  When the fires died out,
people could help themselves to animals weakened by the
fires.  Men alone hunted by the other two methods, which
required specialized techniques and sometimes long-distance travel.  Again, according to the methods employed,

men and women fished.  Both sexes made cloth.  Only women
wove baskets and made pots.  Women gathered.

Although men's participation was equal to and sometimes surpassed the women's in other activities, in agriculture, female participation and productivity were unquestionably higher than men's.  Nevertheless, women did
not have ultimate control over the produce from household
farms where men were heads because men controlled land.
This disadvantage was offset by the social structure.
The region was dominated by the Tonga in the Southern Province and the Lenje in the Central.  Both groups were predominantly matrilineal though, if married, the women lived
virilocally.  Women had access to land in their own matrikin villages.  They could inherit, hold a special place
among their matrikin, and own property independently.
Widowed women could go back to their original villages,
where they had access to land and organized labor through
kin and work parties.  They had ultimate control over
their produce.  Married women seeking some economic independence cultivated fields, in addition to those of the
household, called ntema in Southern and bushikantwala in
Central Province.  They were given land for such purposes
through the husband's membership in the village of domi-
cile.  If they lived close to their matrikin villages,
they got land there.  Such women bought tools or received
them from their matrikin.  Labor was independently bought,
cooperatively obtained, or provided by their matrikin or
children.  Thus, neither tools nor labor were provided
by the husband.  Women had complete control to distribute
or to sell the produce.  A few women cultivating under
these systems were so successful that they bought slaves
and built up herds of cattle (Mvunga, 1978, pp. 160-65;
Muntemba, 1977, chap. II).

This social structure and access to land persisted
into the early colonial period.  Except for the abolition of slavery, the same labor organization, in which
the household was the main unit, also prevailed.  However, the government curtailed other economic activities
such as smelting and hunting in which males had dominated
in precolonial days.  Salt making, weaving, cloth and pot
making were displaced.  Meanwhile, markets expanded.
The mining industry, which later became the major employer and urbanizing force in the country, carried out
marginal operations during this period.  Nevertheless, an
agricultural market existed in the small mining and administrative sector.  In 1908, a British firm, Fear, Colebrook and Coy, negotiated to buy "native maize" from the
railway region (National Archives of Zambia, 1908).  The
idea of the colonizers was to encourage white migrant
farmers, the settlers, to fill the agricultural market
while Africans filled the labor one.  In the first decade of the twentieth century, there were too few set-

tlers in Northern Rhodesia to fulfill this goal. Moreover, settlers found it more profitable to market their
produce in Katanga, Congo, where a larger labor force
existed.  In addition, until 1930 settlers were perenni-
ally undercapitalized; some lacked the necessary expertise.  Therefore, most were farmer-traders who got their
grain and cattle from African producers to resell.  Furthermore, workers in urban centers supplemented the
ration supplied by their employers by buying directly
from producers.

These developments reinforced the predominance of
agriculture, encouraging men to redirect their labor to
agriculture so that now they participated more than ever
before.  The plow began to make its appearance in the
late 1910s.  Some men gained experience with the new
technology by working on settler farms.  A few attended
mission schools, where they learned additional techniques
like the use of kraal manure and the rudiments of horticulture.  Only male producers adopted these techniques.
Here, then, were the beginnings of the changing roles
of both sexes in agriculture.

The above notwithstanding, male participation in
agriculture was checked by capitalist labor demands and
the distribution of the new technology and techniques.
Together with others, Africans in Northern Rhodesia were
required to provide labor for capitalist production in
the Southern African economic region.  The Northern
Rhodesian mining and settler industries wanted to mo-
nopolize the labor of neighboring Africans.  As labor
pressures mounted, men became part wage workers and
part agriculturalists.  Thus, part of the labor released
from precapitalist activities was deployed in wage
employment.

The distribution of the plow and other techniques
was still too limited to make a significant impact on
relations between the sexes in agricultural production.
Although male productivity was increasing, that of women
still surpassed it at this stage.  The social structure
continued to allow women some economic independence.
Old women then living near the growing towns recalled
to me how they traveled to town sometimes two times a
day to sell produce.  Men recalled the women's role in
increasing household productivity.  They told of going
to urban markets to sell their produce as well as that
of female relatives, who were unable to do so because
of long distances (interviews, Central and Southern
provinces, 1975, 1976).

This early colonial period, then, was marked by increased productivity by both sexes.  But the foundations
were being laid for the changing roles of men and women.

The distribution and control of the new technology, now
still in embryo, indicated patterns of economic independence and dependence that became clear in the 1930-1970
period.

1930-1945

In 1929, the government divided land in the railway
region into two categories:  Crown Lands for non-Africans,
for towns, and for present and future mines, and Native
Reserves for Africans.  Crown Lands encompassed 20 miles
on either side of the railway line.  Between 1930 and
1932, Africans were moved into the Native Reserves.  Considerable portions of land in the reserves were not fertile and without the use of fertilizers had low productivity (Trapnell and Clothier, 1937).  Some people were
moved to areas in the reserves where they could not produce maize, the most important crop on the market.  There
were limited water supplies for human consumption and for
stock, and peasants had to adjust to the new environment.
In fact, the year 1931 saw such disrupted production that
Africans produced less than at the close of the 1920s.
Some could not even grow enough for subsistence.  Productivity remained low for the greater part of the 1930s.
In 1933, the chief secretary of agriculture admitted,
"the artificial conditions such as the formation of the
reserves, the spread of communications and demand for
labour have created difficulties which were previously
non-existent"(National Archives of Zambia, 1933-1938).
At the same time, several factors restrained the
government from encouraging Africans to participate more
fully in the agricultural market.  First, there were
limited government funds, particularly in the 1930s.
Throughout the 1930s and 1940s, the government needed to
insure the flow of labor to capitalist enterprises,
especially to settler farms in the area of the railway
region.  Moreover, peasant production was not to threaten
that of settlers.  Settlers used their access to political power to impose financial and technical controls
against peasants.  Thus, in the 1930s the government
limited its operations to the maize belt of the Southern
and Central provinces, effectively only one-third of the
Native Reserves in the two provinces.  In 1936, the government established the Maize Control Board, whose primary aim was to protect settlers against possible African
competition and cushion them in times of overproduction.
The internal market was divided into two reservations:
Pool A, representing 75 percent of the market, was generally reserved for settlers and dominated by the white
maize, whose seed the government imported from  South

Africa; Pool B, only 25 percent, was for Africans. Nevertheless, the existence of the board insured a market, albeit restricted, for Africans. This was particularly
important since African passage through settler lands had
become restricted after 1929. Thus, government encouragement of African agriculture prior to the 1939-1945 war
does not seem to have gone beyond providing the restricted
market and digging a few wells and dams in the late 1930s.
     Some peasants took the initiative in ameliorating
their difficulties. In the Southern Province, a Seventh
Day Adventist primary school had opened after 1910 and
trained men in the rudiments of agriculture. In 1931,
some of the school's former students got together and
formed the Keemba Hill Farming Scheme. They cultivated
individual plots but pooled their technical and technological resources. Initially, they expended their energy
trying to adapt to the new environment and experimenting
with what and how to grow. However, their efforts were
successful in later years. In 1934, the secretary for
native affairs appealed to the Department of Agriculture
to extend agricultural services to Africans. He noted
that a scheme to train African demonstrators had been
proposed for the Mazabuka Research Station, opened in
1929 to help settlers. During the depression, the government had dropped the scheme to train African demonstrators and had not revived it. He commented that Africans in the railway region were determined,with or without
government help, to increase production and that they had
on their own initiative started to alter their methods
of production. He suggested that a training school be
set up; demonstrators would advise and guide producers
particularly to avoid erosion, likely to occur in the now-
crowded sandy soils (National Archives of Zambia, 1934).
     The chief secretary of agriculture opposed these sug-
gestions on grounds of expense and the academic nature of
training schools. However, he agreed to help Africans to
adapt to the new environment and to encourage missions to
continue giving instructions in elementary agriculture.
The reasons he gave may have been genuine, but it would
not be unreasonable to suggest that his main concern was
to protect settlers. In his summary of the department's
future policy, he proposed, among other things, "to refrain from the encouragement of native maize production
in the vicinity of the Railway Line until such time as
the internal market has largely passed of its own accord
into the hands of the native. Thereafter, if export
appears feasible to organise an export trade of native
maize" (National Archives of Zambia, 1933-1938).
     The above developments, then, resulted in checked
African productivity, but they took place against a background of an expanding market. In the late 1920s, the
labor force in Northern Rhodesia started to grow. As the

mines recovered from the depression, the labor force
steadily increased. War demands led to further mining
expansion, which continued after the war, the increase in
mineral production giving rise to the growth of other industries.


1946-1970

    In the postwar period, several factors caused the
government to encourage African agricultural production.
As the urban centers became more developed, most of the
rural areas became poorer and the desire of people to
move to towns rose. The process that started in the
colonial days was reinforced by the more liberal attitudes
of the independent government, which removed impediments
to the flow of people from rural to urban centers. Thus
was created, in addition to an increasingly stabilized
labor force, an urban community dependent on others for
its food requirements. Second, after the war the British
economy was in a weak state. Cash crops were needed to
bolster the metropolitan economy. Finally, agricultural
grievances were an essential element of the rising nationalist movement in the rural areas. From the colonial
point of view, it was necessary to blunt and sublimate
the movement. After 1964, the independent government saw
in agriculture a way to increase national wealth and to
raise the living standards of the rural people.
    Both governments initiated agricultural programs to
raise peasant production, but all the important ones were
directed toward male producers only. This resulted in a
marked increase in productivity by males. In cases where
female productivity did not decrease or actually rose,
male domination, reflected in income distribution, also
accelerated. This was because men controlled the new
technology and techniques. They had easier access to
government finances and markets.
    Over the preceding decades, peasants in the Southern
Province had demonstrated higher productivity than others
in the country. Therefore, most schemes were first introduced there and later reached Central Province, the
next most productive and easily accessible area. The
government established an agricultural school at Monze
in the Southern Province aimed at training extension
workers for the whole country. It was followed by other
agricultural stations and subcenters in the railway region. Extension workers from the station and subcenters
traveled to the villages to disseminate technical knowledge and distribute literature containing agricultural
information.
    After 1964, some agricultural stations became training
centers as well, offering one- to two-week courses on

various aspects of agriculture:  cropping, husbandry,
poultry, farm machinery and management, food storage,
cooperative principles, and female extension.  The stations partly organized the government's Mechanization
Schemes, through which it hired tractors out to producers.
In 1966, the government added radio forums and gave radios
to subcenters and agricultural camps.  Farmers met once
every week when the Ministry of Agriculture broadcast
technical information.
     In 1946-1947, the government introduced the Improved
Farmers' Scheme in the Southern Province.  Before this
date, the government had termed "improved" the African
farmers it allowed to sell through Pool A.  Now the term
had a technical meaning, referring to any producer who
cultivated his individual plot according to the department's instructions.  In 1951-1952, the department extended
the scheme to the railway region of the Central Province.
"Improved" farmers qualified for government loans of money
up to 50 percent to purchase any implement or inputs.
They were visited by extension workers and received bonuses if they followed the methods advocated by the Department of Agriculture through the extension workers.
In 1948-1949, bonuses ranged from 8s. to 15s.  In 1953-
1954, they went up to 15s. to 27s. per acre (Rees and
Howard, 1955, p. 3).
     This scheme was diluted after independence.  The
government now categorized peasant producers as commercial farmers if they sold upwards of 500 bags of maize
and used machinery, emerging farmers if they sold upwards
of 15-20 bags, and subsistence farmers if they cultivated
for consumption only.  Extension workers did not restrict
their activities to any one category, although the first
group received more attention.  Moreover, the new government was more liberal with loans, extending them to cover
fertilizers and other inputs.  In 1967, it established
the Credit Organization of Zambia to loan money to both
capitalist and peasant farmers.
     Between 1947 and 1948, the administration introduced
the Peasant Farmers' Scheme.  First put into practice in
the Eastern Province, it was soon extended to the Southern
and Central provinces.  Under the scheme, the governing
body set aside blocks of land where "peasants" were each
alloted a plot.  They received loans in the form of advanced implements:  furrow and ridging plows, cultivators,
planters, weeders, and the like, and they could get money
loans from a revolving fund that the government established.  Extension workers devoted much of their time to
this category of producer.  The scheme, as indeed that of
the "improved" farmers, had its own drawbacks; for example,
there were undertones of regimentation and the initial
suspicion expressed by Africans who feared loss of more

land. Nevertheless, it afforded peasants who could not
have done so the means to improve their productive forces.
The scheme remained after 1964.

After the war, the government encouraged cooperative
societies to help peasants market produce and acquire and
distribute inputs. After independence, the new government
saw cooperatives "as a means of developing human and
material resources." It encouraged three types of farming
cooperatives. In the first, both land and implements
were cooperatively controlled. In the second, individual
members controlled their pieces of land, but pooled the
implements. The third were poultry cooperatives for
women.

The colonial government excluded women completely
from its direct efforts to alter agricultural production.
Women could not secure loans. Extension workers did not
impart modern knowledge to them. "Women were more aware
of agriculture. But in my days we did not do anything
on women," said Mr. Nyirenda, an extension worker in the
Southern Province, 1949-1951, and in the Central, 1951-
1962. On their visits, extension workers summoned men
(though women could listen) or left word of the next visit
if the man was absent (Nyirenda, 1975). After 1964,
these barriers were legally removed. However, "the rein-
forcement of success" approach which favored commercial
peasants persisted, so that women continued to experience
difficulties in gaining access to government facilities.
Married women could not secure loans without their husbands' acting as guarantors. None of the men I interviewed in either province assisted their wives, particularly when they realized that peasants as a whole were
discriminated against in favor of the rural bourgeoisie.
None of the women I interviewed received loans for implements and inputs. The only loans women received were
connected with poultry.

Although in principle the independent government
extended training facilities to women, their efforts
were slow to be implemented and limited in effect. At
a meeting of some agricultural personnel in the Central
Province in 1965, a member was asked whether the government intended to extend courses to women. The reply was,
"We shall have to see what to do about women courses"
(Keembe Files, 1965). As late as 1974, one Farm Institute in the region gave courses to 288 women, compared to
704 men. While courses given to men ranged across various
aspects of agricultural production, women's courses
covered only poultry, maize, and groundnut production (two
courses), and female extension (seven courses) (Keembe
Files, 1974). Female extension trained women to sew and
knit and helped them establish sewing clubs in their home
areas. Though they may have turned women into better
mothers and wives, these courses could not have supported

their productive agricultural activities. However, the
government did encourage poultry clubs for women, giving
such clubs loans where necessary. Agricultural officers
helped, and poultry clubs mushroomed, particularly in the
Southern Province.

In 1947, the government established Native Trust
Lands. This gave Africans in areas affected by the
earlier land division more patches of fertile land closer
to the lines of communication. But the government did not
designate any land that might in future be required for
white settlement Native Trust Land (Report of the Land
Commission, 1946). The status quo remained to 1970.

Educational policies contributed to the ability of
Africans to improve productivity. Mission schools gave
rudimentary lessons in agriculture at the primary level.
From the 1920s, the government helped design more comprehensive syllabi for agricultural purposes and gave
grants to schools thus engaged. The government itself
started schools that emphasized academic and industrial
training more than agriculture. Producers who had been
to mission schools were reinforced in the postwar period
when extension workers adopted a ".reinforcement of success" approach; peasants who had independently started
to improve their methods and increase productivity received most attention.

Education helped farmers in another way. Producers
needed capital to improve their productive forces. One
of the ways they obtained cash was by combining wage employment with farming. Teachers, clerks, and workers
employed by Native Authorities, organs of local government in the reserves, typically combined their wage employment with farming. The men went into wage employment,
coming home during holidays and at weekends if close
enough. Away, they left their wives to run the farms.

But this method of capital formation was of little
help to women as independent producers. Up until 1964,
a dismally small percentage of women received formal
education. Those who did tended to marry church ministers,
evangelists, or teachers, all of whom were full-time
workers of the church whose wives had to spend some time
in church affairs. Others married government teachers
and clerks who later formed part of the better placed
peasants. Wage labor did not come easy to uneducated
women. There were openings for them as agricultural
laborers at peak periods and as child nurses (nannies).
However, both paid dismal wages, too low to allow savings.
Because they did not go to school, women could not pick
up technical information through literature. There were
more schools after 1964, but they turned out blue and
white collar workers. Those who were not absorbed in
wage labor tended to remain in towns in the hope of future

openings. The government introduced mass literary programs, which made little impact before 1970. Considered
progressive and therefore more suited to receive government technical help, men dominated the radio forums.

Then, too, Native Authorities insisted that the
government honor the land division in every way. They
rejected applications by non-Africans to set up retail
businesses in the reserves. This allowed peasants yet
another way of forming capital, by operating retail businesses in conjunction with farming. Producers in the railway region were particularly adept in combining agricultural and other wage-earning opportunities, and the region became distinguished from most parts of the country
by a higher standard of living. Because of low capital
formation by women, none availed themselves of this way
of realizing savings for increased agricultural production.

The agricultural measures, then, were selectively
distributed. First, only "improved" and "peasant" farmers
benefited from the government schemes before 1964. Because of staff shortages, only those producers close to
the agricultural stations and subcenters were visited.
For financial reasons, the government established few
"peasant" farms. When independence came, the "reinforce-
ment of success" approach continued to place limitations
on peasant participation and ability to raise productivity. Educational and other social and economic developments reinforced government-instigated prejudicial
policies.

The result was that while regional productivity increased, the peasantry became sharply stratified into rich,
middle, and poor peasants. Deriving the most benefits
from the economic and social developments of the period,
the few rich peasants had by 1970 improved their productive forces appreciably; they sold to the market regularly
and enjoyed lifestyles distinctly better than the others.
They corresponded with what the government termed "progressive" or commercial peasant farmers. Middle, or
"emerging" farmers in government parlance, had, in varying degrees, adopted some modern techniques. They met
their subsistence requirements and sold surpluses to the
market. There were two distinct layers among them: the
upper, who sold surpluses more regularly, and the lower,
who did so irregularly. Defined as those who cultivated
enough for subsistence only, poor peasants were few in
the railway region. There were no independent, rich women peasants. They formed the largest percentage of the
middle peasants, particularly in their lower ranks. Women
formed the largest single group among poor peasants.

## DISPOSSESSION AND COUNTERSTRATEGIES

This section will examine more concretely the effects of these social and economic policies on women producers.  To do so, it is useful to consider women in two
categories, married and single.  But first, it is important to emphasize that the policies altered the socioeconomic position of all women decisively and irretrievably.
Like the men, female producers suffered from the Native
Reserves policies, the women's harm being greater because
of distances and other regulations prejudicial to them.
We saw how in the pre-1930 period women had started to
take advantage of the growing interregional and urban
markets.  Between 1930 and 1964, they could not easily
travel to towns to sell agricultural produce.  Those who
were moved far away had no access to urban markets.
Others who were closer to towns relied on men, seeking
passage through settler lands, to go sell their produce
for them, for the official policy frowned on female presence in towns.  Old women passionately recalled to me
this loss of economic opportunity and independence.  Excluded from the market, women depended on male relatives
in wage employment and on males to go to town on their
behalf.  With independence, these constraints were largely
removed and women living near towns or main lines of communication could sell produce.  However, only a few women
living close to the road and railway line linking Kabwe
to Lusaka profitably did so.  Traffic slackened off south
of Lusaka.
Technological developments favored men.  Because they
participated in wage labor, men were better placed to buy
implements and inputs.  Men's greater access to education
meant they could use them more efficiently.  By 1970, of
the women I interviewed only 2 percent independently owned
some modern implements, ox-drawn plows and planters.
Thirty-two percent were able to handle the plow and 5 percent the weeder; 2 percent could apply fertilizer. None
could handle other implements.  Of the women who cultivated independently, 40 percent used ox-drawn plows,
which were mainly hired or obtained through male relatives.
By the 1960s, the swing of the pendulum against women
was further reflected in the cultivated acreage of crops
associated with modern techniques and controlled by men.
This contrasted with the acreage under female control.
In the first group were maize and cotton.  The second
consisted of sorghum, used for local beer brewing.  There
was a third, which represented crops under joint control,
in this case, beans.  In one area in the Central Province,
acreage under male control in 1968 totaled 3,528; 176
acres were under female control, and 303 were jointly controlled (Keembe Files, 1969).
In married households, male productivity rose

while that of women generally fell.  The rate at which
productivity changed corresponded with the level of
technology attained by the household.  In households
where technology was still at low levels, family labor
remained important.  Eager to increase productivity, male
household heads encouraged their wives in the new technology.  They invited them to be present when extension
workers visited.  Sometimes husbands themselves passed
on the new knowledge to their wives.  Women learned to
handle the plow, use other implements, and apply fertilizers and pesticides.  As a result, women's productivity
was high, sometimes equalling that of men, at other times
surpassing it.  When men combined wage employment with
farming, female agricultural productivity unquestionably
surpassed that of the men's.  This situation was more predominant in the pre-1964 period.

At higher levels of technological development, where
the family possessed advanced implements and techniques
and hired labor, men's productivity became higher than
women's.  This happened in rich peasant households.  Here,
women's productivity in agriculture diminished.  By 1970,
the major role of some of the women in this category was
that of cooking for the husband and others working with
him.

Whether productivity increased, stagnated, or diminished, women gradually became more economically dependent
on their husbands, who controlled the more productive
tools and knowledge.  On the production level, women depended on their husbands for the new knowledge.  In order to mobilize family labor to the maximum, men became
more reluctant to secure additional fields for their
wives in the virilocal villages.  On the distribution
level, men felt more justified to tighten control than
was the case in the pre-1930 period.  They controlled
the distribution of agricultural income.  My survey in
parts of the Central and Southern Provinces  indicated
that men uniformly and consistently returned only a
small proportion of agricultural income to their wives,
in amounts varying between one-tenth and one-quarter of
the total income.  Men insisted that they bought household
goods, paid children's school fees, and reinvested some
of the money in agriculture, all of which were joint
marital financial responsibilities.  Women argued that
they could not do their share because of the meager portion their husbands gave them.  "What would women do with
large amounts of money, anyway?" men asked me and their
wives.

The inequitable income distribution was felt most
keenly by women in view of the fact that men kept all
the tools in the event of a divorce.  If the husband
died, his kin inherited the farming equipment.  In the
1964-1970 period, funerals became an undignified scramble

for property by the husband's relatives. Materially, the
unjust distribution of the family income was evidenced
in dress and housing. Men wore decent clothes and shoes,
"because we go to town more often." Some wives still
went barefooted. In polygynous households, the husband
lived in a decent house, the wives in shacks.

Unmarried women relied on inefficient tools and
methods of production, yet married women tended to envy
them, feeling that as independent cultivators with control
over their sales and income, single women had greater
opportunities for raising the material quality of life.
Moreover, they did not have to work for the husband for
a mere pittance. But the married women overlooked the
many disadvantages endured by single female producers.
Because they did not have husbands who wished to increase
family productivity by educating their wives, unmarried
women had less access to technical knowledge. They had
to depend on male relatives. Although social ties were
loosening, unmarried women could still draw on the labor
of some of their relatives. If they owned cattle, they
pooled these with the relatives to enable them to use
plow cultivation. Sometimes they bought fertilizers,
which male relatives applied for them. But my survey indicated that gradually these women came to depend on
hired labor and equipment as their male relatives became
more involved in their own production. None of the women
I interviewed had been given government loans. None
seemed to have sold regularly, although occasionally some
sold as many as one hundred bags of maize. However, as
they grew older, their productivity diminished, their
living standards declined.

My observations suggest that both categories of
women experienced production dislocations. Whether married or single, they gradually became dependent on males:
on husbands to train them and hand out money, or on matrikin and hired male labor to help increase productivity
through the use of more efficient methods otherwise denied
them. And in households where their labor was still
crucial, women provided cheap exploitable labor for the
husbands who controlled the purse.

As the government's and husbands' erosion of their
economic independence and potential grew, women became
acutely aware of their disadvantaged position. One frustrated woman stated,

Men have always been going for training. Very few
of us went between 1964 and 1970. Never before that
date. What they taught us cannot help us much.
Our friends [men] were taught piggery. We were
taught how to make scones. How could that help
us with our farming? Flour was too expensive to
get anyway. Later, you could not even get it.

Here are the words of another informant:

> Now a woman is like a slave.  She works hard.  The
> husband gives her so little in order to buy tractors
> and other implements. When he dies, she loses all.
> Or she works as a slave.  At the end of the year,
> the family sells one hundred bags of maize.  The man
> gives her K20 [about $25].   Following year the
> family sells three hundred bags.  He still gives
> her K20.  What is that but slavery?

The woman uttered these words in a heated argument with
her husband in which he was exonerating male decisions
in matters of income distribution.  The woman was a successful farmer who distinguished himself in the community
by the clothes he wore, including suits, and the good
standard house he lived in.  Quotations like these clearly
indicate the frustrations women have felt in the changed
situation.  What have they done?

Some women attempted to remedy the situation by
taking advantage of their continued access to land.  Soon
after the war, ntema and bushikantwala fields increased,
corresponding with women's growing deprivation.  Out of
sales from these fields, some were able to clothe themselves decently and invest in advanced implements.  A few
contributed to their children's education.  However, evidence suggests that with growing opportunities for expansion from the latter part of the 1950s, most women gradually lost this alternative.  This process began in the
Southern Province.  By the latter part of the 1960s, women in the Central Province also experienced the limitations.  In both less and more mechanized households, a
number of men resented their wives' independent cultivation, which they feared might make it more difficult to
control their labor.  In more mechanized households,
where female participation in agriculture had decreased,
there was always a fear of breakdowns of implements, ne-
cessitating greater reliance on family labor.  In less
mechanized households, men wanted to mobilize family
labor.  Furthermore, where women spent most of their time
in family fields, they were too tired to do much in their
separate ones.  Thus, men became less willing to secure
land for their wives.  As land became scarce in some parts
of the region, particularly in the Southern Province,
women's access to land in virilocal villages was curtailed further.  Where women insisted on retaining their
additional fields, men reacted by maintaining that traditions be respected and not allowing their wives to use
household implements.  I came across only one case in which
the husband claimed that he let his wife use household
implements he said were his.  The wife was quick to re-
mind him that he used hers in return.  Men did not share

their knowledge with women.  Even though they were better
equipped in modern methods, they persisted in not working
with their wives in these separate fields.  Consequently,
the acreage was small and the yield low and poor in
quality.

These few women who continued to cultivate additional
fields hired labor and equipment, which required capital.
This, as we saw, did not easily come to them.  Some could
send to their matrikin villages for implements and labor,
but foreigners and women from other parts of Zambia did
not have this resource.

Some women expressed their discontent by withdrawing
their labor from household fields, particularly at peak
labor periods.  Local women utilized this most effectively.
During the rainy season, they went back to their matrikin
villages, where they had access to land in their own
right.  At harvest time, they went away again.  This practice was greatly resented by men, who had to either increase the women's share of income or sue for divorce if
the pattern was frequently repeated.

Local men labeled the women's reaction "laziness"
and "insubordination."  They were quick to point to foreign women who worked from dawn to dusk and yet "behaved
well."  However, foreign women did so because their options were limited.  In fact, the men's remarks under-
score the disadvantaged position of foreign women.  When
what they considered exploitation persisted, both local
and foreign women felt justified in divorcing their husbands.  Thus, the changing economic base adversely affected social relations.  But temporary withdrawal of labor
or even divorce did not guarantee permanent respite for
married women.  Back in their natal villages, they faced
the production difficulties of single women.

Some women, married or single, turned to those crops
and other economic activities they felt did not require
much capital outlay and expertise and over which they
could have complete control.  Some started to grow vegetables for sale; others attempted to raise poultry; they
also increased acreage devoted to groundnuts.  All these
activities had traditionally been associated with women.
But the women experienced difficulties.  First, there
were not many perennial rivers in the reserves of the
railway  region, and producers found it difficult to
grow vegetables during the dry season.  Furthermore, there
were transport and marketing difficulties.  A government
horticultural officer explained:

> There is a problem on vegetable sales in that we
> have no market for  vegetables in Keembe areas.  So
> it is hard for farmers to be waiting on the roads,
> in that they get lifts on the roads.  Also they

are wasting money using lifts from Keembe areas
going to copperbelt and many other towns where
they can find people to buy their produce. (Keembe
Files, 1970-1972)

Another agricultural assistant reminded the department
of the problem of marketing, adding, "it is better to think
of the market before considering to keep birds" (Keembe
Files, 1969b). Because birds are perishable, only women
very close to urban centers or the main lines of communication availed themselves of this opportunity for improving their lot. They were not the majority. Then, too,
men started to move into vegetable and groundnut growing
by providing the tools for their wives. As with other
cash crops, this sort of farming entailed some measure
of male control of produce and distribution. However,
by 1970, this process was not yet marked.
     Finally, as with other peasants, women were threat-
ened by the emerging local rural bourgeoisie, who com-
manded more efficient productive forces. Between 1964
and 1970, they started buying plots near towns where they
worked. Many went in for vegetable growing and poultry.
They dominated the urban markets, thereby further under-
cutting women's efforts.
     A number of women turned to beer brewing. The suc-
cess of this depended on their distance from towns and
main lines of communication. The closer to town, the
greater the competitive threat from bottled beer and
imported brewed beer. In the 1964-1970 period, there
was an impressive swing in consumption to these two,
which caused some women to move into the bottled beer
business. They did this successfully, given the high
demand. Women farther from towns and main roads found
brewing local beer a lucrative activity. But the frequency and quantities allowed women to make enough just
for day-to-day requirements. For a more secure standard
of living, they looked to agriculture and male relatives.
     The precarious life resulting from changing agricul-
tural fortunes led many poor female peasants to make
"temporary loans" of land to which they had access as members of their matrikin villages. Such women did not always succeed in reclaiming their land and the arrangement
sometimes resulted in permanent loss of land. Moreover,
as population increased in those areas with greater economic opportunities, land became scarce, and although
land sales were not legal, some women sold their land
outright.
     Finally, women sought recourse by migrating to towns,
where they hoped for better economic opportunities. How
successful or unsuccessful they became needs further research, though my data suggests that some of the ways

open before 1964 were fast closing to them.  In colonial
days, the government did not encourage women to migrate
to towns.  Some Native Authorities even passed regulations
forbidding such movement.  However, some women managed
to escape and lived as "shabeen queens," women who ran
prostitute houses in the compounds.  Some were prostitutes
themselves.  But by 1970, towns had reproduced their own
prostitutes.  Other women worked as child nurses.  This
option was still open to them in 1964-1970, although most
employers preferred workers farther from the railway line,
who, they felt, were easier to control.  Third, women became traders, an option discussed by Ilsa Schuster in her
paper.  How long women can seek respite by running to towns
remains to be seen. Generally, urban life for women in the
informal sector is fast becoming precarious.


CONCLUSION

     I have traced the changing fortunes of women in the
most agriculturally endowed part of Zambia.  I have argued
that between 1964 and 1970, agricultural productivity was
closely linked to government policies and attitudes.
This was because in the colonial and neocolonial economy,
the government played a significant role as controller
of lending and marketing facilities, of technology and
technical knowledge.  Active government involvement during
this period raised productivity for some peasants but
placed handicaps on others.  Women were the majority of
the latter group.  They lagged behind in advanced technology and modern knowledge, and their productivity consequently stagnated or diminished.  Second, men controlled the new technology and knowledge.  Thus, even where
female productivity rose appreciably, men controlled the
distribution of household income.  Wives did not receive
a fair share.  Women in rich and upper middle-class households experienced this more sharply, for poor peasant
husbands did not have much to share anyway.  Because of
the changing circumstances, women's standard of living
stagnated or fell.  Where it rose in married households,
it depended on the husband's continued support.  Overall,
women became some of the region's poorest inhabitants.
     Peasant women became sharply aware of their deprived
status.  Some sought respite, but their attempts were
not always successful.  Married women's flight back to
their natal villages did not guarantee higher productivity
and better quality of life.  At most, it granted them
freedom from what some termed "a life of slavery."

REFERENCES

Keembe Files. 1965. Minutes of the Broken Hill Rural
Intensive Conservation Committee Held at Keembe
Farm Institute, 14 October.
_____. 1969a. Agricultural Officer, Keembe, to Dis-
trict Agricultural Officer, Kabwe, 30/1/69. Farming, Gen/1/14.
_____. 1969b. Report by the Agricultural Assistant,
Chibombo, 9/9/69. Crops/Gen/21.
_____. 1970-1972. Horticultural Officer, Keembe
Agricultural Station to Horticulturalist, Lusaka,
23/2/70, Report on Vegetable Growing in Keembe Areas.
A/AS/60. Progress Report, General.
_____. 1974. Uncatalogued, Farmer Training Programmes.
Muntemba, M.S. 1973. "The Evolution of Political Systems
in South-Central Zambia, 1894-1953." M.A. thesis,
University of Zambia.
_____. 1977. "Rural Underdevelopment in Zambia:
Kabwe Rural District, 1850-1970." Ph.D. dissertation, University of California at Los Angeles.
Mvunga, M.P. 1978. "Land Law and Policy in Zambia."
Ph.D. dissertation,University of London.
National Archives of Zambia. 1908. Fear, Colebrook
and Coy to Administrator, North-Western Rhodesia,
25.8.08. BS2/20, Cotton Growing and Maize Trade.
_____. 1933-1938. Chief Secretary of Agriculture.
Memorandum on the Future Policy and Organisation of
the Department of Agriculture, 1933. Sec. 1/58.
Policy of Organisation of the Agriculture Depart-
ment.
_____. 1934. Secretary for Native Affairs to Chief
Secretary, No. 121-55/2/9, 12/2/34. ZA 1/9/55/9,
Proposed Agricultural School, Reserve XII.
Nyirenda, E.R. 1975. Interview of 7 May.
Rees, A.M.M., and R. Howard. 1955. An Economic Survey of
African Commercial Farming among the Sala of Mumbwa
District of Northern Rhodesia. Lusaka.
Report of the Land Commission. 1946. Lusaka.
Trapnell, C.P., and J.N. Clothier. 1937. The Soils,
Vegetation and Agricultural Systems of North-Western
Rhodesia: Report of the Ecological Survey. Lusaka.

## 5. Marginal Lives: Conflict and Contradiction
## in the Position of Female Traders in Lusaka, Zambia

*Ilsa Schuster*

Research in the past few years has shown an important change in the economic activity of African women
which has produced an impact on the social relationships
of women toward each other and toward men (Obbo 1975;
Hansen, 1975; Nelson, 1978; Schuster, 1979; Hafkin and
Bay, 1976). Trade in particular is conspicuous in the
economic activities of urban women. Study of its forms
in various societies suggests the existence of similar
patterns and constraints. Thus, it is said, because
wives have definite financial obligations as providers to
their families, women trade more out of a sense of necessity than privilege. The proceeds of trade provide marginal subsistence. While women organize and participate
in group action, such activity is limited in scope (Hafkin and Bay, 1976, pp. 6, 7, 12, 13, 15).
   The female traders of Lusaka present an interesting
case study in this new area of inquiry. In Zambia, unlike West Africa, there is no deep-rooted tradition of
female trade, and extensive involvement in such activity
is a recent phenomenon. Trade in Lusaka has arisen as an
important local response to the major social upheaval
brought about by mass migration. Lusaka's social and
economic systems, reflecting those of the nation-state
Zambia, of which Lusaka is the capital city, are in a

Field work was conducted between February 1971 and September 1974, initially under a two-year predoctoral grant
from the National Institute of Mental Health and subsequently under a grant from the University of Zambia.
An additional period from October 1975 to August 1976
was spent in Lusaka. I wish to thank Drs. Bonnie Kel-
ler, Claire Robertson, and M.S. Muntemba and participants
in the Symposium on Women and Work in Africa, held
April-May 1979 at the University of Illinois-Urbana-
Champaign, for their helpful comments.

state of flux.  Political change in the national arena
has brought in its wake major demographic change.  As a
result, whole populations have had to adjust the social
and economic arrangements by which they order their
lives.  During the early stages of such changes, when new
arrangements are as yet in the making and social and economic conditions are fluid, values, attitudes, and behavior patterns tend to be ambiguous.  Ambiguity is reflected in such a high degree of conflict and contradiction that these become the norm.  The female traders of
Lusaka lead marginal lives, both as individuals and as
a group in society.  As witnesses to rapid social and
historical changes wrought upon their nation, they are
both victims and beneficiaries of the developing socioeconomic system.  Having left the familiar world of the
rural village, they have entered the new world of the
city.  But their lack of education and proficiency at
skills required for employment in a Western type job
denies them the possibility of enjoying many of the modern amenities of the city, and often their primary concern is merely to survive.  "Survival" is used here in
its literal rather than metaphoric sense:  the majority
of traders work for food to fill stomachs, clothes to
protect modesty, and, if they are unmarried, a crude
form of shelter.
    "Marginal" is used in a dual sense.  First, the un-
educated, unskilled, impoverished women of Lusaka are
economically marginal.  That is to say, they make no
substantial contribution to economic production in town
and in fact cannot do so, given the nature of the urban
economy.  Second, these women are socially marginal in
the sense that they occupy an ambiguous position in the
eyes of the wider society.  They lack the high socioeconomic status of educated career women in the modern sector and the well-defined--if inferior--status of rural
women who must produce subsistence crops.  I suggest that
the first and second types of marginality are function-
ally related and mark an important change in the position of women.  I further suggest that these processes,
the economic marginalization of women out of production
and their increasingly ambiguous position in society, are
widespread in contemporary Africa.  The processes are
rooted in European colonial attitudes about the incorporation of men into modern production systems, which
African governments continue to emphasize, in both
urban and rural development plans.[1]
    The aim of this paper is to show the conflict and
contradiction in the attitudes of the wider society toward these women, its reflection in their ambiguous
position in society, and its embodiment in the personal
lives of the traders.

## THE SETTING

Zambia gained its independence from Great Britain in 1964. In the years immediately before and after this date, there was a widespread feeling throughout the country that its citizens would soon enjoy what they called "the fruits of independence." In anticipating the new dawn, symbolized by the name kwacha (dawn) given the new currency, ever-increasing numbers of people began migrating to Lusaka, itself a symbol of the new-found freedom that was to come at the end of "the yoke of colonial oppression."

Colonial Lusaka had never suffered the extremes of sex ratio imbalance that were characteristic of the copperbelt (Ohadike, 1975). Nevertheless, there always had been substantially more men than women in Lusaka during this period. During the 1960s, this imbalance was gradually corrected as year by year women migrated from the rural areas and from other Zambian cities to Lusaka (Ohadike, 1975).

By the mid-1970s, the population of the city had nearly doubled to half a million. An unprecedented number of women and dependent children had come to live in Lusaka, and the sheer weight of their numbers indicated a demographic change that would have a major impact on socioeconomic organization. Clearly, the women could not fulfill familiar rural economic roles in the new urban environment. Perhaps even more importantly, there were now too many women intending to stay in town for them to be accomodated in previously familiar ways.

Before the era of balanced sex ratios, the most common survival strategy the women in town used was to enter into a more or less temporary "marital" union with a man. In exchange for her domestic and sexual services, the man would provide her and the children born of their union with food, clothing, and shelter (cf. Gutkind, 1974, pp. 108-9). Given the opportunity, she would supplement the diet of the household with produce from a small kitchen garden (cf. Wilson, 1940). A woman who did not wish, or was not able, to enter into such a dependency relationship with a man supported herself through various forms of trade, including beer brewing, prostitution, and the selling of certain foodstuffs.

The last option must be examined more closely, for the significance of female trade in Zambia during the period before independence is disputed. Some informants, Zambian and European, maintain that women did, in fact, engage in market trade during the colonial period, that female traders served as political mobilizers for various political parties during the struggle for national independence, and that these traders were respected as a force-

ful social group.  Other informants remember a more
limited role for women traders in that period, an impression suggested by researchers.  Nyirenda's brief study of
Luburma, Lusaka's oldest and largest African market
(1957, pp. 37, 43, 49, 50), is consistent with the observations of informants who maintain that the activities of
Lusaka's female marketeers in colonial days were irregular and limited to the sale of their domestic supplies
in the dry season; during the rains they sold mainly
forest and garden produce.  Analysis of the female trade
on the copperbelt, based on Miracle's data (1965, pp.
322, 333-34), collected in the colonial period, shows the
same tendency.

Contemporary informants, both within and outside the
marketplace, maintain that Zambian women in the colonial
period traded mainly out of desperation rather than preference, that most female traders were of non-Zambian
origin, and that female traders were generally regarded
with contempt by "the masses" as being "no better than
prostitutes because they talk with strangers."  Certainly,
there never existed in Zambia the strong, positive tradition of the West African market women.  When women in
Zambia did sell fresh produce grown by commercial farmers,
they competed with adult men, who were the overwhelming
majority of sellers.


THE RISE OF WOMEN'S TRADE

After independence, a greater need developed for
women to earn money.  Demographic change in the sex ratio
has meant greater competition among women for the limited
resources available to the uneducated, unskilled urban
population.  Thus, for example, it is not as easy as it
once was for a woman to find a man willing to support
her in the urban style to which she aspires.  While the
most common survival strategy of women continues to be
dependence on a man, it is increasingly held to be un-
satisfactory even by the women who practice it.  This is
because there is not as much flexibility for women in
choosing among men as there once was, so women have become more victimized.  They must accept a level of financial neglect that had not been necessary for urban women
in the past.  Men remain unreliable supporters and earn
low salaries.  As Hansen (1975) has shown, more of Lusaka's married women would like to work than actually do
find work.

Prostitution in the Western sense is not a common
occupation in Lusaka as it is, for example, in tourist
cities like Nairobi or ports like Dar es Salaam.  It is
heavily stigmatized in Lusaka and is considered by the

women themselves to be the least desirable occupation.
While there is some incidence of the exchange of sexual
intercourse for money, it is considered embarrassing, and
women retain the right to refuse a man (cf. Schuster,
1979, pp. 146-47).

Work in the formal sector of Lusaka's economy is
considered the most desirable occupation for a woman to
find.  Thus, for an uneducated, unskilled woman, a job as
a cleaner in a public institution is relatively prestigious and secure.  But there are many fewer jobs for
unskilled women than there are job seekers, so relatively
few are formally employed.  There is also little work to
be found as house servants, since this form of employment still tends to be a male occupation, as in colonial
days.  Increasingly, with the growth of an indigenous
elite, there are opportunities for young female migrants
who work as child-minders ("nannies").  Normally, such
opportunities are available only to those with elite
relatives, and they receive only token salaries.

Under these harshly limited circumstances, trade
has emerged as the most significant strategy for uneducated, unskilled women to earn money in town.  It has become the women's most common--most widely accepted and
acceptable--occupation.  In rapidly expanding Lusaka,
opportunities for trading have opened up in all sections
of the city.  Shanty towns grow up in pockets within the
city and at great distances surrounding the city.  This
growth creates a potential consumer market.  Though impoverished, shanty-town dwellers must eat and drink, and
mechanisms for food and beer distribution must be developed.  Authorized inner-city and suburban marketplaces
expand to cope with the burgeoning population.  In the
late 1960s, an industrial area also grew up in a specially zoned district of Lusaka.  It lacked a formal, legal
provision for feeding the workers.  Elite residential
areas develop far from the center of town, creating consumer needs by wives of house servants, who would buy
locally instead of walking many miles to the central
markets, given the choice.

Female entrepreneurship has thus come to take various forms.  The basic categorization turns on the issue
of legality.  Trade in Lusaka is either legal, which is
to say licensed, or it is illegal, or unlicensed.  My
impression is that women's unlicensed trade is the far
more common variety, although it is virtually impossible
to document statistically.[2]  Women's licensed trade is
confined to authorized marketplaces, limited to the sale
of fresh produce and to cooked meals at "restaurant"
stalls, whereas illegal trade takes place throughout
the city and is limited only by the resources of capital
and the personal strength, energy, imagination, and dar-

ing of the individual trader.

Illegal trade can be classified as based in the home or in public (outside the home). Home-based trade is either fairly regular, as in the case of the brewing of beer or gin, or it is highly irregular. Sometimes it is dependent on personal luck in securing a surplus of a household necessity, such as cooking oil or soap, which are in chronic short supply in Lusaka. Sometimes it is a product of advance planning, such as a trip south to the Kafue River to buy fish for personal use and for sale. Sometimes it is a service such as healing and giving abortions, dependent on reputation and density of personal networks. Nearly all illegal home-based trade is found only in shanty towns.

Illegal public trade is found all over Lusaka. Some of it is regular and itinerant. Women sell fried chicken or mice outside taverns and bars. Some itinerant trade is seasonal. Women squat on busy downtown sidewalks to sell a basinful of fresh mangoes or boiled maize. Some itinerant trade is based on craft. Squatting in the parking lot of a suburban shopping center, women sell crocheted doilies or clay pots to Europeans. Other illegal trade is not itinerant, but, rather, based in a specific location. Illegal markets on well-traveled crossroads grow up. Some markets are based on the sale of raw produce, as in elite residential neighborhoods. Other markets are based on the sale of cooked foods, as in the industrial area.

Illegal trading activity is difficult, for women who engage in it risk arrest by the police. Arrested women must pay fines, which produce enormous hardship for the woman and her dependants. They take the risk for several reasons. The trade may be too intermittent and on too small a scale for them to buy a license. Alternatively, the trade may be illegal--as, for example, brewing is. Or no license is offered for a particular type of trade-- for example, selling fried mice outside taverns.

Legal, licensed trade is obviously the more desired entrepreneurial activity of Lusaka's "businesswomen." This trade is confined to marketplaces, of which there are two types. The first type, also the most desired, is the marketplace that is authorized by Lusaka's City Council. The council has poured tens of thousands of kwacha into tarring and fencing these markets and, in some, constructing concrete block stalls, roofed in tin as a protection against the sun. In these busy establishments, traders expect to make a profit, however small. The second type is the authorized market in an unauthorized shanty town. The council refuses to grant the neighborhood itself as legal, but, by granting licenses to traders in its marketplace, gives it a quasi-legal

status.  Few shanty-town marketeers expect to make profits through their entrepreneurial activity.  For them,
trade is a strategy for sheer physical survival in which
nonmonetary exchange transactions are an important economic activity.  Despite its lack of profitability, women
prefer it to itinerant trade.  Itinerant trade is a soli-
tary activity, whereas shanty-town market trade involves
cooperation and mutual support among the women, which increases their strength as individuals coping with the
stresses of poverty.

One of the most important aspects of marketplace-
based trade, particularly in fresh produce, is its new
domination by women.[3]  Whereas men predominated in the
colonial period as traders in fresh produce and a few
continue selling in Lusaka's wealthiest old market, today
the fresh produce trade has been almost totally monopo-
lized by women.  As the Zambia Daily Mail reports ("Well
done, women" 20 October 1971),"Men have since 1964 been
losing the grip and recognition for the right to pre-
dominate in the market."  In the new shanty-town markets,
market managers do not permit men to sell fresh garden
produce.


AMBIVALENT ATTITUDES OF THE GOVERNMENT

Zambian society exhibits an extreme ambivalence toward female traders.  The ambivalence exists at different
levels of society.  At the level of the central government, ambivalence is not specifically directed to women
as traders, but to the role that urban women, on the
one hand, and private entrepreneurial activity, on the
other hand, should play in the state.

National politicians extol the virtues of the working woman, encouraging the uneducated to try their hand
at trading.  They stigmatize the urban poor housewife as
a "lazy parasite" while soliciting political support in
the marketplace among the female traders.  Market women
are expected to join UNIP, the national political party,
and they are pressured into joining the UNIP Women's
Brigade, which, indeed, gets most of its grass-roots
strength from urban market women.  Yet the same politicians who, in one breath, flatter marketeers as "developers of the nation" and require their presence at political rallies in the next breath, instruct them to return
to their homes and not to interest themselves in politics when demonstrators, expressing their own opinions
and interests, prove politically embarrassing.  And, sub-
mitting to male authority, they obey, salvaging self-
respect by grumbling and belittling men (Schuster, 1979,
p. 165).

Ambivalence toward private entrepreneurial activity
derives, at least in part, from the philosophy of Dr.
Kenneth Kaunda, Zambia's president since 1964.  Dr.
Kaunda is against capitalism because the capitalist system is based upon man's greed.  But he is also against
communism and does not envision a society in which all
means of production and distribution are state controlled.
In his philosophy of "Humanism," citizen and state cooperate for the betterment of all.  Zambia's economic system can thus best be described as inconsistent.  At times,
policies are procapitalist, requiring Zambian citizens
to take over retail trade from foreigners (rather than
nationalizing distribution), and at other times anti-
capitalist, requiring large private firms to sell controlling shares to government.  "Humanism" is said to
benefit "the common man," but there is disagreement within the society as to who should be considered "the common
man."

Government ambivalence toward capitalists at the
national level filters down to the local, city level,
where it seriously affects produce traders.  Clearly, it
is in the interest of city and national government to
insure the distribution of food in the urban areas,
especially because chronic shortages of basic commodities
create social tensions and a frustrated and deprived
consumer public.  Small-scale retail trade is encouraged
as an aid to distribution of consumer needs.  Taxes and
market fees contribute to city council coffers.  Town-
planning councils periodically designate new marketplaces
as cities grow.  Such areas are inadequate for serving
the burgeoning population, however, so that illegal trading is inevitable.

Yet, the notion of illegal trade itself is a product
of government's ambivalence.  The presence of illegal
traders squatting around the city is thought to make the
city look poor, untidy, and to call attention to distribution problems.  The modern capital city of a progressive developing country should hide such evidence of its
poverty, it is thought.

Illegal traders also symbolize lack of control of
its citizens and their social and economic problems by
the government.  Government considers this a problem because, well within the memory of today's young adult migrants, the ruling party had promised so much in the years
immediately before and following independence.  Previously, the failure to raise the African standard of
living was attributed to racist colonial policies.  A decade after independence, colonial policies can no longer
be blamed.  Instead, the politically sophisticated urban
population today tends to blame the policies of the present government for the shortages, distribution problems,

and the low standard of living.  Suppression of traders
under the guise of protecting consumer health and maintaining quality standards is really government suppression of testimony to the failure of its "humanistic"
economic policy.  Fines paid by illegal traders contribute to city council coffers; confiscated food items contribute to full stomachs of policemen.  These may be two
economic reasons, complementing political reasons, for
harassment of illegal traders.


THE EFFECT ON THE MARKETPLACE

     The contradictory attitudes of government toward
trading both structure and limit the success that traders,
both legal and illegal, can hope to achieve.  Since all
traders are seen by the local and national government as
"greedy capitalists" whose profits are made at the expense of "the common man," there are active policies to
restrict market practice and keep the marketeers tightly
controlled, which have the effect of insuring their economic marginality.
     Price fixing is one mechanism by which government
controls trading activity.  Nearly all popularly consumed fresh produce is price controlled to guard against
what government considers the danger of excessive profit
making.  Traders are expected to own scales and sell
their produce by weight.  Government bureaucrats called
"price-checkers" patrol the markets and report sellers
who charge more than the controlled price or who sell by
volume rather than by weight.  Such "cheaters," as they
are called, are fined.
     Women must sometimes pay nearly as much for their
produce as they are permitted to sell it for.  Sometimes, turnover is so low that they do not sell out before government lowers the retail price, and they are
forced to sell at a loss.  Fines can put them out of
business.  The use of scales to weigh produce is deeply
resented and resisted, whenever possible, by trader and
consumer alike.  The practice of giving basela, an added
amount to favored customers, reported from colonial
times, continues despite government interference over
the issue of weights and measures.
     Thus, even in the legal marketplaces, the atmos-
phere is often sullen and somber.  There is very little
active hawking; gaiety derives largely from music from
portable radios, not from the hustle and bustle of the
busy market full of competing sellers.  There is much
tension and suspicion, for a customer may really be a
price-checker in disguise.  Competition among sellers
can not be based on variations in price, or even varia-

tions in what is offered, for nearly every trader offers the same items for sale. Since traders can not legally undercut the prices in order to sell out, there is some variation in quality as the produce is in varying states of freshness. But the only significant basis for competition is the extent to which an individual trader is willing to offer credit. This she does with extreme reluctance.

Limiting the number of marketplaces and the number of stalls within marketplaces is another way government controls and restricts trade. In shanty towns, competition for a place to trade is very keen. Once local residents agree to set aside an area for trade, the first action they take is to elect a manager who, together with the local chairman of UNIP, pressures home-based traders to move into the marketplace. Since the number of stalls is limited, and since women are harassed by the UNIP youth if they try to trade from their homes once a marketplace is set up, they put themselves on a waiting list for a stall while trading, if they must, beyond the shanty town. If a stall holder misses a day in the market and does not pay the daily market fee, her place may be given to a woman on the waiting list. To prevent this, traders enter into friendships in which they mind each other's stalls during absences. Without such cooperation, they cannot stay in business.

Another important form of cooperation in these poor marketplaces derives from the combination of the desperate poverty of the traders and the low turnover of produce they sell. They enter into exchange transactions with each other, bartering vegetables among themselves, together cooking them in the marketplace over shared charcoal fires and taking them home to their families for the evening meal. Such exchange transactions cut loss through spoilage and are a basic strategy for survival for those for whom existence itself is precarious. Thus, while there is more organized group action by legal traders for whom profit making is a goal and a hope, there is more nonmonetary economic cooperation among women for whom mere physical survival is the primary goal.

This simple kind of economic cooperation as a survival strategy is also found among Lusaka's illegal brewers in the shanty towns. Economic cooperation within transient friendship networks was also observed among female brewers in Mathare Valley, Nairobi (Nelson, 1978).

Markets in Lusaka are sectioned off according to type of trade. Thus, for example, tobacconists have their section, tinsmiths, tailors, grocers, charcoal sellers, bicycle repairers all have their own areas. Enhancing the separation of the world of the marketplace

from the community, each market erects a fence as soon
as possible.  Produce sellers have their own section in
the marketplace, and a certain amount of personal cooperation among them emerges as a result of propinquity.
Sellers spend about eight to ten hours a day in their
section of the market, in close and constant physical
proximity.  Tending the stall takes up very little time
except for busy Saturday mornings at month's end, when
salaried workers get paid.

Under the circumstances, the traders' most constant
and frequent social interactions are with each other,
gossiping, advising each other, commiserating.  Small
acts of cooperation exist on a daily, even hourly basis,
such as supervising each others' toddlers.  Less frequently, more important acts of cooperation occur, such
as when an elderly tribeswoman acts as banachimbusa
(female instructor) to her fellow trader's daughter at
the time of the daughter's initiation.

Government interference in their trade has had the
positive side effect of creating a consciousness of common self-interest among female traders who are based in
marketplaces.  They organize protests against government
policies through their membership in the (male-dominated)
African Marketeers and Fisheries Union, their membership in the UNIP Women's Brigade, or their membership in
a particular local marketplace.  They demonstrate against
price fixing, against the use of scales, against harassment.  Within the union, they threaten to quit and form
their own union if "useless" male members do not help
them fight their cause.  But their demonstrations, while
highlighting their visibility and raising to the level
of conscious mass awareness their presence as a force in
society, also highlight their powerlessness.  They are
even made to appear ridiculous, since government and
media correlate their resistance to standardization with
"ignorance" and "backwardness"; they are admonished to
be "modern."

Control of illegal traders by government authorities
is more severe than control of legal traders.  From time
to time, mounted police appear, either to make purchases
or to arrest the illegal trader and temporarily confis-
cate supplies.  Police swoops--a common sight in Lusaka--
can prove a financial irritant to an illegal male cloth
seller or an illegal male watch repairer.  But to a woman
selling a basin of tomatoes or mangoes, the "temporary"
confiscation of her supplies represents a total loss of
capital investment, especially when the police eat the
evidence of her illegal activity, as often happens.  Thus,
government ambivalence dampens rather than encourages the
system by which fresh produce is distributed to the urban
population.

Traders who are not based in markets and traders
in illegal, unauthorized marketplaces do not participate
in organized protests.  Itinerant traders, intermittent
traders, and most home-based traders operate as individuals.  They do not have the opportunity of participating
either in group action or in cooperating economic networks on a regular, organized basis.  We have seen how
traders in particularly impoverished shanty-town markets,
where there are sometimes more traders than customers,
have developed patterns of cooperation based on friendship networks.  But they participate in political activity  only when the government sends in a truck to take
them to a rally.  They do not protest their own plight
in an organized manner.


AMBIVALENT ATTITUDES AT THE GRASS ROOTS

Ambivalent attitudes toward female traders are expressed not only by government authorities but also at
the grass-roots level of society.  Traders are admired
because they follow the popular national slogan of "self-
help."  Rather than weep and complain about the harsh
conditions of urban life, they are taking positive action
to help themselves and their dependents.  They are seen
as "modern" at the grass-roots level, despite their
resistance to the use of standardized weights and measures
and fixed prices.  And to be a modernizing force in
society is to be respected.
The grass-roots acknowledgment of new roles for urban
women is reflected elsewhere in society.  Newspaper
stories of successful marketeers--that is, women who have
managed to maintain stalls in the markets for a period of
years--appear from time to time.  The emphasis is on how
hard work brings happiness and success to the women.
Market women are courted by the ruling political party;
their support to government programs and political decisions is solicited and invariably, since there is no
choice, granted.  Many shanty-town housewives quietly
envy traders, especially if the housewives' husbands do
not give them adequate funds for food and clothing.
Yet, there remains a lingering suspicion about the
morality of female traders.  Town women in general are
suspected of being morally deficient, women who work outside the home even more so.  A kind of suspicious ambivalence is apparent in the attitudes expressed by urban
poor husbands toward female entrepreneurship.  To the
question "should women trade?" they answer "yes."  Their
reasons are that women must help develop the nation, and
they must help men by earning money for the family.
These are generalized and impersonal reasons, often more

reflective of society's viewpoints than of personal ones.
Thus, many men agree that women should trade, adding the
caveat "but not my wife." Frequently, however, men
answer "no." Their reasons are that women belong at
home and that they should not talk to strangers with whom
they might then be tempted into arranging a sexual
liaison. Some men say that jobs are scarce and men should
have the few that exist. This particular argument was
used especially by male produce sellers, with an obvious
lack of impact.

Trade in fresh produce is one of the few areas of
economic activity that women have been able to take over
from men despite the ambivalence felt by society at
large. There seem to be two reasons for the women's
achievement. One is the deep cultural association of
women as the producers and distributors of foodstuff.
While it is clearly impossible for women to grow food
for the urban market--such activity is left to commercial farmers--the women could make a case for their having
a niche in its distribution. Their system of exchange,
especially in the poorest shanty towns, is a means by
which food is distributed even without a ready cash flow.
Their constant emphasis on respectability is the second
possible reason for their successful takeover. Traders
are deeply concerned with projecting an image of respectability. "We are not prostitutes" is a theme heard over
and over again among the market women interviewed.

THE MARGINAL STATUS OF FEMALE TRADERS AND ITS IMPACT ON
PERSONAL LIFE

Denied the high social status of financially independent educated elite and subelite career women, no longer
accepting the inferior status of the rural producer or
the vulnerable position of dependent urban housewife, the
female trader is in a marginal position. This marginal
status is both caused by and reflected in the ambivalence
of the government and the public toward traders' work,
their goals, and their personal lives. Both supported
and condemned, the women occupy an anomalous position,
which has profound consequences for their lives as women,
as wives, and as traders. Many characteristics of the
women become tinged by their ambiguous social position:
their image, dress, behavior, respectability, financial
security, and aspirations.

Individually and collectively, market women seek to
develop an image of poor-but-respectable. Selling style
is one technique. A respectable woman is supposed to be
reserved, even passive and shy. Sellers are quite
passive, rarely trying to attract customers in the aggres-

sive way familiar in markets in other countries.  In
some markets, selection procedures for applicants for
stall space also help promote the image of respectability.
The woman applies to the market manager, who visits the
UNIP branch chairman in the community in which she lives.
The UNIP official attests to her character.  In other
markets, women penetrate through friends and relatives
already trading, who offer character references.

Membership in the UNIP Women's Brigade helps as
well, since brigade leaders have steadily worked to transform the cultural image to that of the ideal woman: a
tradition-minded conservative who has moved from village
to town to join the forces of modernization and development.

Few market women have access to reliable modern
means of birth control and so, unlike educated counterparts, still produce--or intend to produce--large families.  Indeed, they realistically see large families as
their most important social security in old age.  Fertility remains an important measure of respectability
in Lusaka, and so, by virtue of their numerous offspring, traders command respect.

The role of clothing is another technique by which
the respectable image is maintained, but clothing is also
a mark of ambiguity.[4]  Clothing for urban Africans is as
important a clue to status and image as it is for the
most fashion-conscious New Yorker or Parisian.  On the
copperbelt in the 1950s, Kalela dancers, for example,
wore immaculate and well-tailored European clothes as
a means of identifying with the African middle class and
its "civilized" way of life (Epstein, 1978, p. 37).
In the early 1970s, traders made a point of wearing
"traditional" dress and headscarves.

Lusaka's female traders claimed to wear such dress
to express their identity as traditional-minded, modest
women.  They identified with the majority of Zambians
and especially the UNIP Women's Brigade, who condemned
Afro wigs, hot pants, and miniskirts that were the "uniform" of the educated young women.  This might seem
paradoxical.  The traders wanted to be considered
"modernizers"--so the question is, why didn't they follow
the example of the Kalela dancers?

Change in fashion provides a clue.  Over the course
of five years, fashions changed as hemlines lowered and
elaborate hair plaiting replaced Afro wigs.  Fashion
differentiation among traders then occurred.  In the most
prosperous section of the main downtown market that
catered to European and Asian trade, young women adopted
the modern look and it became difficult to differentiate
typists from vegetable sellers--a barrier that, only a
few years earlier, had seemed absolute. The majority con-

tinued wearing traditional clothing.  The answer to the
paradox may well be simply the poverty of the traders.
Traditional two-meter lengths of cloth were much cheaper
than tailored clothes.

The traders made a virtue of necessity, claiming
moral superiority over more educated women.  But as
locally produced fashions became accessible to them,
traders in a position to do so abandoned traditional
attire.  Even the ubiquitous headscarf was abandoned by
those who had friends who could plait their hair.  In
choosing modern attire, female traders, who appear so
obsessed with the desire to cultivate a respectable image,
might at long last be repeating the old pattern of the
1950s noted for the Kalela dancers:  identifying with the
African subelite.  This identification comes at a time
when entree into subelite status is becoming more difficult as the Zambian economy weakens and class lines
harden.  This may also explain how traders seek means to
create differences among themselves in order to enhance
personal status.  Thus, there is potential for intra-
group conflict correlated with increasing economic differentiation, and the limited solidarity that exists at
present may well be transitory.

It is a truism that all people normally want respect.  When respect is not given by society, members of
despised occupational groups form relations of solidarity that give them a measure of self-respect (cf. Nelson,
1978, on the female beer brewers of Nairobi).  On the
one hand, all petty commodity traders have low social
status, even within the low-income group in Lusaka.
Within the low-income group, salaried workers, especially
those who wear uniforms, have higher status and hence
command more respect than traders, so that female
cleaners employed by institutions have higher social
status than female traders.

On the other hand, since the income and exchange
transactions of traders enable them to feed and sometimes
clothe their dependants independently of men, compared
with housewives they command the gruding respect of the
community of urban poor.  Traders affirm the cultural
notion that one of women's major roles is the provision
of food, whereas unemployed housewives who must beg
their husbands, relatives, neighbors, or--as a last re-
sort--husband's employer for money for food are not respected as women, since they have not provided food.  It
is widely believed that women should somehow find the
means to provide food.  Trade is more dignified than begging and certainly more successful than gathering wild
foods in the fast-disappearing bush.  Street begging is
illegal in Lusaka.

Yet, in the conflicting elements of the Zambian

value system, the highly regarded urban woman who is
truly worthy of respect has a husband who willingly and
generously provides for her needs and those of their
numerous children.  Betty Kaunda, wife of President
Kaunda, is the model noncareer-minded housewife, typify-
ing and frequently expressing this view.  But this image
has its own pitfalls.

One pitfall, or problem, for wives is that the respect given a man by other men--and even many other
women--does not depend on his role as a willing and
generous provider for his family of procreation.  Rather,
it depends on his generosity in buying drinks for his
friends at a bar, the number of women he is able to keep,
and, sometimes, the support he provides his own relatives
within his family of orientation.  Interestingly, this
does not change with education (Schuster, 1979).

The system of expectations between men and women,
between women and other women, and even of an individual
woman in her various roles, thus lacks complementarity.
This lack of complementarity produces conflict between
men and women, between women, and within an individual in
her personal roles.  In her personal life, she wants a
husband to provide for her in a way that she knows that
men generally do not.  Yet, she is intensely ambivalent
about men who, in fact, behave the way she wishes her own
husband would.  Generous providers are regarded--if only
half-consciously--as somehow womanly or as fools.  Women
are unsure of whether a woman should by right depend on
a husband's income, what a husband should provide for the
household budget, what the wife should provide, and how
she should provide it.  Should she work, for example in
trade?  Should she gather at least some food in the bush?
Should she enter into networks of exchange in relationships with others?

The housewife whose husband is generous is assumed
to have powerful magic charms.  She uses these charms
to make her husband a good provider against his natural
inclination.  She is therefore powerful and he is weak.
His relatives agree with her and try to work countermagic
so he will strengthen and help them instead of his wife.
The use of charms is assumed in this belief system.

Respect, admiration, and fear are given to powerful
people, and this is why housewives who have to beg for
food money or for food itself are not respected, for they
suffer the torment of being married to a powerful man
instead of themselves being powerful.  They are therefore
not as respected as traders, and, in fact, they envy
traders.  The issue of respect for a woman trader as
against a woman as a housewife thus has a variety of subtle implications.

Hafkin and Bay (1976, p. 6) say, "Wives and husbands

in Africa usually have separate incomes, with clearly
defined financial obligations to their children, their
spouse, and the spouse's lineage." But this is not true
in Lusaka. Neither working women nor housewives are
quite certain what their role as providers should be.
Traders themselves vary considerably in the allocation of
financial responsibility in their households. Men control their own incomes and give their wives a percentage
of their salaries as the mood suits them. Normally,
however, traders expect their husbands to provide housing
and a monthly stipend for such staples as maize meal,
sugar, tea, salt, and charcoal cooking fuel. Clothing is
an area of conflict. Many traders agree that if their
husbands spent less money on beer and gin, they would
not have to trade, imagining that they could live con-
tentedly on the husband's income. But no female trader
knew exactly what that income was. Yet, many felt it
was their right to know. They frequently expressed the
opinion that the government should pass a law stating
that a wife has the right to collect her husband's pay-
check. Thus, in a sense, her very act of trading is
accepted, in a kind of forlorn way, as a testimony to
male drunkenness and callous irresponsibility.

There is, of course, a range of variation in success
in petty trade among women, and success affects perception of status by society at large. Some female shop
owners began their careers as small-scale traders. The
most successful, whose incomes equal and sometimes sur-
pass those of subelites, are often multiple divorcees.
They are respected if they have borne a number of children who survive into adulthood. Their fertility and
financial success indicate the same kind of extraordinary
power that is possessed by the wife whose husband is a
generous provider. They are fully conscious of their
charismatic power and correlate its growth with the diminishing of their emotional dependency on a husband.
"I know that as long as I was married I could never
really make it," says a woman who owns a string of bars
around Lusaka. Her view if quite different from highly
educated Zambian women who, though not married, often
say that they long to be--if only they could find the
appropriate husband.

The overwhelming majority of traders have no possibility of expanding entrepreneurship. Those whose
itinerant activity is sporadic can hope for a stall;
those with stalls can hope, at best, to keep them. It
is much more likely for a woman to lose her stall and
slip into a daily survival struggle than it is for her to
accumulate a profit for reinvestment in her business.
The constraints against which she works--for example, by
being cheated by wholesalers and being unable to pass off

her loss to consumers by raising prices, by paying fines,
by having to cease working for a day because attendance
is required at demonstrations, at funerals, at the hospital, at police headquarters, or because produce is in
short supply--all these mitigate against development of
a standard of living beyond precarious subsistence levels.

The most sensitive indications of the marginal
quality of the lives of Lusaka's female traders, their
ambiguous position in society, and their internalization
of society's contradictory and conflicting attitudes and
values, are their aspirations for their daughters'
futures. Middle-aged traders expect that conditions of
life will be such that one of their oldest daughters will
join them in market trade if she has not already done so.
In fact, some long-established "restauranteurs" in
Lusaka's oldest African market inherited or share stalls
with their mothers. But for their younger daughters
and their granddaughters, they hope for a different way
of life. Nearly all young traders whose children are
young hope that the children will finish secondary
school, if not university. They want their daughters to
become nurses, primary school teachers, typists. As they
are themselves active participants in urban economic
life, they are relatively realistic in their understanding of the requirements for entering white-collar employment in the formal sector. This realism contrasts with
shanty-town housewives who, while vaguely aspiring to a
better life for their daughters, are fanciful about
specific kinds of modern occupations open to women and
the educational and training requirements for such occupations.[5]

Yet, while nearly all traders expressed the desire
for their daughters to be educated and employed in the
modern sector, they were also committed to raising them
in a traditional manner. Thus, nearly all insisted that
their daughters undergo female initiation in the short-
ened school-holiday version that has become popular in
both town and countryside. They were very ambivalent
about the relative importance of marriage versus career
for their daughters. Some worried that if their daughters married they would come under the control of husbands who would take their salaries and not let them give
money to their mothers and young brothers and sisters.
Others felt that marriage should be the primary goal for
their daughters, although they hoped their daughters
would work for a few years before marrying. All accepted
the notion that a wife must subordinate herself to her
husband, and all wanted their daughters to be trained
in traditional wifely virtues and responsibilities. Yet,
they freely volunteered the opinion that the institution
of marriage was in need of drastic reform, that adherence

to many traditional customs produced untold suffering
for women, and that they were themselves victims or potential victims of customs.  But since they felt that
they were also victims of urban life, at the end, all
they felt able to do was cling to their dignity in the
conduct of their daily lives.


SUMMARY AND CONCLUSIONS

The female traders of Lusaka provide a case study
of the way rapid social change results in marginal
status, especially when there is little connection to
traditional roles.  As a result of mass migration of
women to cities, some found that they had to support
themselves in order to survive.  The rapid growth of
Lusaka creates demands for all kinds of trade; as produce traders, women fill a niche in the urban economic
system.

Both the government and the general public react
inconsistently to this new entrepreneurial spirit in
women.  Their service to the nation as traders is both
praised as vital and vilified as exploitative.  As
women, they are both admired for their independence and
dismissed as immoral.  Their trading activities are
severely controlled by regulations and by politics.

The marginal status of the traders is apparent in
all aspects of their lives:  their passivity and appearance at work, their limited hope for improvement, their
ambiguous role as both wife and provider.  Since trading women do not occupy a traditional place in society,
their incomes are not earned to meet definite financial
obligations to their families.  Trading among women
evolved as a strategy for survival in the city, a dignified alternative to begging or returning to the rural
areas.

The conflict and contradiction in Zambian society
toward female traders is part of a more general ambivalence toward all urban women.  Subelite women, better
educated and better paid, are also subjected to contradictory attitudes and pressures (Schuster, 1979, 1981b).
Like their poorer counterparts, their role in nation
building is praised while their personal status and independence is both admired and feared.  All urban women
internalize society's ambivalent attitudes and exhibit
conflicting and contradictory values in their personal
lives that reflect their ambiguous position in society.
Thus, they are concerned with being respectable but are
ambivalent about what constitutes respectability (Schuster, 1981a).

Underlying this ambivalence of roles is, perhaps, an

even deeper ambivalence toward sexual power as it is
played out in married life.  Thus, the underlying dynamic
of the difficult position of Lusaka's female traders is
very much the same as that of urban women whose lives,
from a financial point of view, are far less marginal.

Shared problems among urban women do not result in
group action.  Lusaka's complex society is in the process
of becoming too economically differentiated for action to
succeed, despite recognition by women of their similar
problems.  Elite and subelite women virtually never act
as an interest group.  Group action is limited to legal
marketplace-based traders around circumscribed issues and
does not extend even to women who trade in other circumstances.  Nor does it seem reasonable to expect concerted
action in a society in such a state of flux.  The very
fluidity of the structure inhibits such development, since
ambiguity toward them produces at once hope and despair
in the women.


NOTES

1.  See, for example, Staudt (1978) and Brain (1976),
which show these processes for rural women in Kenya and
Tanzania, respectively.

2.  There are no statistics on the informal economic
sector available from government sources.

3.  At the time of the market study in 1973, there
were about eight markets in Lusaka.  Interviews were conducted in five of these: a new and quasi-legal shanty-
town market (Chipata), a relatively older quasi-legal
market (George), a site-and-service scheme legal market
(Mandevu), a relatively old and well-established city
council market (Luburma), and a newer city council market
(Matero).

Because the study of traders was part of a larger
study of adaptation to change by Lusaka's young women,
the majority of interviews were conducted of women aged
thirty and under.  Slightly older women were occasionally
included.  Thus, the age range of the 78 interviewees
was thirteen to thirty-nine; 19 percent twenty and under,
61 percent thirty and under, 20 percent over thirty.
Twenty different Zambian ethnic groups were included, as
well as citizens of neighboring countries:  Zimbabwe,
Malawi, Zaire, and Botswana were represented.  Of the
group, 83.3 percent were rural born, 16.6 percent urban
born, and 81 percent were married, 10 percent single, and
9 percent divorced.  Interviews were conducted by the re-
searcher and three university student assistants:  Juli-
ana Chileshe, Beatrice Mulamfu, and Annie Mubanga.  The
majority of interviews were conducted in three of the

most important Zambian languages: Chinyanja, Chibemba,
and Chitonga.  Others were conducted in English and other
languages in which the assistants were competent.  Informal interviews were conducted with home-based and
itinerant traders throughout the years of the field
work.
    4.  Responsibility for the provision of clothing is
a source of ambivalence in married life.  Wives generally
feel it should be the husband's responsibility, but in
Lusaka 54 percent of the traders shared this responsibility with their husbands.  However, 16 percent of the
husbands were unemployed.
    5.  Formal interviews with shanty-town housewives
were conducted as part of the larger research design,
which also included a study of the first generation of
educated women.

REFERENCES

Brain, James L. 1976. "Less than Second Class: Women in
    Rural Settlement Schemes in Tanzania."  In Women
    in Africa, ed. Nancy J. Hafkin and Edna G. Bay,
    Stanford: Stanford University Press.
Epstein, A.L. 1978.  Ethos and Identity: Three Studies
    in Ethnicity.  London: Tavistock Publications.
Gutkind, Peter C.W. 1974.  Urban Anthropology: Perspec-
    tives on "Third World" Urbanization and Urbanism.
    Assen: Van Gorcum.
Hafkin, Nancy J., and Edna G. Bay, eds. 1976.  Women in
    Africa: Studies in Social and Economic Change.
    Stanford:  Stanford University Press.
Hansen, Karen. 1975. "Married Women and Work: Explora-
    tions from an Urban Case Study." African Social
    Research 20: 777-99.
Miracle, Marvin. 1965.  "The Copperbelt Trading and
    Marketing." In Markets in Africa: Eight Subsis-
    tence Economies in Transition, ed. Paul Bohannan
    and George Dalton. Garden City, N.Y.: Doubleday,
    Anchor Books. Pp. 285-341.
Nelson, Nici. 1978.  "Women must help each other."
    In Women United, Women Divided: Cross Cultural
    Perspectives on Female Solidarity, ed. Patricia
    Caplan and Janet M. Bujra.  London: Tavistock
    Publications. Pp. 77-98.
Nyirenda, A.A. 1957.  "Africal Market Vendors in
    Lusaka with a Note on the Recent Boycott." Rhodes-
    Livingstone Journal 22:31-63.
Obbo, Christine. 1975.  "Women's Careers in Low Income
    Areas as Indicators of Country and Town Dynamics."
    In Town and Country in Central and Eastern Africa,

ed. David Parkin.   London: Oxford University Press
    for the International African Institute. Pp. 288-93.
Ohadike, Patrick. 1975.   "The Evolving Phenomena of
    Migration and Urbanization in Central Africa: A
    Zambian Case." In Town and Country in Central and
    Eastern Africa, ed. David Parkin. London: Oxford
    University Press for the International African
    Institute. Pp. 126-44.
Schuster, Ilsa.   1979.   The New Women of Lusaka.   Palo
    Alto: Mayfield Publishing.
_____.  1981a."Constraints and Opportunities in
    Political Participation: The Case of Zambian Women."
    Paper presented at the workshop "Women in the African
    Political Process." Meetings of the African Studies
    Association of the United Kingdom, School or Orien-
    tal and African Studies, University of London, 22
    September 1981.
_____.  1981b. "Perspectives in Development: The Prob-
    lem of Nurses and Nursing in Zambia." Journal of
    Development Studies, special issue on African Women
    in the Development Process.
Staudt, Kathleen. 1978.   "Agricultural Productive Gaps:
    A Case Study of Male Preference in Government Policy
    Implementation." In Development and Change 9:439-57.
Wilson, Godfrey. 1940.   An Essay on the Economics of
    Detribalization in Northern Rhodesia.   Livingstone:
    Rhodes-Livingstone Institute.
Zambia Daily Mail, 20 October  1971.

# 6. Colonialism, Education, and Work: Sex Differentiation in Colonial Zaire

*Barbara A. Yates*

The link between education and economic activity is
close. Western-style education in colonial Zaire (Belgian Congo), as elsewhere in the world, provides cogni-
tive skills and indoctrination to the necessary social
values for participation in the modern economic sector.
Moreover, formal educational credentials are frequently
the predominant badge that defines the entry level to
the labor force. When the Belgian Congo became an independent republic in 1960, none of the several hundred
Congolese students attending the two universities or the
half-dozen postsecondary institutes was female. Furthermore, none of the 800 cumulative academic secondary
school graduates was female.[1] The most educationally
advanced Congolese female was a senior in an academic
high school.[2] Not surprisingly, Congolese women had
few nontraditional career opportunities.

These low participation rates of Congolese females
in schools and employment were attributed by the
colonial establishment to the African womens' reluctance to attend school or to participate in the emerging
modern economy. These conclusions, however, are too
simplistic. Western colonizers brought with them a set
of notions about proper activities for women. While
sharply differentiated sex roles have been a perennial
theme in the Judeo-Christian tradition, Belgian Africa
represented an extreme case of the influence of Christianity, especially that of conservative Catholicism,
on educational practice and career opportunities. Belgium, from its inception in the early 1830s, was a re-
pository of conservative European thought. England, it
has been said, had the Reformation and France had the
Revolution, but Belgium had little intellectual ferment.
In Belgium, social patterns were little affected by the
upheavals of the Industrial Revolution and the accompany-
ing scientific age. The rural and working-class background of most missionaries who served in the Congo also

reinforced their conservatism, especially among Catholic
missionaries from rural Flanders, a stronghold of conservative Catholicism.

There were, of course, traditional differences in
the roles of African men and women.  These sex role
differences were extensive because of the great number
of ethnic groups in an area as huge as the Congo.  Congolese women thus were caught in a double bind; they
suffered from the dual differentiation of both the traditional and colonial societies.  Whether conservative
Western concepts concerning appropriate gender roles
were more restrictive than the various traditional
African concepts they were meant to replace is a subject
in need of further research drawing upon anthropological
literature.

This study, however, focuses upon the superimposed
colonial system.  Whatever the local traditions, Belgium
colonialism introduced the Western-type school and the
modern economic sector and gave preeminence to conservative Western concepts about gender roles--even in
agriculture, where Congolese women had clearly defined
managerial responsibilities.  European educators sponsored a deliberate pattern of sex-differentiated roles
whose norms were embodied in the life of schools.  As
would be expected, strongly emphasized patriarchal traditions led to stereotyped linkages between sex differences in access to education, on the one hand, and employment in the modern sector, on the other.  Finally, as
would also be expected, sex differentiation during the
colonial period has implications for the contemporary
life of Zairian women.


CHRISTIAN PATRIARCHY AND THE "CIVILIZING" TASK


Belgian colonialism was dominated by the "Big
Three": the Roman Catholic Church, the colonial administration, and the large corporations.  Through political
tradeoffs, schools became the special preserve of the
Church; at independence, nearly all of the 1.6 million
Congolese pupils in school attended Catholic (77 percent) or Protestant (19 percent) institutions.  The
residual enrollment was in state vocational schools
(established beginning in 1897), in secular primary and
secondary schools (beginning in 1954), or in training
programs financed by commercial firms (beginning in
1908)(George, 1966).

The predominance of missionaries as educators made
their aims, values, and lifestyles central to the establishment of sex differentiation in education and work.
Missionaries, bolstered by the government, sought to im-

plant Christian patriarchy and white supremacy among
Congolese peoples.  Missionaries dreamed of establishing
a Christian nation in Central Africa.  Nevertheless,
there would be Christianization without general Westernization.  Converts would be discouraged by admonition
and by the nature of their education from seeking employment in the "immoral" towns and would be encouraged to
remain agriculturalists (or homemakers), who would
exemplify new moral precepts in a hitherto pagan environment.  A class of male "native intellectuals" was resisted, a policy based upon conclusions about the dele-
terious religious and political effects of "literary"
education in older colonies, such as India and Sierra
Leone.  Recipients of academic education were said to
lose their religious interest and to acquire an anti-
colonial outlook as well as to exhibit an arrogant desire for assimilation.  Consequently, until after World
War II, secondary (as distinct from postprimary) education for African males was limited largely to Bible
schools and seminaries preparing them for missionary
service.

To attain Christianization without  Westernization,
the missionaries altered African culture selectively.
They were not opposed to all African customs, despite
their litany of derogatory comments designed to loosen
the purse strings of metropolitan supporters.  It was
those customs that flouted the basic moral tenents of
Christianity--polygyny, traditional religious beliefs,
and premarital sexual relations--that were especially
abhorred by churchman (Yates, 1980a).  Consequently,
missionaries strove first to establish the monogamous
family and to instill Christian influences within
African homes.  These strategies were epitomized in the
statement of a pioneer Belgian missionary leader: "We
missionaries are here to make the Congolese nation a
Christian and civilized people.  However, a people is
composed of families. . . . When the young Congolese
boy and girl are civilized and Christian, we will unite
them into a Christian family from which will come the
Christian people" (Cambier, 1900).  For creating a new
type of society, as distinguished from merely creating
new mines and plantations, women with a new character
were as essential as men.  As a Belgian Jesuit admonished, "It is Christian mothers who make a Christian
society" (de Pierpont, 1906).  Missionaries viewed the
taking of a pagan wife by male converts as a major cause
of spiritual and moral backsliding; the unschooled country girl led a man back to paganism, while a sophisticated town girl led him into debauchery (Gabriel, 1914,
p. 14).[3]

In order to achieve the new Christian state, mis-

sionaries carefully delineated roles by race and gender.
The conduct expected of European missionaries provided
role models for the African of appropriate behavior between the sexes. While expectations varied between Protestants and Catholics, all agreed to follow the "teachings of the Bible where all authority comes from God
through the father" (Comhaire-Sylvain, quoted in Boserup,
1970, p. 60).

The Swedish Missionary Society, for example,
affirmed that its male clergy "united in their person
various, but similar, roles toward the Congolese" with
whom they had close contact--the roles of "father, employer, teacher and maybe even owner,"--as when pupils
were ransomed from slavery (Axelson, 1970, pp. 248-49).
Depending upon the methods of evangelization, a male missionary supervised construction and maintenance of the
station, farming, and the purchase and distribution of
supplies. He preached in the station church or chapel
and in rotation among nearby villages. Many strove to
reduce the vernacular to a written form and then translated the Bible and the catechism, wrote lessons, and
selected and trained young men as religious assistants.
In truth, the missionary was a patriarch; he guided the
work of subordinate female missionaries and African male
assistants and established the rules by which the
Christian community should live.

Catholic priests welcomed female missionaries who
would devote their efforts to preparing local girls to
become Christian wives of male converts. Belgian Jesuits
attributed the failure of the early Portuguese mission-
aires in the Congo and Angola to the lack of sisters for
this duty (Laveille, 1926, p. 124).

The principal task of female missionaries (whether
single Protestant or Catholic women or Protestant wives)
was to teach in the elementary schools; secondary teaching and theological training were by and large white
male domains. Non-Western attitudes were blamed for the
restriction of European women to elementary teaching.
As the American Baptist Committee on Education explained,
it was "because they excel in this work, and because in
it their influence is less likely . . . to be seriously
weakened by the prejudices of oriental society against
independent life and action on the part of women" (Committee on Education, 1894, p. 200). But preconceptions
concerning women's proper roles in actuality were inte-
gral ideas to Christian patriarchy and Western culture
brought into the Congo. Despite their indispensability
to the apostolate, female missionaries had to remain
subservient and refrain from any threat to priestly
hegemony.

Missionaries expected African men to take on the

ideal character traits of white women: industriousness,
docility, obedience, gentleness, and passivity--of
course in relation to Europeans, especially to males.
African women were to display the same humility but also
toward African males. While the African wife was to be
the foundation of her Christian family, devoting her time
to tending the hearth and bearing and rearing a generation of African Christians, she would be subservient to
her husband.

As with boys, schooled African girls were not to be
assimilated into white society, not even those who later
entered convents. Neither girls nor boys were to be educated in the European pattern, "which would create in them
new needs and useless servitides." For girls, "civilization is not shown to them in a glass of frothy wine or a
beautiful gown nor in unknown or refined food" (Guillemé,
1896, pp. 405-6). Rather, girls, like boys, should follow the "best" local customs in dress, food, and lodging.

Both Christian missionaries and the colonial government attacked the traditional sex division of labor in
agriculture, and their consequent activities in agricultural education embodies this obtuseness. In the
Congo, women traditionally were the major producers of
food, especially in the non-Muslim areas of the West and
the South.[4] The new patriarchal aim, however, would move
women out of the fields; men should do the heavier work
because women were overworked while men were lazy. Absence of a "proper" division of labor, the Jesuits (the
principal agricultural educators) contended, helped to
make "all improvement in agriculture impossible" (Van
Wing, [1918], p.19) and so it was males who received
seeds, training, and supervision in farming.

Christian patriarchy was allegedly a blessing to
African women, for it would rescue them from polygyny
and would confer vaguely stated benefits of Western civilization, such as "a healthy and comforting morality,
which among other things, gives to the woman her real
situation in nature. Polygamy will be replaced by the
Christian family with all the rights that it confers"
(Devos, 1904, p. 349).

These Christian "rights" of women were discussed
endlessly by male missionaries. Remarking at the time of
World War I that there was hope that in two or three
generations the population around the Jesuit missions in
the Lower Congo would be Catholic and therefore well on
the way to "civilization,"a leading Jesuit emphasized
that, among other things, it would be necessary "to establish the rights of fathers of families over their
children" and "to introduce more and more personal property by agricultural cultivation" (Van Wing, [1918],p.37).
Missionaries assumed that enhanced "personal property by
agricultural cultivation" done by men would augment male

property and that somehow there would be a "trickle down"
effect to other members of the new Christian family.
However, the Jesuits reported a "strange phenomenon":
men, even Christian converts, refused to cultivate traditional crops, although they were willing to grow new European crops, such as rice and sweet potatoes (Van Wing,
[1918],p. 19)[5] The reason perhaps was not so much laziness, as the missionaries claimed, as resistance to uncom-
fortable sex roles.  When agricultural education came to
be provided by the state (1908), it was limited to males,
who frequently deserted these schools for a more academically oriented program.  When only an agricultural school
was accessible, frequently it was used by young men to
acquire the literacy skills necessary for urban employment (Deheyn, 1957, pp. 1-22).


PATRIARCHIAL GOALS AND SEX DIFFERENTIATION IN EDUCATION

     Given all these deeply rooted attitudes, the pro-
vision of educational opportunities inevitably mirrored
Western patriarchal goals.  The school became a powerful
agency for socializing Africans into conservative Western
views, especially about family life and occupation.
Boys' postprimary and secondary education before World
War II centered upon preparation of religious assistants
for evangelization and secondarily on training subalterns
for the administration.  After World War II, the education of secular elites was added to the preparation of
priests, pastors, and subalterns.
     While the purpose of the education of males would
shift after World War II as political change came to the
continent, the primary objective of girls' education at
all levels remained unaltered from the opening of the
first Western-type school in 1879 to independence in 1960:
training Christian wives and mothers.  The aim of education for girls was to implant Christian morality, an
awareness of "proper" family relationships, and a favorable disposition toward children's learning their religious duties.  Accordingly, apart from the "sacramental"
duties of wifehood, African girls needed to prepare formally for few new roles through attendance at schools.
     These differential educational goals for boys and
girls were reflected and reinforced in access to schooling, in curricula, in the language of instruction, and
in educational participation rates.  The development of
education in the Belgian Congo can be conveniently divided into three periods:  (1) the Leopoldian period (1879-
1908), when the Congo basin was the personal fiefdom of
Leopold II, king of the Belgians, (2) the early parliamentary period, beginning in 1908 with the formal transfer of sovereignty from Leopold to the Belgian Parlia-

ment, and (3) the post-World-War-II period until the
Congo became independent in 1960.

## The Leopoldian Period

The colonial educational system took form during the
Leopoldian period. Neither the initial legislation, the
1890 and 1892 Education Acts and their implementing ordinances, nor the 1906 Concordat with the Vatican mentioned girls. The latter legislation promised state sub-
sidization to Catholic educators for the training in
colonies scolaires and mission schools of orphaned, neglected, and abandoned boys as French-speaking artisans,
agriculturalists, or soldiers (Congo, 1890, 1892). Protestant schools received no subsidies until after World
War II. Beginning in 1897, a handful of secular state
vocational schools (écoles professionnelles) were also
established for boys, only to train noncommissioned officers, artisans, clerks, male nurses, and plantation
workers for the colonial administration.
While neither the 1890 and 1892 Education Acts nor
the 1906 Concordat referred to girls, nonetheless separate Catholic-run and state-supported (Moanda and Nou-
velle-Anvers) and government-authorized (several dozen
locations) mission colonies scolaires for girls were
established, beginning in the late nineteenth century.
They were to teach primarily domestic skills and Christian virtues. These schools were viewed by Catholic missionaries as "nurseries of virtuous young girls," hard-
working and well instructed, "where our boys can find
faithful and devoted wives. Isn't this a work par excel-
lence for extending the Christian religion and making it
flourish in an infidel country?" (Missions d'Afrique,
1898, p. 360). Executive orders required district com-
missioners to be sure, in recruiting pupils for these
schools, that they sent an equal number of boys and girls
from each tribe so that they could later be joined in
Catholic marriage (Kervyn, 1912, p. 287).[6] Sex differentiation in the content of vocational education was vi-
vidly expressed by a visitor to King Leopold's Congo:
"Boys are taught to cultivate, to work with wood and iron,
to bricklay, to make bricks and tiles, and to construct a
house; the girls learn to sew, wash clothes, cook, and
keep house" (Verhaegen, 1898, p. 153).
Though education for artisans was sponsored by the
colonial administration for boys and missionaries designated home economics as the principal skills for girls,
general literary education and teacher training under
missionary auspices for both boys and girls eventually
arose. When missionaries opened schools in the late
nineteenth century, Congolese demanded to be paid to
learn reading and writing, perceiving no intrinsic or
economic value in such skills. But as railway construc-

tion opened up the interior and as Congolese became acquainted with the lifestyles of the literate West African craftsmen who had been brought in to assist with railway construction and colonial administration, local attitudes toward literacy changed from indifference to curiosity and finally to enthusiasm. Villages began to request that schools be established; enrollments soared. The new African interest in literacy led to intense intra-Christian rivalry for converts; schools were used as inducements to enter the mission orbit. Protestant and Catholic missionaries scurried to prepare more male teacher-evangelists and catechists in order to compete for villages. Some Protestant missionaries concluded that religious goals were fostered by teaching the wives of their evangelists at least to read. These wives could then assist with village schools as well as teach dressmaking to girls. Neighboring Catholic missions were not to be outdone and conferred the direction of village work upon married catechists, whose wives had been trained by the sisters. Between 1898, when the railway was completed from Matadi (the seaport) to Leopoldville (the beginning of the navigable portion of the Congo River), and 1903, enrollments increased from approximately 9,000 to 27,000.[7]

The general education curriculum was very rudimentary in these schools. While religion was at the heart of every mission school program and character-building manual labor was required of all pupils, the girls' curriculum was more meager than the boys'. At the better elementary schools, boys were exposed to the three R's and perhaps a smattering of geography and French. Catholics lagged behind Protestants in providing girls with opportunities for literacy, partly because of the Catholic aversion to coeducation (single-sex schools became a continuing feature of Belgian colonial education) and partly because most Catholic orders forbade male catechists or priests to teach girls any subjects other than religion.

Generally, Catholics viewed literacy as nonessential to religious goals and their missions in the Leopoldian period seldom offered reading and writing to girls. Indeed, Catholic education for girls could best be described as resocialization, rather than instruction. Reading and writing were regarded by some Catholic missionaries as actually dangerous for girls. "To learn to read and write is usual for all our boys. But the majority of our female savages have none of it and it is reported even that certain ones, who have learned to read, neglect the care of their homes" (Missions belges, 1907, p.328).

Protestant schools provided more literacy education for girls because of the imperative for Bible reading and because of the coeducational nature of some Protestant schools. Some Protestant missionaries believed that if the school was taught by a missionary rather than by an African male, it was good to have boys and girls

together; the boys would be spurred to better achievement by competition from the girls and at the same time
become more respectful of the girls' ability (Congo Missionary Conference, 1906, p. 80).  Moreover, Protestant
Bible schools usually required men to bring their families; these schools also admitted single women, who subsequently were encouraged to marry evangelists or pastors.
But Protestant missionaries nonetheless directed their
main efforts to the conversion of boys and to training
the most obedient and religiously pious of them as evangelists.  Only after their staffs had expanded and station construction was completed did the intra-Christian
rivalry lead Protestant missionaries to give more time
to educating girls.[8]

     Another continuing feature differentiating education
for boys and girls was the medium of instruction (Yates,
1980b, pp. 257-79).  Although the Education Act of 1890
emphasized the teaching of French, the administration
endlessly berated Catholic headmasters of boys' schools
for ineffectiveness at this task while remaining uncon-
cerned that schools for girls taught no French.

     By the early twentieth century, then, sex differences
in education and in subsequent career opportunities were
well established.  By 1908, more than 46,000 Congolese
attended school.  Although educational statistics were
not consistently disaggregated by gender, probably well
under 15 percent of pupils in 1908 were female.  The
management of knowledge would be such that girls would
receive less literary training than boys and that girls
would be limited to domestic science courses and teacher
training, while boys would prepare for artisan, military,
nursing, clerical, teaching, and religious careers.  Only
boys (albeit a very limited number) would have access to
French language training.  This distribution of know-
edge would be partly controlled through the provision of
single-sex schools.  Most importantly, the objectives of
Belgian colonial education were firmly fixed during the
Leopoldian era:  men belonged in the fields, the shop,
the pulpit, and the marketplace, while women belonged in
the home as good Christian wives and mothers.  Men in
limited numbers were schooled to enter the army, the colonial administration, trading firms, the railway, and the
missionary enterprise; women who ventured outside the
home were limited to the elementary school and the convent.

## Educational Legislation of the 1920s

     The colonial Charter of 1908, which formally trans-
ferred sovereignty from Leopold II to the Belgian Parliament, incorporated the existing legislation on schools.
While opportunities for both boys and girls grew slowly
as more schools were opened and more years were added to
existing programs, differential opportunities based upon

gender persisted and became explicit and official in the
1920s.  Codifying educational practices of the previous
four decades, the Education Code of 1929 recognized three
levels of schooling: two-year village schools (grades
1 and 2), three-year upper primary schools (grades 3-5),
and three-year postprimary vocational schools (grades 6-
9).[9]  While the two-year village schools could be coeducational, this code stated expressly that boys and girls
in government-subsidized upper-primary schools had to be
separated beginning with grade 3.  Protestant schools,
being unsubsidized, were not subject to the 1929 code;
consequently, some of their schools continued to be coeducational, although many followed the government curriculum (Report of the First Education Conference, 1934;
Report of Second Education Conference, 1934).

The general curriculum for girls continued to be
a watered-down version of that offered to boys (Liesenborghs, 1940, p. 262).[10]  The section on girls' education
in the code was introduced with the statement, "The domestic education of women is a factor of first importance
in the elevation of a race and in the development of its
needs" (Organisation de l'Enseignement, 1929, p. 10).

The code provided that in grades 1 and 2 in village
schools, some of which were coeducational, instruction
would be the same for both sexes with the exception of
"manual labor"; girls were limited to light gardening,
while boys participated in stock raising and in the construction and repair of buildings.  Beginning with grade
3 (when segregation by sex was required by law in government-subsidized schools), time devoted to the three R's
was reduced for girls in order to add needlework, sewing,
and child care.  While French was offered to boys as an
elective (and was the language of instruction in schools
to prepare male clerks), only Congolese languages were
used in girls' schools.

Opportunities for boys and girls in vocational education continued to diverge in the interwar years, as
opportunities steadily widened for young men.  Three
kinds of postprimary job-oriented programs for boys were
provided in the 1929 code: clerk schools (écoles de can-
didats-commis,  subsequently called écoles moyennes),
normal schools (later called écoles de moniteurs), and
vocational schools (écoles professionnelles).  The clerk
schools prepared young men to be office workers, customs
agents, tax collector aides, or railway conductors.  Normal schools prepared primary teachers for mission schools.
In the vocational schools, four options were offered to
boys: (1) woodworking (carpentry, cabinet making, join-
ery), (2) general mechanics (blacksmith, locksmith,
foundryman), (3) metalworking (plumbers, metalworkers),
and (4) agriculture.

The educational legislation of 1929 also reinforced
the domestic role of women under the guise of vocational

education. Postprimary vocational schools for girls remained limited by the 1929 code to elementary school
teaching (écoles de monitrices) and to home economics and
agriculture (écoles ménagères-agricoles). The normal
schools prepared elementary teachers and later aides to
European social workers in the new foyers sociaux (government-subsidized Catholic adult education centers for
married women). The home economics and agricultural
"vocational" schools led only to the hearth, not to employment in agriculture or in careers using marketable
skills in domestic science; domestics in European households were generally males.

The agricultural portion of the curriculum in these
postprimary home economics and agriculture schools differed from that in the postprimary vocational agriculture
sections for boys. The girls' schools ignored tillage
and focused on household work and on the care of the sick
and injured; they taught nutrition, meal planning, hygiene, syrup and oil making, confection making, conservation of meat and fish, preparation of butter and cheese,
the making of soap and starch, the fabrication of pots
and the weaving of mats, housecleaning and the destruc-
tion of vermin, and sewing, washing, and ironing. The
"agricultural" curriculum for girls focused on vegetable
gardening, medicinal plants, and the care of barnyard
animals (such as upkeep of chicken coops, pig stys, pig-
eon cages, and rabbit hutches). In the vocational agriculture schools for boys, the emphasis was upon export
and plantation crops, soils, irrigation, horticulture,
animal husbandry, and agricultural machinery. While the
boys became qualified for employment in commercial agriculture, the girls had little alternative to homemaking
and gardening.

Work in hospitals as midwives and nurses' aides now
became acceptable for a few young women. The colonial
medical service and the missions opened a handful of
schools to train hospital personnel, including the soon-
to-become prestigious male medical assistants; several
sections to train female midwives and nurses' aides were
also opened.

During the interwar years, colonial educators in
Belgian Africa concentrated their efforts on training a
religious rather than a secular elite in nongovernment-
subsidized seminaries, Bible schools, and convents.
While the White Fathers in the eastern Congo had pioneered
the preparation of Congolese priests in the late nineteenth century and nuns in the early twentieth century,
a shift in Vatican policy in the 1920s toward Africaniz-
ing the clergy led to a significant expansion of schools
to train priests and nuns.

Despite legislative provision for the postprimary
education of girls, few opportunities actually were provided. During the interwar years, most of the expansion

in girls' enrollment (as well as for boys) took place in
village schools (grades 1 and 2). Here, the emphasis
was on bringing more young people under missionary gui-
dance through the attraction of rudimentary literacy.
On the eve of World War II, no more than 20,000 girls
attended primary school and fewer than 2,000 were in
postprimary schools, whereas over 50 percent of the boys
of school age attended formal classes. Catholic missions
had only twenty-four postprimary schools for girls in all
the Congo; nine écoles de monitrices, twelve écoles
ménagères-agricoles, and three écoles médicales (Goetschalckx, 1953, pp. 6-73), plus several dozen convent
schools for training nuns scattered over an area the size
of the United States east of the Mississippi. In addition, there were several dozen Protestant postprimary
home economics and teacher-training schools, the latter
frequently coeducational. The few programs for nurses'
aides and midwives, conducted by the colonial Medical
Service and the missions, enrolled probably no more than
one hundred girls. Data are sparse, but we can estimate
on the basis of the number of Congolese nuns in 1960 that
there were probably as many girls enrolled in convents
preparing for religious vocations as in all these government-subsidized postprimary programs.

Belgian commentators conceded that these first postprimary programs for girls did not really constitute
secondary education but were useful mainly in filling
the time between primary school and marriage (usually at
fourteen to sixteen years). Even after girls began
attending primary school at the usual European ages,
upon completing five years of primary education they were
still not old enough to marry; further schooling might
keep them out of mischief until they could find husbands
(Liesenborghs, 1940, p. 263).

Changes After World War II

World War II brought many changes to the Congo. New
educational programs were initiated after the war in two
phases. First, the Education Code of 1948 (Congo belge,
1948) established the first full six-year academic
secondary schools for black males as preparation for
university studies, and in 1954 the Catholic-run Lovanium
University opened with a solely male Congolese student
contingent. Second, after 1954, secular state primary
and secondary schools were established; these institutions now replicated the practice in Belgium of "parallelism," whereby parochial and secular schools coexisted
and competed for pupils.

The patriarchal ideal, however, persisted. Missionaries were still asserting that one duty of the mission-

ary educator was to instruct the people in their rights
and duties according to the precepts of Christ:  the
abolition of polygyny, the establishment of the monogamous family, as the primary unit of civilization, the in-
culcation in males of "their responsibilities as heads of
families," and "enlightening" the African woman "on the
mission of being a wife and mother in a new Christian
society" (Mottoule, 1950, p. 74).

The 1948 code embodied no new aims for girls' education; they still were to become "good wives and mothers."
The code stated that government would have preferred that
education of boys and girls proceed at the same pace.
However, education for girls lagged because of the (1)
"social organization" of native communities, (2) the
"atavistic servitude" which burdened the Congolese female, (3) the generally lesser "intellectual receptivity"
of girls, and (4) the "prejudices" and "opposition" of
Congolese families to the education of girls.  Consequently, "we cannot think of developing the instruction
of girls at the same rate nor on a plan as widespread
nor according to a curriculum as complete as that for
boys" (Congo belge,  p. 26).

Indeed, the 1948 reorganization widened the sex
disparity in educational opportunities, especially in
general academic education and in teacher training.
The 1948 code stated that the instruction of girls must
be "educative and practical."  Not only was full academic secondary education denied to girls, but primary
education was further differentiated by gender.  Beginning with grade 3, primary schools for boys were now to
be of two types; a three-year "ordinary" program and a
four-year "select" program, and latter leading to the
new six-year academic secondary schools.  Girls' upper
primary schools were to be only of the "ordinary" type.
While the 1948 code provided for the first full academic
secondary schools for boys using French as the language
of instruction, the teaching in all girls' schools was
still to be only in the vernacular.  Academic courses
for girls continued to be partly replaced in the time-
table by sewing and housecleaning, under the rubric
travaux féminin.  While manual labor for boys involved
development of school gardens, girls continued to do
only "light work" in these plots and now were to clean
the classroom.

Moreover, curricular differences for boys and girls
in secondary teacher training became even more rigid.
The 1948 code stated bluntly that the teacher-training
curriculum for girls was to be "more simple and more
practical" than that for boys.  Teacher training for
girls (écoles de monitrices) continued to emphasize home
economics and child care, just as did the primary schools

for girls in which these graduates would teach.

The reorganized educational system embodied a commitment to improve the schooling of girls as much as was "possible and opportune." In actuality, this meant the ubiquitous presence of home economics. A new three-year secondary home economics program (écoles moyennes-ménagères) was established for daughters of évolués-- chiefs, government clerks, medical assistants, teachers-- who would marry the new secular male elite being trained in the academic secondary schools. The aim of the new secondary home economics schools was "to create a class of young girls capable of making a good appearance [de faire bonne figure] in the world of native évolués, as much from the standpoint of education (e.g., savoir-vivre, care of the home) as from that of instruction." To prepare this new feminine "elite," the schools instituted a transitional classe de sixième préparatoire, in which students could complete their sixth primary year and qualify to enter the new secondary schools of home economics.

New postprimary programs in elementary-school teaching and in hospital work were also created by the 1948 code for girls (and boys) who completed the "ordinary" primary cycle. The 1948 code provided for the establishment of two-year postprimary schools to train apprentice teachers (écoles d'apprentissage pédagogiques), with sections for boys and girls. Girls who were at least sixteen years of age might enroll in the reorganized two-year schools for nurses' aides (écoles d'aides-infirmières) or midwife aides (écoles d'aides-accou-cheuses).

The main change for girls following from the 1948 code was reorganization of domestic science instruction. While the new secondary home economics schools were for daughters of évolués, the schools at the bottom of the educational ladder (écoles ménagères periprimaires and écoles ménagères du deuxième degré) were designed to draw into the missionary orbit girls who had not attended primary school at the usual age. Many of these girls came directly from the "bush." In the Lower Congo area, these schools included only engaged girls, reflecting the missionaries' continuing desire to abolish cohabitation by engaged couples. The postprimary écoles ménagères-agricoles of the 1929 code, which had prepared the female elite of the interwar years, dropped the agricultural label and became simply postprimary schools of domestic science (écoles ménagères postprimaires) catering to girls who had completed the "ordinary" five-year primary program and were of normal school age. As before, such schooling kept them "properly" occupied until marriage.

Thus, by the early 1950s, academically oriented

female students or daughters from évolué families could
enter (after primary school, including the sixième préparatoire) the secondary teacher-training schools
(écoles ménagères moyennes), together the apex of female
education.  Students who finished these programs, usually
about age fifteen, could teach in a primary or postprimary homemaking school or become aides to European
social workers in the foyers sociaux.  Yet, by 1952 there
were only ten of the new secondary écoles moyennes ménagères and only twenty secondary teacher-training schools,
which together enrolled just over 1,000 girls (Goetschalckx, 1953, p. 2).  The less gifted girls followed the
"ordinary" upper-primary cycle and the younger ones could
then go on, even after the fourth grade, to the two-year
apprentice-teacher training schools (écoles d'apprentissage pédagogiques) or to nurses'-aide or midwife aide
schools.  Those who were left over entered the postprimary homemaking schools (écoles ménagères postprimaires)
if they were of normal school age.
     Catholic educators reported that it was only in
1952, after being partly empty for years, that girls'
postprimary schools finally were filled (Goetschalckx,
1953, p. 2).  The better postprimary and secondary
schools for girls in towns suddenly began to have waiting lists.  Curiously, at the same time évolué families
were reported to be dissatisfied with the amount and
quality of education available for girls.  In 1952, the
Council of the African Quarter in Leopoldville had unanimously asked that Congolese girls be given equal educational opportunities.  Indeed, in the early 1950s
several hundred daughters from educated Congolese families took the ferry across the Congo River to attend
school in Brazzaville, where it was said they would at
least learn French (Congo belge, 1954, p. 235).
     Further expansion of educational opportunities for
both boys and girls came in the mid-1950s after a Liberal-Socialist coalition government in Belgium replaced
the Catholic Party in power.  The new minister of colonies established the first secular primary and secondary schools for Congolese--on a coeducational basis--
and inaugurated a secular university at Elisabethville.
The introduction of "parallelism" expanded opportunities,
particularly in secondary education.  "Select" upper
primary sections in parochial schools finally were provided for girls (as preparation for academic secondary
education) and girls finally were admitted to Catholic
six-year programs of general academic secondary education
and to the senior technical high schools (usually, to
the normal or nursing sections).  The original midwife
schools were replaced by a three-year school for maternity nurses (écoles d'accoucheuses) with higher standards, requiring at least four years of general secondary

education for admission.[11]  For the first time, girls
could receive an education in which French was both a
subject and the medium of instruction.  While girls
could in principle now prepare for study at the university, at independence in 1960 there were few "select"
primary sections for girls, even in the principal provincial centers, and no Congolese women in the universities.
    In the mid-1950s, for the first time thought was
given also to creating vocational schools (écoles d'
auxilliares and écoles professionnelles) to prepare girls
for jobs in commerce and industry (Moffarts, 1957, p.
120).  The few schools created specialized in clothing
and textiles (métiers féminins).
    The election of a non-Catholic coalition in Belgium
in 1954, however, did not equalize opportunities for
schooling between the sexes nor change the goals of
education for girls.  Appointed by the Liberal-Socialist
Coalition, the Coulon Education Commission, which visited
the Congo in 1954, criticized education for girls, not
so much because of sparse academic opportunities but because it did not even teach home economics efficiently
(Congo belge, 1954, p. 238).  An official provincial
director of education, serving under the coalition
government, maintained even in 1957 that the "atavism of
servitude" imposed on the Congolese female by her own
culture could best be overcome by educating her "to
occupy in a dignified manner her place in the true [i.e.,
Christian] home" (Moffarts, 1957, p. 120).


EDUCATIONAL OUTCOMES AND OCCUPATIONAL CONSEQUENCES

    Eighty years of Belgian colonial education in a
Catholic-dominated system was immensely successful in
reinforcing the social relations of conservative Christian patriarchy.  Access to schools and educational
attainment for girls were affected by the legal differentiation into single-sex schools, by the restriction of
curricular choice for those schools, and by limitations
on the use of a European language for instruction.
    Enrollments in schools were sharply differentiated
by gender:  of the 1.6 million primary pupils in 1959-60
(the last school year before independence), only a fifth
were female, and of the 29,000 students in secondary
schools, under 4 percent (less than 1,000) were girls
(Young, et al., 1969, p. 13).  The Belgian Congo had one
of the highest Third World enrollment rates for males and
one of the lowest for females.[12]  All in all, in 1960
there were some 350,000 girls in primary schools, but
probably no more than 10,000 girls attended any postprimary or secondary school, about 1.5 percent of girls

of secondary school age (fifteen to nineteen).  Over half
of the postprimary and secondary enrollments were in
normal schools or in postprimary apprentice teacher-
training programs.  There were only seven vocational
schools (métiers féminins), with an enrollment of 430
girls, and sixteen hospital schools, with about 350
girls.  About 200 girls were taking academic general
secondary programs, mainly in the urban centers of Leopoldville and Elisabethville.  Thus, less then 9 percent
of two million Congolese girls aged five to nineteen
years were attending a formal school at independence.

Sex differences in educational participation were
closely related to occupational outcomes.  Specific
educational credentials were required for entry to
skilled occupations, especially with government, which
was a major employer.  The sex-differentiated Belgian
colonial education system meant that career opportunities
for Africans in the modern sector were much broader for
males than for females and that jobs were stereotyped
by gender.  For example, by 1960 males could enter
several score occupations which required postprimary,
secondary, or higher education.  In religion alone, there
were 600 Congolese priests, 400 Congolese brothers, and
600 ordained Protestant pastors (Slade, 1961, p. 33;
Lemarchand, 1964, p. 126).  All 136 of the prestigeful
assistants médicaux were male (Craemer and Fox, 1968,
p. 3,5), as were the agricultural (250)and veterinary
(15) assistants (Young, et al., 1969, p. 15).  There is
no evidence that any of the more than 11,000 Africans in
the administrative services (Hoskins, 1965, quoted in
Golan, 1968, p. 3) were female, nor were many of the
thousands employed in industry.[13]  It should be noticed
that opportunities for boys or young men were limited
by white views on the proper role of black males in
colonial society.  Other than the priesthood and ministry, the modern Congolese man was to have at best a sub-
altern position within the administration, the military,
and the commercial firms.

The black female was to be even lower in the colonial hierarchy; women and girls were prepared for the
home and for the more humble occupations in the modern
sector.  On the eve of independence, Congolese women were
employed mainly as Catholic sisters (745) and as mission
elementary school teachers (several thousand) (Young,
1965, p. 13).  In 1959, there were only 15 Congolese
maternity nurses and 485 assistant midwives (Public
Health Service, 1960, p. 48).  Even though both boys and
girls were prepared for religious vocations, for school
teaching, and for hospital work, their job titles (e.g.,
male nurse-maternity nurse, moniteur-monitrice, Catholic
brother-sister) varied, as did their tasks.  Catholic

nuns did not have the same tasks nor the same status
as Catholic brothers.  Monitrices were not employed in
the more prestigious schools (those for boys only), as
were male moniteurs.
Colonial attitudes toward women and work in the modern sector and the success of colonial education in
limiting opportunities for Congolese women were well
illustrated by reports on female education and employment in the three largest urban centers of the Belgian
Congo.  In a study of Stanleyville in the 1950s, the
differences between economic and social opportunities
of African men and women were found to be probably more
acute than those found in other African urban areas.
"Most women had little or no involvement in either wage-
earning or trading and were largely confined to work in
and around their homes" (Pons, 1969, p. 214).  Moreover,
Congolese women in Stanleyville also had little contact
with Western education or culture, as compared with
Congolese men.  "Only two or three" Congolese women could
conduct even the "most ordinary conversation" in French,
less than 5 percent worked for wages, only about 15 percent had ever attended school compared with 50 percent
of the men, and only about 35 percent of girls under
sixteen years of age in the city were then attending
school, as compared with nearly 80 percent of the boys.
Few Congolese women ever visited the center of the
"European town."  In addition, there was virtually no
attempt on the part of évolués' wives to emulate the
dress and public behavior of European women (Pons, 1969,
pp. 214-15).
The few women in Stanleyville who had received
schooling were in great demand as wives for educated
male évolués, but their supply was so scant that the
"overwhelming majority" of men, even those with secondary
education, married illiterate women.  Even the few educated women were in a difficult situaton.  Evolué males
complained such women were not sufficiently educated,
while uneducated men usually regarded women with some
education "as less trustworthy than others" (Pons, 1969,
p. 217).
A study of Elisabethville (Lubumbashi) almost two
decades later found similar results with regard to women
and work.  Out of a total adult female population of
66,000 in the city, it was estimated that there were
only seventy female professionals, including nurses and
schoolteachers (Gould, 1978, p. 133).
The propriety of women's working and especially the
experiment, begun in 1953, of employing Congolese women
in textile-related industries was discussed at a meeting
of Catholic business leaders (Association des Cadres
Dirigéants Catholiques des Enterprises du Congo Belge)

in Leopoldville in 1958.  Several general attitudes prevailed in the discussion.  Certain occupations were found
more suitable for women than for men, such as "domestic
service and shorthand typists."  However, few Congolese
women were capable of holding these jobs "best suited
to their abilities" because of their lack of education
and vocational training.  Thus, those women who wanted
to work could find no jobs other than unskilled ones in
factories (Capelle, 1959, p. 56).  Whether  Congolese
women belonged in textile factories, where, despite their
lack of formal vocational training, they operated sewing
machines on the production line or folded, ironed, and
packed products, was discussed in economic and moral
terms.  Economically, women were potentially cheaper to
employ than men because the firm did not have to pay
family and housing allowances.  But it was feared they
would not be as punctual or disciplined as men because of
their lack of education, and since most were illiterate,
only a few could be utilized as forewomen-timekeepers.
Moral concerns, however, were paramount.  While the
assembled Catholic industrial leaders agreed "in principle" that is was "unjustifiable antifeminism" to deny
access to wage-earning occupations to women and counter
to the "social teachings of the Church" to pay women
different wages than men for the same task, nonetheless,
the Congolese woman's place was in the home, either that
of her father or that of her husband.  Working in factories meant that a woman's "moral standards" were
"bound to suffer."  It was "unanimously agreed" that men
and women should be separated in factories and that it
was preferable that supervisors be European women.  Although the shop foreman could be a man, he should not
have African women working directly under his supervision (Capelle, 1959, p. 58).

The assembled Catholic business leaders concluded
their discussion by expressing their opposition to allowing women to engage in any kind of work, especially heavy
work, "harmful to their physical health" and "types of
work incompatible with their family duties," such as
night work and long hours.  While calling for Congolese
schoolgirls to be "initiated to the problems of factory
life," the Catholic business leaders insisted upon "the
need for social policy" to safeguard the "woman's family
duties" and not to compel married women to take a job to
balance the household budget.  They remained especially
opposed to the employment of women in cases where moral
precautions were inadequate (Capelle, 1959, pp. 58-59).

Thus, the outcomes of colonial education affected
the lives of Congolese women in at least three ways.
First, Belgian colonial practices reinforced gender as
a legitimate basis for differential treatment.  Sex-
segregated schooling[14] and the related sex-segregated

structure of jobs made it manifest to children and adults
that there was something profoundly different in what
males and females could and should learn and in what work
they could and should perform.  Second, colonial education superimposed upon diverse traditional African views
Western concepts of appropriate roles for men and women.
The sex-segregated school system was depended upon to
insure that women would be in the home and not in the
fields, the office, the pulpit, or the workplace.
Finally, Belgian colonial policies and practices in education affected women through omission.  The transplanta-
tion of Christian patriarchy fostered economic marginality among women of the Congo in the modern sector.
Women's opportunities to learn modern skills such as
literacy (especially in French) or marketable trades
were scanty.

IMPLICATIONS OF COLONIAL EDUCATION FOR MODERN ZAIRIAN
WOMEN

Sex differentiation in schooling during the colonial
epoch continues to affect the lives of women in Zaire.
First, the gap between male and female participation in
education and the modern economy may widen as stringent
budgets require cutbacks in educational investment and
government employment (Young, et al., 1969, p. 12).  As
expansion of places in these institutions slows down,
aspirations remain constant and competition for these
places becomes more intense.  The percentage gains in
school enrollments made by women since independence
could diminish.  Such reductions in opportunities for
women probably would be justified on the "colonial" basis
that women belong in the home and that investment in their
further schooling in a period of stringent budgets is
extravagant.
Second, the experience of racial and ethnic minorities generally has been that it is difficult to equalize
opportunity once some groups obtain an initial lead.  For
example, at independence, there were no Zairian physicians,
male or female.  Through scholarships offered by Western
nations, several hundred Zairian practicing male medical
assistants (as well as younger men) were sent to Europe
for medical training, and by the early 1970s there were
almost three hundred Zairian physicians--all male (Young,
et al., 1969, p. 15).  Even if quotas for women were to
be established in medical programs at Zairian universities, it would be decades before there could be appreciable representation of women in the medical profession.
Third, eighty years of sex stereotyping of curricula
(home economics for girls and artisan training for boys)
and of occupations (trades for men and elementary school-
keeping for women) hold back efforts to broaden roles--

as in many societies.  When secondary education finally
was offered to girls in 1948, the few females enrolled
were in home economics, elementary teacher training, and
nursing.  This pattern persists.  In a study of professional women in Lubumbashi (Elisabethville), almost two
decades after independence, women still were engaged
mainly in four occupations, as nurses, teachers, directors of health clinics or home economics schools, and
university assistants--the latter the only new occupation
(Gould, 1978, p. 133).[15]

Few data are yet available about the effect of educational and occupational stratification by sex on the
self-concept and motivation of young Zairian women.  Research in Western societies indicates that women continue to congregate in "female" occupations because they
receive more social approval and fewer negative social
sanctions.

Fourth, particularly unfortunate was the undermining
of womens' position in agriculture.  Typical of the Belgian Congo experience was the dichotomy in agriculture
between food production and export crops.  Colonial
agricultural policy focused on the development of export
crops and colonial agricultural education concentrated
on the preparation of African males to assist with the
task.  While female pupils were required to garden, they
were seldom trained in modern farming techniques, despite their predominant role in domestic food production.  This worldwide colonial blunder especially handicaps contemporary schemes of rural development in many
Third World countries, which are now becoming food im-
porters.  Devoting disproportionate resources and attention to the rural male "can be attributed most readily
to a tendency of some project planners and authorities
to see African women in Western terms--i.e., essentially
as domestic workers whose primary responsibility should
be in the home and not in the fields" (Lele, 1975, p. 77).

During eighty years of Belgian colonial rule in Central Africa, schools were used to socialize men and women
to those European norms of Christian patriarchy that prevailed in Belgium, a distinctively conservative country.
Christian patriarchy was taken to the Congo by colonial
administrators and missionaries and only now are developers recognizing the economic--and  human--costs.  As
Judith Van Allen has noted, "African women have paid
dearly for carrying the white man's burden" (1976, p.26).


NOTES

1.  The number of high school graduates was estimated by the author in 1960-61 after interviews with the
director of secondary education at the Bureau of Catholic

Education and the UNESCO statistical advisor at the
Ministry of Education, both in Leopoldville.  Higher education figures were ascertained from graduation lists
provided in 1960-61 by the registrars of Lovanium University, the State University at Elisabethville (Lubumbashi), and the postsecondary institutes.
        2.   In early 1961, I interviewed this student,
Mlle. Sophie Kanza, the daughter of the then mayor of
Leopoldville.  She became the first Congolese woman to
receive a high school diploma when she graduated from
the Lycée du Sacré Coeur in June 1961.
        3.   Prostitution was evidently also an avenue of
employment for some Congolese women.  Catholic missionaries constantly harangued the government to enact more
stringent laws on adultery and promiscuity for both
whites and blacks, especially in the towns.  By the beginning of the twentieth century, mulatto boys were being
admitted into the state colonie scolaire at Boma.  Soon,
a school for mulatto children was also opened by the
Belgian Holy Ghost Fathers in the Kindu region, shortly
after construction of the railway in that area was completed.  (See Dorman, 1905).
        4.   For example, Axelson (1970, p. 259) reports that
in 1893 women exclusively cultivated the ground and produced food in the Lower Congo. Boserup (1970, p. 60) indicates that 68 percent of farm work in the Congo was
performed by females.
        5.   An interesting modern parallel is reported in an
American magazine.  East Coast air travelers complained
of dirty airplanes.  Management consultants found that
maintenance men were using brooms instead of vacuum
cleaners, which they considered "the tools of women."
The solution was to make the machines heavier, paint them
grey rather than pastel, and label them "industrial vacuum cleaner."  A "military-style competition" was undertaken to see who could best disassemble and clean his
new industrial tool.  The plan was successful.  "It's
now macho to vacuum efficiently."  (From the New York
magazine, quoted in MS., August 1978, p. 24.)
        6.   Boys at the colonie scolaire at Boma, for ex-
ample, were regularly transported at government expense
to the nearby Catholic-run girls' school at Moanda to
choose wives.  The boys and girls sections at Nouvelle-
Anvers were in close proximity.
        7.   Estimated by the author from annual reports in
missionary journals.
        8.   For example, of the fourteen women, including
wives, who were accepted for the first class in 1908 at
the United Congo Evangelical Training Institution at
Kimpese, the most advanced Protestant school in the
Congo, only five could read or write, while all nineteen
men were literate. (See Hawker, 1911, pp. 315-24).

9. A commission, appointed after World War I, reviewed colonial education. The recommended plan appeared as Projet de l'Enseignement (1925) and was put into practice by a code of government regulations, Organisation de l'Enseignement (1929). The former appears in English translation in Scanlon, (1964, pp. 142-60). See also the royal decree of 19 July 1926 regulating vocational education (Congo belge, 1926b), implemented by an Ordinance of 11 September 1926 (Congo belge, 1926a). This legislation did not create schools but, like the 1929 code, formalized existing practices.

10. A schoolmistress at Ibanj frankly admitted that when a sewing class for women began in 1901, "the object was not so much to teach sewing as it was to get them together for prayer and song." (See Sheppard, 1905, pp. 162-63). It is interesting to note that missionaries in Kenya wrote to their supporters to send cloth cut into postcard size so that it would take a year to make a dress and thus provide ample time for the women to hear many gospel messages. (See Connolly, 1975, p. 68).

11. These new schools for maternity nurses gave a three-year specialized program that included science courses but mainly ward work in obstetrics, pediatrics, and surgery, including the sole delivery of at least twenty-five babies.

12. For example, by 1962 there were eleven female African college graduates in East Africa (See Hunter, 1963, p. 102). UNESCO data indicate that in 1963 girls made up approximately one-third of the primary and secondary enrollments in most African countries (See figures quoted in Evans, 1972, p. 213, n.1).

13. When in Kinshasa in 1960-61, I was struck by the absence of female secretaries in government offices or salesclerks in stores. I observed female clerks only in the few modern supermarkets.

14. In pedagogical writings, discussion of the relationship between single-sex schooling and differential psychological and social outcomes (e.g., self-concept, academic achievement, role models) is frequently contradictory and ambiguous. Belgium itself still has one of the highest percentages (88 percent at the terminal secondary level) of single-sex schools in the industrialized world. See Comber and Keeves (1973, pp. 71-75).

15. Indeed, the Economic Commission for Africa estimates that well over 50 percent of all mass education offered to women is related to domestic programs. This is true even when women have over 50 percent participation in food production, animal husbandry, and marketing (U.N., Economic Commission for Africa, 1975, p. 68). In the Congo, well over 80 percent of women in school were in domestic-science related programs.

REFERENCES

Axelson, Sigbert. 1970. Culture Confrontation in the
    Lower Congo. Falkoping, Sweden: Gummessons.
Boserup, Ester. 1970. Woman's Role in Economic Develop-
    ment. New York: St. Martin's Press.
Cambier, Scheutist Father Superior Emeri. 1900.
    "X/20/99 from Luluabourg." Missions en  Chine at au
    Congo, August, pp. 485-86.
Capelle, Gerard. 1959. "Emploi de personnel féminin dans
    les entreprises du Congo belge." Bulletin of the
    Inter-African Labour Institute 2:46-61.
Comber, L.C., and J.P. Keeves. 1973. Science Education
    in Nineteen Countries: International Studies in
    Evaluation. Vol. 1. New York: Halsted Press.
Committee on Education. 1894. "Annual Report for 1893."
    Baptist Missionary Magazine, July, pp. 185-210.
Congo, Etat indépendant du. Gouvernement central. 1890.
    Bulletin officiel de l'Etat indépendant du Congo
    [Brussels], pp. 120-22.
_____. 1892. Bulletin officiel de l'Etat indépendant
    du Congo [Brussels], pp. 18-19, 188-95, 241-43.
Congo belge. 1926a. Bulletin administratif, pp. 376-78.
_____. 1926b. Bulletin officiel, pp. 712-17.
_____. Ministère des Colonies. 1954. La Réforme de
    l'enseignement au Congo belge (Mission Pédagogique
    Coulon-Deheyn-Renson). Brussels.
_____. Service de l'Enseignement. 1948. Organisation
    de l'Enseignement Libre Subsidié  pour indigènes
    avec le concours des sociétés de missions chréti-
    ennes. Dispositions Générales. [Brussels].
Congo Missionary Conference 1906. A report of the third
    General Conference of Missionaries of the Protestant
    Societies working in Congoland. Held at Kinshasa,
    Stanley Pool, Congo State, 9-14 January 1906.
    Bongandanga: Congo Balolo Mission Press.
Connolly, Yola Evans. 1975. "Roots of Divergency: Ameri-
    can Protestant Missions in Kenya 1923-1946." Ph.D.
    dissertation, University of Illinois.
Craemer, Willy de, and Renée C. Fox. 1968. The Emerging
    Physician. Stanford, Cal.: Hoover Institute on War,
    Revolution and Peace, Stanford University.
Deheyn, Jean-Jacques (Director of Technical Education).
    1957. Réalisations et objectifs de la Belgique en
    matière d'enseignement agricole au Congo Belge."
    Bulletin Agricole du Congo Belge 68, no. 1:1-22.
de Pierpont, Ivan, et al. 1906. Au Congo et aux Indes:
    Les Jésuites belges aux missions. Brussels: Bulens.
Devos, A. 1904. "Principes de civilisation." Mouvement
    des missions Catholiques au Congo, December, pp.348-
    50.

Dorman, Marcus. 1905.  A Journal of a Tour in the Congo
    Free State. Brussels: Lebeque, and London: Kegan
    Paul, Trench, Trubner.
Evans, David R. 1972. "Image and Reality: Career Goals of
    Educated Ugandan Women." Canadian Journal of
    African Studies 6, no. 2:213-32.
Gabriel, Frère. 1914. Essai d'orientation de l'enseigne-
    ment et de l'éducation au Congo. Anvers: Stockmans.
George, Betty. 1966. Educational Developments in the
    Congo (Leopoldville). Washington, D.C.: U.S. Gov-
    ernment Printing Office.
Goetschalckx, E.P. 1953.  Situation des écoles post-
    primaires pour autochtones 1952-1953.  Leopold-
    ville: Bureau de l'éducation Catholique.
Golan, Tamar. 1968. Educating the Bureaucracy in a New
    Polity. New York: Teachers College Press.
Gould, Terri F. 1978. "Value Conflict and Development:
    The Struggle of the Zairian Woman."  Journal of
    Modern African Studies 16, no. 1: 132-34.
Guilleme, White Father Maturin. 1896.  Missions d'Afrique
    des Pères blancs, September, pp. 405-6.
Hawker, George. 1911.  An Englishwoman's Twenty-Five
    Years in Tropical Africa.  New York: Hodder and
    Stoughton.
Hoskins, Catherine. 1965.  The Congo Since Independence.
    London: Oxford University Press.
Hunter, Guy. 1963.  Education for a Developing Region:
    A Study in East Africa. London: Allen and Unwin.
Kervyn, Edouard. 1912. "Les missions Catholiques au
    Congo belge." La Revue Congolaise, pp. 284-307.
Laveille, E. 1926. L'Evangile au centre de l'Afrique,
    Le Père Emile Van Hencxthoven, S.J., fondateur de
    la Mission du Kwango (Congo belge) 1852-1906. Lou-
    vain: Museum Lessianum.
Lele, Uma. 1975. The Design of Rural Development: Lessons
    from Africa. Baltimore and London: Johns Hopkins
    University Press for the World Bank.
Lemarchand, Rene. 1964. Political Awakening in the Bel-
    gian Congo. Berkeley and Los Angeles: University
    of California Press.
Liesenborghs, Oswald. 1940. "L'Instruction publique
    des indigènes du Congo belge." Congo 21, no. 3
    (March): 233-72.
Missions belges de la Compagnie de Jésus. 1907. Septem-
    ber, p. 328.
Missions d'Afrique des Pères blancs. 1898. December, p.
    360.
Moffarts, M. 1957. "Enseignement secondaire." Problèmes
    d'Afrique Centrale no. 36 (2nd trimester): 120.
Mottoule, L. 1950. "Les Missions et le développement
    économique du Congo." L'Eglise au Congo et au

Ruanda-Urundi. Brussels: Oeuvres Pontificales mis-
    sionaires.
Organisation de l'Enseignement Libre au Congo belge at
    au Ruanda-Urundi, avec le Concours des Sociétés des
    Missions Nationales. 1929. Brussels: Dison-Verviers.
Pons, Valdo. 1969. Stanleyville: An African Urban Com-
    munity under Belgian Administration. London: Oxford
    University Press.
Projet de l'Enseignement Libre au Congo belge avec le
    concours des sociétés de Missions Nationales. 1925.
    Brussels.
Public Health Service, Department of Health, Education
    and Welfare. 1960. Republic of the Congo, A Study
    of Health Problems and Resources. Washington, D.C.
    U.S. Government Printing Office.
Report of the First Education Conference (18-23 December
    1931). 1934. 2nd ed. Kimpese, Belgian Congo: mimeo-
    graphed.
Report of Second Education Conference (25 July-2 August
    1933). 1934. Kimpese, Belgian Congo: mimeographed.
Scanlon, David C., ed. 1964. Traditions of African
    Education. New York: Teachers College Bureau of
    Publications, Columbia University.
Sheppard, Mrs. 1905. Missionary, April, pp. 162-63.
Slade, Ruth. 1961. The Belgian Congo. 2nd ed. London:
    Oxford University Press.
United Nations. Economic Commission for Africa. 1975.
    Economic Bulletin for Africa 11, no. 1.
Van Allen, Judith. 1976. "African Women, 'Modernization,'
    and National Liberation." Lynne B. Iglitzin and Ruth
    Ross, eds., Women in the World. Santa Barbara, Cal.:
    Clio Books.
Van Wing, Joseph, S.J. [1918]. Le Vingt-cinquième anni-
    versaire de la Mission du Kwango. Brussels: Bulens.
Verhaegen, Pierre. 1909. Au Congo: Impressions de Voyage.
    Gand: Siffer.
Yates, Barbara A. 1980a. "White Views of Black Minds:
    Schooling in King Leopold's Congo." History of
    Education Quarterly 20, no. 2 (Spring): 27-50.
_____. 1980b. "The Origins of Language Policy in
    Colonial Zaire." Journal of Modern African Studies
    18, no. 2:257-79.
Young, M. Crawford. 1965. Politics in the Congo. Prince-
    ton, N.J.: Princeton University Press.
_____, William M. Rideout, Jr., and David N. Wilson.
    1969. Survey of Education in the Democratic Repub-
    lic of the Congo. Washington, D.C.: American Coun-
    cil on Education.

## 7. Reinventing the Past and Circumscribing the Future: *Authenticité* and the Negative Image of Women's Work in Zaire

*Francille Rusan Wilson*

Ester Boserup's <u>Woman's Role in Economic Development</u> uses precolonial Zaire to exemplify female farming systems as an economic mode of production in Africa (1970, pp. 16-18). This division of labor in which women do most tasks associated with cultivation was predominant in the entire Congo region. The precolonial Congolese woman's specific status was dependent on the social and political organization of her group, but there were a number of fundamental similarities among most groups. Women generally had independent rights to cultivate land and to dispose of its produce. They could also inherit and pass on rights in land and other real property to others. From an economic standpoint, precolonial matrilineal and patrilineal systems both allowed women to have access to the basic means of agricultural production and gave them control over the surplus they might generate. Adult women were an economic asset to the family and the clan; they were not luxury items. Because of their critical role in food production, women's status in precolonial economies was relatively high compared with that of their late-nineteenth-century European counterparts.

Trade, especially in agricultural products, was a largely female endeavor. But unlike trade in West Africa, trade in the Congo was never a major economic enterprise for men or women. Systems of transportation and communication, never well developed except for river traffic, were greatly disrupted in the nineteenth century. The extension of Arab slaving; warfare between settled peoples and migrating groups who were pushing northward and eastward from Angola and Zambia, as in the Lunda-Chokwe wars; and the military occupation of the Belgians came in successive and overlapping waves in the latter half of the nineteenth century and left great political, social, and economic fragmentation.[1]

It would be a fruitless exercise to attempt to de-

termine whether men or women were more exploited under
the colonial Belgian regime.  The explicit purpose of
the Congo Free State and the Belgian Congo was to produce the greatest amount of profit possible for private
shareholders.  I will argue, however, that the particular character of the exploitation caused African women
to be at an increasing disadvantage vis à vis men despite of and even as a result of their continued pre-
dominence in agriculture.  This disadvantage was caused
by economic policies and abetted by an ideological
assault on the status of women.  At the ideological
level, Belgian administrators and missionaries campaigned
vigorously against matrilineal systems of descent and
female farming.  Female farming was attacked because it
allegedly made men indolent.  This approach allowed administrators to justify forced labor on the grounds that
Congolese men had to be "educated" to appreciate the
true value of labor (Boserup, 1970, p. 60; Miracle and
Fetter, 1970, p. 246).  Actually, female farming facilitated the rapid proletarianization of the Congolese man.
    The colonial economic system benefited from female
farming in three major ways.  First of all, it allowed
men to become wage earners without completely disrupting
food production.  Second, the wages paid in the mines
and plantations were too low to support a family, making
considerable contribution by women necessary.  In order
to insure that this contribution would be in food for
local consumption, colonial authorities did not allow
women to live in mining areas or to grow their own food
on the plantations in the early years.  The wage policy
was possible only because the so-called subsistence
sector directly subsidized the colonial economy (Boserup,
1970, p. 77-80; Peemans, 1975, p. 151).  Finally, colonial policy artificially restrained agricultural trade
and peasant initiative through a state monopoly over
cash crops, and through the practice of raiding villages
for foodstuffs (Peemans, 1975, p. 151; Miracle and Fetter, 1970, pp. 245-50).
    The new cities of the Belgian Congo quickly became
male enclaves.  At first, legal restrictions prevented
men from bringing their families, and single men found
few unattached women.  In the copperbelt, the proportion
of wives to workers was eighteen per hundred in 1925
and rose only gradually to eighty-three per hundred in
1955, despite the relaxation of restrictions to combat
serious labor shortages (Young, 1965, p. 205; Miracle
and Fetter, 1970, p. 205).  Low wages in the mines and
other industries caused Congolese families to depend on
contributions from the rural areas to support urban
workers.  In the cities, petty trade was not initially
lucrative because of the low wage level and disincen-

tives to surplus food production.  Peasants soon discovered that bringing a crop to the market exposed them
to punitive raids in which all their surplus was seized,
thus exposing them to the risk of starvation between
harvests.  The unbalanced urban sex ratio and the re-
straints to trade meant that many of the single urban
women (and some of the married ones) were forced to rely
upon prostitution for the greater part of their incomes.
Prostitution, with its implications of breakdown of the
traditional system of social control, caused cities to
become increasingly identified in the popular mind as
bad places for women.  The terms for the single woman,
femme indépendante, femme libre, and femme célibataire,
became commonly used as synonyms for "prostitute."  At
the same time that the city became identified as sinful,
rural areas were becoming stereotyped as shameful and
backward (Comhaire-Sylvain, 1968, p. 39).  Congolese
women had the unenviable choice of being scorned as
prostitutes or being scorned for continuing outmoded
"uncivilized" practices.

The deterioration of the status of women in the
colonial period was greatly abetted by the educational
system (see Barbara Yates's paper, above).  There were
few opportunities for female education, especially in
rural areas.  The few girls' schools that existed offered
only courses in "domestic science."  On the eve of independence, the disparity between the levels of male and
female education was quite marked.  The male literacy
rate was the highest in Africa, although almost no one
went beyond the third year of primary school.  On the
other hand, few women could even speak the rudimentary
French needed for many urban jobs.  In 1960, only 1 percent of the women who lived in Kananga (ex-Luluabourg),
the fourth-largest city, could speak French, as opposed
to 25 percent of the men (Young, 1970, p. 982).

Women as a group were much less able to manipulate
the outward symbols of "civilization," language, manners,
and access to the money economy.  While this difference
is evident in many other African countries, it was extreme in Zaire, and only the settler colonies of British
and Portuguese Africa are really comparable.  Furthermore, the increasing deterioration of women's economic
independence, the rural isolation, and the absence of
meaningful education for women caused a loss of status
in the traditional sector.  Zairian men and women began
to view women's roles in the rural areas as noneconomic
because they did not produce cash incomes.

The notion that women were economically peripheral
in colonial times is still current in Zaire.  This
notion with its implicitly negative view of female
farming continues to be accepted under authenticité

(authenticity). Ida Fay Rousseau echoes this sentiment in her comparison of women's education in Zaire and Sierra Leone when she states that "education of women did not concern Belgium because women were economically marginal and did not serve a practical function for Belgians in the enterprise of exploitation" (1975, p. 46).

In point of fact, as I have suggested, the economic exploitation of the peoples of Zaire was accomplished in large part through the exploitation of the traditional agricultural sector. "Under the Leopoldian regime [1885-1905], the State tried to attract foreign capital to develop large transport and mining enterprises, but severely restricted the actions of foreign commercial companies and petty traders. It instituted a State monopoly over the agricultural surplus for export" (Peemans, 1975, pp. 150-51). During serious world crises such as World Wars I and II and the Great Depression, the prices paid to peasant producers approached zero (Young, 1965, pp. 216-24). Real income paid as wages steadily declined from 1911 until the 1950s. Transfers from the agricultural to the industrial sector in the form of low-wage labor and low-cost food helped the export-oriented industrial sector produce a surplus, which it exported abroad and reinvested in expansion. In order to keep industrial wages low and still guarantee an unlimited labor supply, it was necessary that rural income remain low.

Attempts of Zairian peasants to protest their continued exploitation were suppressed. The number of days of mandatory unpaid labor steadily increased between the world wars, as did the effort required to raise the cash necessary to pay taxes on all households and unaffiliated adults. By the end of World War II, 10 percent of the male population had been in jail, chiefly for violation of forced labor requirements (Young, 1965, pp. 223-26). Whole villages had fled into the bush to avoid the agricultural agents and tax collectors. Year after year, the official explanation for active and passive peasant protests was the continuing inability of Congolese men to grasp the importance of farming export crops. This counterfactual explanation has found its way into the literature on development in Zaire, as in the description of the failure of the largest compulsory farming scheme, the paysannat, in the 1974 country report on Zaire by the World Bank.

The deep-rooted attitudes which accompany the traditional division of labor was one of the reasons for the failure of the "paysannat" experiment promoted by the Belgian administration, the other reason being the clan ownership of land.

An attempt to change men into traditional cultivators met with resentment and resistance, and
agriculture reverted to the traditional pattern
as soon as coercion disappeared. On the other
hand, the traditional division of labor leaves
men free to take wage employment and leave farming to the other family members. (International
Bank, 1974, p. 12)

The paysannat "experiment" was a twenty-year-long
scheme of compulsory and heavily supervised crop rotation in Belgian-created collective villages or paysannats,
designed to greatly enlarge the area and volume of cotton cultivation. First proposed in 1936, the promise of
individual land titles was made to those peasants who
found themselves involved in the scheme. The paysannat
were tremendously unpopular in most areas because they
did not take actual soil conditions into account when
assigning holdings, as did the traditional system.
Prices paid for the crops outside the areas most suited
for cotton rarely made resettlement attractive without
force, and peasant farmers constantly deserted the paysannats because clear titles to the land were never provided and their tenure was always in doubt (Harms, 1974,
pp. 16-17; Young, 1965, p. 226). The failure of the
paysannat system was due to the unwillingness of the
colonial administration to make cotton farming profitable
to Africans. There are numerous examples throughout
the African continent of men who grow cash crops within
female systems. Cotton prices were very favorable to
peasant production during this period, and outside Zaire,
African men were quick to introduce cotton on their own
initiative. There is no reason today to believe that
Zairian men would not have grown cotton themselves if
it had been profitable (Young, 1965, pp. 91-92, 223-26,
66-68).
By the 1950s, the need for an unlimited low-wage
labor supply had decreased, as the larger businesses
found that wages were a relatively small portion of
their costs. Wages began to increase in real terms for
the first time, but the level of employment began a
steady decline. Women did not fully share in the so-
called golden age of the Congolese working class. Because of settler pressure, rural wages and farm incomes
did not rise as quickly as urban wages (Peemans, 1975,
p. 152). Urban wages doubled but employment dropped
sharply. Plantations were the only sector showing an
increase in workers. The failure of the nonagricultural
labor force to expand and the consequent limits to the
growth of a consumer economy played a large part in the
social and political disorder that immediately followed
independence. The number of those employed in Kinshasa

declined from 87,000 in 1959 to 58,000 in 1961 (Young,
1970, p. 986).

The legal rights of women in Zaire today were developed in the colonial period. The Belgians imposed
their own legal codes, which made most women legally the
dependant of a male head of household. All households
were subject to colonial taxes and the head of house was
required to carry an identity card that listed the names
of all the dependants not subject to taxes living within
the household. The right of Africans to live and even
gather in certain areas was dependent on possession of
this card issued by colonial authorities and the carte
de travail, or worker's pass, which was issued by employers of wage workers. The right of association was closely
regulated and monitored. If an African wished to form
or belong to an association that was not an ethnically
based mutual aid society or an approved European-sponsored
alumni or church group, he or she had to have this membership listed on the identity card and endorsed by the
proper colonial official. Very few women, including
those married women who paid individual taxes as merchants, possessed identity cards. Even women who were
unmarried adult wage earners were listed on the card of
the presumed male head of household, their father, uncle,
brother, or son if they lived within a family structure
(Comhaire-Sylvain, 1968, pp. 14-15). Because of these
restrictions, the first non-ethnic women's organizations
to develop in the colonial era that were outside of
missionary control were clubs made up of femmes libres,
women living outside of the jurisdiction of a man who had
their own identity cards and who were mostly prostitutes.
Other femmes indépendantes, single and divorced petty
traders, and the tiny number of wage workers did not form
associations until after independence, when the rules
regarding freedom of association were swept away (Comhaire-Sylvain, 1968, pp. 44-51). The first Congolese
women's clubs were recreational and social. They were
often sponsored by and/or named after a popular orches-
tra or beer. During outings, the club members wore
identical outfits in the latest styles. They were able
to go to places that respectable women did not go--bars
and nightclubs--and soon became trend setters in fashion
and manners.

Women's organizations flourished throughout Zaire
in the immediate postcolonial period, 1960-1965, despite
some tendency to link all women's associations with prostitution. After independence, all sorts of women's organizations, including trade unions, were voluntarily
established. Suzanne Comhaire-Sylvain's excellent study
of women's organizations in Kinshasa in 1965 reveals
that the majority of women in Kinshasa belonged to some
sort of organization after 1960, and that these organi-

zations were increasingly feminist, nationalist, and
interethnic. Some groups were founded by the tiny number of educated women and others by women who were the
wives of political figures. However, the evidence that
Comhaire-Sylvain presents seems to indicate that most
of the organizations were started by women with little
or no education and that their membership was pre-
dominately women who did not speak French. Four of the
best known of these organizations, with branches in other
parts of the country, had an approximate total of a
thousand members each in 1965 (Comhaire-Sylvain, 1968,
pp. 253-88). Women were also active in the political
struggles that began soon after independence. In 1960,
the Femmes Nationalistes appeared as fighters among the
rebels in the northeast. In return for their aid, the
rebel army promised them places on the governing council
in the town of Maniema (Young, 1970, pp. 982-83). Women
in Kinshasa also demonstrated for various causes through
1965.

After independence, the city did not offer as many
options for women's employment as for organizations.
Declining real income and rural unrest cut deeply into
what women could earn as petty traders. It was difficult for women lacking in education to compete with the
growing numbers of unemployed men even for domestic
work. Studies done in 1945, 1965, and 1970 show surprisingly little change in the material conditions for
women's work.[2] Prostitution continued to be a major
occupation for single women in urban areas (Young, 1970,
pp. 982-83).

The decision to become a prostitute in Zaire had
serious social and legal consequences. Prostitution
was not considered a morally acceptable occupation for
women by any of the peoples of Zaire. Women who became
prostitutes risked social approbation and the loss of
formal and informal support from their kin. Economic
realities often caused adjustments in moral attitudes,
but it would be a mistake to assume that prostitution
had the same moral status as petty trade. Prostitutes
who were able to give support to their extended family
were tolerated. Prostitutes who seemed rich and clever
might even be called movie stars--vedettes. Fontaine
suggests that in Zaire, women's status was related to
a moral hierarchy in which marriage was the ideal.
Single women having sexual relations with men were considered "better" if they were mistresses than if the
relationships were based solely on money. Women who
were most like European prostitutes were referred to
derogatorily as chambres d'hôtel (La Fontaine, 1974,
p. 109).

THE RECOURSE TO AUTHENTICITE: 1965 TO THE PRESENT

Authenticité as a political philosophy may be most
simply described as an explicit rejection of imported
ideologies and a call for the return to traditional
Africal values and institutions. Hence, its philosophical roots may be found in Negritude and in the African
nationalist movements of the late 1950s. Before 20 May
1967, when authenticité was rhetorically enshrined as
the personal gift of President Mobutu to the Zairian
people, its explicit aims were associated with the
radical and even revolutionary forces within the country
who opposed Mobutu and his allies (Wilson, 1974, p. 40;
Nzongola-Ntalaja, 1976, p. 8). It was Lumumba, Mulele,
trade unionists, and students who first called for economic nationalization, reorientation of public values,
and the changing of names from colonial to their authentic African forms. By the time of the Mobutu coup d'état
on 24 November 1965, there was considerable mass support
for the changes that authenticité seemed to promise. In
eastern Zaire, most of the towns were under the control
of the "second independence" movement, which promised
to deliver the "real" independence that had been delayed
and betrayed by "corrupt politicians" who were "foreign
puppets." Mobutu's development of authenticité as governmental policy fully capitalized upon the legitimate
political and economic grievances and the nationalist
sentiment of the Zairian people.
    In practice, authenticité has been a device for con-
solidating power and legitimizing antidemocratic principles as traditional African values. Today, it is
clear that authenticité has been used to obtain mass
support and to distract attention away from the pressing
economic and social problems that confront Zaire.

> The mystification [of authenticité] itself con-
> sists in the effort to strip all progressive
> ideas of their true meaning so they can be used
> in their emptiness to cover up the true neocolonial
> practices of the ruling class. In this regard,
> the people's campaign against the alliance between
> foreign exploiters and their corrupt national
> leaders became a potent weapon against all politi-
> cal opposition and a rationale for the extreme
> centralization and bureaucratization of governmen-
> tal functions characteristic of a Bonapartist
> state. The system of privilege and corruption
> against which the people had fought has remained
> intact. (Nzongola-Ntalaja, 1976, pp. 6-8).

Under authenticité, all organizations have been

suppressed and reorganized under the single party,
the MPR (Popular Revolutionary Movement).  Like the
others, women's groups were first banned and then a few
official women's organizations within the party were
created.  The situation now is very similar to the
colonial regulations.  Only mutual aid, church-sponsored
organizations and recreational clubs are allowed to
exist outside the party structure.  These groups must
receive permission from the authorities and their activities are closely monitored.  The hundreds of women's
groups that flourished between 1960 and 1965 have been
disbanded.

The rhetoric and reality of authenticité is pater-
nalistic, authoritarian, and self-serving.  The political structure of the past is depicted as a totally
male hierarchy with an absolute chief who ruled the
childlike masses through the force of his superior per-
sonality, will, and intellect.  It was men who provided
the material needs of the community--alone.  According
to a popular saying, in the home men reigned, women
governed.  The woman's principal role in the authentic
past was to have as many children as possible and to
provide education in the basic values of the tribe.
Women had no authentic historical roles that were economic or political.  This notion and the idea that all
decisions were made by a village chief without consultation with others is a gross distortion of complex
structures of governance, which varied greatly between
and within ethnic groups in the precolonial Congo.
Authenticité accepts the Belgian characterization of
precolonial agriculture as shameful and backward.  Women's work in agriculture is described only in the most
negative of terms.  Rural women are described as having
been degraded and despised, mere beasts of burden, before the ascension of Mobutu in 1965.  Thus, the Belgian
philosophy that women made no economic contribution as
farmers became the philosophy of the Mobutu regime.  The
colonial period does come under criticism for making
women its first victim by denying them education and by
destroying the traditional meaning of the bridewealth,
but the assault on the Zairian family by the plantation
and forced labor system does not come under sustained
analysis or particular criticism.  The spontaneous response of Zairian women to the opportunity to form
political organizations between 1960 and 1965 is not a
part of the authentic past because women owe all of their
emancipation to the generosity of the head of state
(Salongo, 1976; Bureau Politique, 1975).

Under authenticité, the entire responsibility for
maintaining the morality of the system rests with women.
Men do not have moral responsibilities.  All of the prob-

lems of morality, particularly those in the cities, are
blamed on women who have neglected their authentic responsibilities for the lure of foreign ideas.  For example, the official news agency AZAP declared in a
widely reprinted press release in May 1975 that men must
not be considered primarily responsible for prostitution
because it was well known that women could resist temp-
tation better than men!  It concluded by saying that if
a prostitute had relations with a man, it was because
she wanted to, not because she needed the money.  Following much the same logic, AZAP called for more girls'
schools, on the grounds that having to travel long distances tired girls and encouraged them to become prostitutes.

There are two authentic images of women.  The ideal
woman is a mother and housekeeper firmly under the authority of her husband, kinsmen, and ultimately the president himself.  This identification of woman with mother
is stressed in all official publications.  International
Women's Year (IWY) was changed to International Mama's
Year in Zaire (Gould, 1978, p. 136).  Conversely, the
word for men has not been officially changed to "Papa"
because there is only one père de la nation. "La Maman
Zairoise" does have one important difference from her
authentic counterpart in the past.  She has been emancipated through the sole and personal efforts of "Le
Guide."  Furthermore, she now has a wide range of acceptable opportunities open to her, all of which are appropriate to her natural talents as a teacher, nurse, and
seamstress.  The authentic woman does not go to night-
clubs, bars, or movies and does not dress in a shameless
fashion.

Existing alongside the image of woman as ideal is
the image of woman as prostitute and breaker of traditions.  There is a major contradiction in this image.
The successful courtesans continue to be the trend-
setters in fashion, manners, and much of what is considered both exciting and civilized (La Fontaine, 1974,
pp. 97-98).  Even Mobutu's female praise singers adopt
the latest styles favored by the femmes libres. This
contradiction has been strengthened by the president's
seeming sanction of mistresses by claiming that having a
mistress is a form of polygyny and therefore authentic.
Nevertheless, the official line is that women lure men
into immoral acts with perfume and charms.  As a result,
the way to improve society is to reform women and to
police their behavior.  The following resolutions for
a morale révolutionnaire were adopted at the official
IWY conference in Kinshasa, 20 May 1975.

1.  The unconditional support of the efforts of
    "the helmsman" to
    a.  suppress nightclubs and whore houses
        [maisons de tolérance]
    b.  regulate and limit the hours of bars
    c.  support decent dress for the Zairian mother
    d.  suppress prostitution
2.  Severe sanctions for reactionary women who con-
    tinue their ways
3.  The need for women to show patriotism and re-
    volutionary consciousness
4.  The creation of feminine brigades to educate
    women in their role as mother and educator
5.  Strict censure of music, theater, books, movies
    and artists
6.  Ban on all pornography
7.  Severe sanctions for pornographers
8.  Limit and reorganize all orchestras
9.  Reform the civil code to protect the family in
    line with the principles of authenticity
10. An appeal to the President for a statute guaran-
    teeing the rights of widows and children in
    case of the death of the head of house. (Bur-
eau Politique, 1975, pp. 40-42).

All but the last resolution actually represented approval
of governmental policies already undertaken.

Today, legal protections for Zairian women, particularly married women, are few and rarely enforced.
The combination of Belgian law and authentic law has
been codified to strip women of many of the rights they
actually held in the past.  Married women legally need
their husband's permission to work, and if this is with-
drawn, they can no longer stay in a salaried position.
This is a potent if rarely used threat.  My own interviews with women who had more than a secondary education
indicated that this threat was occasionally carried out
and frequently invoked.  A married woman who works
does not receive housing or a family allowance even if
she is separated or divorced or if her husband is unemployed.  A married woman also needs her husband's
permission to get a passport or maintain a bank account.
Nonetheless, despite these legal and ideological dis-
incentives to women's work, women's non-wage work accounted for at least 10 percent of the real income of
families in Kinshasa and greater percentages in other
cities in 1974 (International Bank, 1974, p. 15).

By far the most serious legal problem a woman faces
in Zaire is her absence of rights after the death of
her husband.  Unlike the custom in many other African
countries, in Zaire, a woman's having had a Christian,

Moslem, or civil marriage does not much affect the distribution of property at death.  The combination of
the Belgian legal code and "traditional" laws has resulted in a distressing hodgepodge of some of the worst
aspects of both in regard to the rights of widows.  Not
only are many of the Zairian statutes inappropriate for
the urban, increasingly nuclear, and oft-times interethnic Zairian family, but there is abundant evidence
that magistrates often ignore the actual ethnic laws
and cite statements from the philosophy of authenticité
when determining cases.  Thus, the additional protection
matrilineal women would appear to retain often gets
swept away by the entrenched attitudes of magistrates
and the legal system (Manzila, 1974).  These magistrates
take the position that women are under the economic protections of their own kin and have no rights to real
property accumulated during marriage.  This is a distortion of traditional laws.  Under traditional law, land
was owned collectively; it could not be sold but might
be alienated by the collectivity (Harms, 1974, pp. 1-2).
Since no individuals owned land, usage rights were important and, in general, men and women retained rights
to land use in their birthplace and their adult home.
Women generally retained the right to real property
accumulated through their own efforts, as in the sale
of excess foodstuffs.  At present, when the husband
dies and there is no male adult child who is legally
entitled to inherit under customary law, the widow may
be forcibly ejected from her home and stripped of all
property except her clothes.  Property which is the result of the profits of petty trade can be seized by the
husband's kin if the husband followed the common custom
of giving his bride a small symbolic sum to begin her
trading career (Bureau Politique, 1975, p. 41).  Customary practice would have required the return of the
initial sum, not the profits.

     This practice of impoverishing widows has been
generally recognized as an aberration of custom, but
reforms have been very slow.  The legal code was in the
process of a long-awaited reform and modernization in
1976, but there was little indication of just how this
situation would be remedied.  Authenticité has created
a whole new category of prostitute in the hundreds of
widows of all ages and social classes who join the labor
force each year as a result of the failure of the current
regime to provide other occupations and the inability of
their families to support them.  Divorced women also face
legal disadvantages.  In order to qualify for the family
allowance paid to all male wage earners, the woman must
maintain her innocence while proving her husband's
guilt, not an easy task when the president declares

adultery authentic. Alimony or pension awards can not
be made unless only the wife has grounds, and they tend
to be extremely low when granted. My interviews indicated that legal divorce was rare and that only in the
most flagrant cases of mistreatment would the woman's
family agree to repay the bridewealth and undertake the
necessary legal costs. To say that this situation makes
married women in Zaire insecure is an understatement.
It was a constant theme in my interviews and in the
women's press. This insecurity was alluded to in the
tenth resolution of the IWY seminar. A new marriage
statute was necessary, according to the transcript of
the seminar, to put an end to the "degrading practices"
that were forced upon widows (Bureau Politique, 1975,
p. 41). By 1976, Mobutu himself distinguished between
widows and other prostitutes when attacking prostitutes as being responsible for the economic as well as
the social decline of the country.[3]

Women in Zaire have not taken lightly the serious
deterioration of their status and their ability to work.
However, they have been forced to employ indirect means
of putting pressure on the government because of its
hostility to criticism and change. Because Mobutu claims
that the full emancipation of women was achieved on a
specific day in 1970, he sees open criticism as an explicit challenge to him. Women can and do claim that
the desires of the president are not being carried out,
and when enough pressure is applied, the government
generally responds, albeit rarely in as complete a way
as the women had hoped. In 1975, women were given a
bit more latitude to debate publicly the consequences
of their emancipation. Most of the articles that appeared
in newspapers, magazines, and scholarly journals followed
the party line, but a few offered careful criticism
that exposed many of the contradictions within Zaire
today. For example, in one newspaper article, an unsigned
married woman denounced the return to polygynous practices as a scheme by rich city men to increase their
prestige and exploit women. She pointed out that the so-
called recourse to polygamy was not a true readoption of
traditional practices because the women involved did
not actually become second wives. She claimed that
polygyny's return was itself inauthentic because only
those customs that aid the country's advance should be
revitalized (Salongo, 1975).

Women have challenged the doctrine of authenticité
even in the rarefied atmosphere of the presidential es-
tates outside the capital. The IWY seminar at Nsele
was attended by 921 women invited from all regions of
the country. Delegates included virtually all women
who were party officials, trade unionists, workers in

the government, members of religious organizations, and
the wives of high party and governmental officers.  Although traders were not invited as a specific group,
many of the most influential and wealthy of the market
women were in attendance.  It is likely that most of
these women were commissaires du peuple, a low-ranking
but important party functionary similar to a ward leader.
Because of the great amount of agitation over economic
problems, the president himself asked--or agreed--(this
point is in dispute) to meet with a small group of the
delegates to receive their views.  This group was chosen
by the ranking women, who were said to emphasize the
need for harmony and pleasantries.  This harmony was
not achieved, for the president asked the women to speak
frankly and a number of the traders were openly critical
of the general economic conditions and the legal rights
of women.  Le Guide Clairvoyent became enraged, denounced the women as ungrateful, and stormed out of the meeting.[4]  The most immediate and obvious result of this
meeting was an increase from one to three in the number
of women commissaires d'état (a cabinet-level position).
One of these women was a popular activist from outside
of the capital.  The final text of the complete resolutions included the personal promise of Mobutu to end
all social inequality and to create more jobs for everyone.  However, the seminar can not be seen as an un-
qualified success because at the same time that these
concessions were made, Mobutu further consolidated his
personal exploitation of the economic assets of the
country by giving all of the social services in the entire country to his wife.  The appropriation of all of
the state-run hospitals, clinics, women's training
schools, and all other services and their conversion
to the personal ownership of his late wife, La Citoyenne
Mama Mobutu, was justified on the grounds that she was a
good person and had maternal feelings.  The delegates duly
approved this outrageous action in three flowery resolutions (Bureau Politique, 1975, p. 40).

Few women in Zaire have the opportunity to take
their grievances directly to the president.  A more ad
hoc and individualistic means of protest by women is
simply to refuse to marry.  This strategy is increasingly
popular despite the marginal role of the unmarried
woman in society.  Women argue that if one lives with a
man without marrying him or, better yet, is the girl
friend of one or two wealthy men, any property accumulated is legally one's own.  The successful mistress of
the wealthy man is called the deuxième bureau, or
"second office."  The decision to become a deuxième
bureau is not without risk, for very few women are
actually able to achieve economic independence in this

way.  The women who do  succeed provide a powerful incentive for their sisters and are much envied and
imitated.  Several of the university women I interviewed
felt that female university graduates were in such demand as companions that it was possible to delay marriage without too much loss of social status while accumulating the means to avoid the older widow's sobering
fate.  The women who chose absolute respectability felt
that working would provide them their cushion against
prostitution if they were careful to give generous
gifts and even a large part of their salaries to their
own kin. Because of the insecurity of women within marriage, marriages are increasingly unstable in urban
Zaire.  The economic conditions demand that a couple pool
its resources to survive, but the social and legal
realities behoove the woman to make her investment in
herself or her kin.
     While the evidence of women's insecurity and mar-
ginality in present-day Zaire is compelling and depress-
ing, we should not actually view women workers in Zaire
as defeated.  As a philosophy, authenticité has attempted
to limit women's entrance into the labor force by stressing the image of housewife/mother as the ideal.  Men
have tended to accept this because it both enhances
their image and limits competition at a time of rising
unemployment.  Families have not always resisted the
impoverishment of widows because it allows a kind of
windfall inheritance of land and houses in the urban
areas.  Congolese were not permitted to own land in the
cities until independence, and this method offers the
kin network a means of acquiring land without paying
for it.  However, several studies of the attitudes of
Zairian women toward work indicate that neither female
students nor working women have accepted the limited
role offered them (Verheust, 1972; Luhakumbira, 1975;
Mbo, 1975).  Articles have also appeared on the inade-
quacies of the legal code and the relevance of feminist
thought (Manzila, 1974; Mulumba, 1974; Mikanda-Vundowe,
1966).
     The government of Zaire has also attempted to use
the image of the woman as prostitute to deflect criticism
of increasingly serious economic conditions.  The social
reality that many working women are at least partially
dependent on some form of prostitution for family income
reinforces the government's claims that prostitution
and women's participation in the work force are connected.
But the increasing importance of women's contributions
to family income not only makes the society in general
more sympathetic to part-time prostitution but reduces
the government's credibility when it claims to have
fully emancipated women.
     The economic situation in Zaire has steadily deter-

iorated since the research for this paper was completed
in 1976.   I have necessarily concentrated on urban areas
for the postindependence period because data on rural
areas is almost wholly lacking. There is no doubt, however, that since 1960 the agricultural output of the
country has declined and that agriculture in particular
and the rural areas in general have been neglected in
the allocation of resources.   Women in rural areas have
been less touched by the application of new legal codes
than by the breakdown of the transportation infrastructure and raids on harvests by the army, which have
caused peasants in many areas to produce for personal
consumption  only.   The role of the rural woman in the
economy remains important, but the infrastructure is
more limited than it was in the colonial era.   Living
costs in the cities far exceed the incomes of salaried
workers today.   The World Bank reported that the typical
family budget in 1978 in Kinshasa was three times the
salary of a semiskilled worker.   Similar disparities
existed in other cities.   Real income in 1977 was at
lease 60 percent lower than in 1970.   In this grave
economic situation, trading has become the major source
of supplemental income and varies from "petty trade by
women to corporations owned or controlled by public
officials."   Corruption of public officials, banditry,
and civil disorders reached proportions that required
the president to declare 1979 "The Year for Raising the
Level of Morality" (International Bank, 1980, pp. 23,2).

Thus, as Zaire continues into its third decade as
an independent country, the ideological image of women
workers has not much changed from the Belgian stereotype
of primitive farmers and corrupted city women.   The
Zairian woman's ability to make an economic contribution
to her family may actually have declined because of the
stagnation of the agricultural sector and drops in real
income for wage earners.   The severity of economic conditions in Zaire makes it highly unlikely that the
official attitude toward women's work will change.   But
the ability to use women as scapegoats will possibly
decline, as fewer and fewer people are willing to attri-
bute the over one-half cut in real income in a decade,
the virtual disappearance of medical supplies, the rising
unemployment, and growing crime rate to the presence of
prostitution.   The ideological image and present-day
reality of working women reflects the general economic
plight of the country.   Authenticité is not a development strategy, or even any longer a nationalistic response
to colonial domination.   It is structure for control that
has achieved its goal at the cost of the economy and
the well-being of its citizens.

NOTES

    1. The best English-language histories of the
Congo tend to concentrate either on European aspects or
on the larger kingdoms. Slade (1962) and Vansina (1966)
are the most comprehensive examples of the respective
traditions.
    2. Comhaire-Sylvain (1968) is an analysis of two
studies she made of women in Kinshasa in 1945 and 1965.
La Fontaine (1974) based his article on his 1970 study
of women in Kinshasa.
    3. Public speeches made May through July 1976
and broadcast on radio and television.
    4. Field interviews with participants during May
1976 in Kinshasa.

REFERENCES

Boserup, Ester. 1970. Woman's Role in Economic Develop-
    ment. New York: St. Martin's.
Bureau Politique du Mouvement Populaire de la Revolution.
    1975. Année International de la Femme au Zaire.
    Kinshasa.
Comhaire-Sylvain, Suzanne. 1968. Femmes de Kinshasa:
    Hier et Aujourd'hui. Paris: Mouton.
Gould, Terri F. 1978. "Value Conflict and Development:
    The Struggle of the Professional Zairian Woman."
    Journal of Modern African Studies 16: 133-40.
Harms, Robert. 1974. Land Tenure and Agricultural De-
    velopment in Zaire, 1895-1961. Land Tenure Center,
    No. 99. Madison: University of Wisconsin.
International Bank for Reconstruction and Development.
    1974. Economic Report on Zaire. Nairobi.
    _____. 1980. Zaire: Current Economic Situation
    and Constraints. World Bank Country Study. May.
La Fontaine, Jean. 1974. "The Free Women of Kinshasa:
    Prostitution in a City of Zaire." In J. Davis, ed.,
    Choice and Change. Atlantic Highlands, N.J.:
    Humanities Press.
Luhakumbira Lando. 1975. "Situation et Intégration de
    la Femme dans une Entreprise Industrielle--Cas de
    la Gecamines." Unpublished sociological paper,
    Université Nationale du Zaire, Lubumbashi.
Manzila Lutambu Sal'A'Sal. 1974. "Le Statut Juridique
    des Biens Mariés." Zaire-Afrique 81: 21-30.
Mbo Massanga. 1975. "L'Adaption de la Femme Zairoise
    au Travail Salarié." Unpublished paper, Université
    Nationale du Zaire, Lubumbashi.
Mikanda-Vundowe, Suzanne. 1966. "Féminisme Congolaise
    Aujourd'hui." Congo-Afrique 2: 71-78.

Miracle, Marvin, and Bruce Fetter. 1970. "Backwards-
     sloping Labor Supply Functions and African Economic
     Behavior." Economic Development and Cultural Change
     18: 240-251.
Mulumba Katchy. 1974. "De la Pension Alimentaire
     Allowée à une Femme Divorcée." Zaire-Afrique 82:
     97-107.
Nzongola-Ntalaja. 1976. "The Authenticity of Neocolo-
     nialism: Ideology and Class Struggles in Zaire."
     Paper presented at the African Studies Association,
     Boston.
Peemans, J. Ph. 1975. "The Social and Economic Develop-
     ment of Zaire Since Independence: An Historical
     Outline." African Affairs 74: 148-179.
Rousseau, Ida Faye. 1975. "African Women: Identity
     Crisis?" In Ruby Rohrlich-Leavitt, ed., Women
     Cross Culturally. Chicago: Mouton.
Salongo. 27 October 1975; 22 May 1976.
Slade, Ruth. 1962. King Leopold's Congo. London: Ox-
     ford University Press.
Vansina, Jan. 1966. Kingdoms of the Savannah. Madison:
     University of Wisconsin.
Verheust, Therese. 1972. "La Jeune Fille Kinoise Face
     à la Profession." Zaire-Afrique 70: 593-606.
Wilson, Ernest J. III. 1974. "State Ideology and State
     Administration in Developing Countries." Unpub-
     lished.
Young, Crawford. 1965. Politics in the Congo. Prince-
     ton, N.J.: Princeton University Press.
_____. 1970. "Rebellions in the Congo." In Robert
     Rotberg and Ali Mazrui, eds., Protest and Power in
     Black Africa. Oxford: Oxford University Press.

## 8. International Development and the Evolution of Women's Economic Roles: A Case Study from Northern Gulma, Upper Volta

*Grace S. Hemmings-Gapihan*

This paper provides a brief description of economic change in a rural community in Upper Volta. The study is based on field data gathered from 1976 to 1978 in Northern Gulma, located in the northeastern portion of Upper Volta.[1] At that time, the purpose of my research was to identify the adaptive strategies developed by the local population in response to the disastrous drought of the early 1970s. However, it became clear that the society was undergoing profound socioeconomic transformations that had intensified during the years of the drought. Even though this period of economic change concurred with the drought, it was apparent that ecological crisis was not the sole vector of change. The local population had been subjected to droughts for many generations. In fact, the villagers recalled a terrible drought during the 1940s. Though droughts had taken the same form for centuries, merely varying in intensity, survival strategies of the local population had varied according to the historical context of the crisis.

The specific historical context of the latest drought offered a set of solutions previously unknown to the local population, the adoption of which has had profound effects on the social economy of the village. In assessing the effects of the drought, I concluded that international intervention was a greater stimulus for change than the drought itself. This paper briefly examines the sociohistorical context within which the drought occurred, as well as the effects of international response to the drought on the local village economy. Although the paper outlines general economic change, special attention is paid to the economic roles of women.

Studies of economic change often focus on the participation of young men in nontraditional forms of economic activity, that is, activity not centered in the village, including wage labor (migrant or other), cash crop production destined for export, or other forms of remunerated activity. Even studies addressing themselves to women

often emphasize women's continuing participation in the
traditional economic sector.  Such studies fail to explore the crucial aspects of the role of women in socioeconomic change.  Scholars assume that the traditional
sector remains unchanged and that women continue to participate in it despite "advances" made by men.  Rarely
is attention paid to the restructuring of social or productive units that is necessary to free the labor of the
young men who participate in the modern economy.  Women
play pivotal roles in the internal socioeconomic transformations without which the modernization of the rural
economy would be impossible.  These women are discussed
here not only as participants in but as generators of
economic change.  The detrimental effects of the resultant change on the lives of village women will be discussed.

The paper provides a brief summary of the colonial
and precolonial period, followed by an account of the
effects of the drought on the village economy and an
analysis of the social mechanisms involved in its transformation.  It concludes with a discussion of the possible
effects of these changes on the social relations of production within the village.


ECONOMIC AND POLITICAL HISTORY OF THE REGION

Northern Gulma is a sparsely  populated region with
a population density of ten inhabitants per square kilometer.  The neighboring Mossi region has a population
density of about forty inhabitants per square kilometer.
Large expanses of Gulma territory still remain unpopulated and most of the villages number less than 200 inhabitants.  In the past, these unpopulated regions were
attractive to Fulani herders in search of uncrowded
grazing areas.  Many pastoralists have settled in the
area.  There are also pockets of Mossi settlements in
the more densely populated regions of the west.  Their
numbers have grown in the years since the drought.

The relative infertility of the soil, aggravated by
a lack of a perennial source of water, is the reason
given for the seasonal and sometimes permanent migration
of single families.  Most families remain as long as
possible in one area.  When the land is no longer fertile, a family will move to the nearest most fertile
village to request land for farming.  Land is sufficiently abundant in the region such that access to use
rights to land is virtually unlimited.  Despite the relatively high mobility of certain individual families,
the villages are permanent.  The inhabitants are organized on the basis of membership in patrilineal descent

groups, which give exclusive title to land and to religious and political offices. Each village chooses its rulers from among the male members of the oldest residing lineage segment.

In precolonial times, the radius of mobility of individual families was limited because of the threat of slave hunters and wars. During colonial times, tax evasion provided people with a powerful incentive to move from village to village, avoiding the census takers. However, fear of impressment into colonial forced labor camps restricted the radius of population movement.

Precolonial Northern Gulma consisted of a confederation of kingdoms. The village chiefdom, dodieba, was at the base of the traditional political structure. Several village chiefdoms made up a kuamba. The chief of the kuamba bore the title of jisindjianu and paid tribute to the head of the founding dynasty of Gulma kingdoms, the yadja, residing in Fada N'Gourma. The jisindjianu was totally independent of the kingdom of Fada N'Gourma (Madiega, 1978).

The Gulmantche were sedentary farmers who cultivated cereal and raised a small number of livestock. The agriculture of the region was characterized by hoe technology and shifting cultivation. Division of labor, then as now, was based on sex and age. Farming was shared by all members of the household. Extended families worked collective plots of land, growing millet and sorghum. In addition, various members of the family cultivated individual plots of common farm products. Before the introduction of large-scale cultivation of peanuts as a cash crop, women grew individual plots of millet and peanuts, while men grew cotton and tobacco. A number of other vegetables and grains were grown in small quantities.

Women were in charge of all food-processing activities, including the search for water and wood. Old men and women were exempted from communal farming. Old women, however, continued to cultivate individual fields of millet and bambara groundnuts. Small livestock were guarded by children, while cows were entrusted to the neighboring Fulani. Men engaged in hunting and warfare.

Patrilineages were divided into segments. Each segment, which may have comprised several extended families (three generations of male agnates, their spouses, and their children), resided in one compound. In the past, these compounds formed a single unit of domestic economy that produced and consumed its own food and all the materials required to reproduce the household. If at any time one of these household units was short of food (usually because of natural disaster or prolonged illness of its members), the head of the compound appealed

to heads of other compounds, members of the same patrilineage, for food. Members of the same patrilineage were
expected to provide each other with food in times of
stress, though not on a regular basis. The members of
the units of domestic economy provided for their own
needs most of the time. In times of natural disaster,
entire regions were stricken and all the families within
the patrilineage were destitute. In these cases, cloth
and horses were taken as far as Niger and sometimes even
farther to be exchanged for millet. The threat of ecological disaster was constant. Even in years of adequate rainfall, a region or a village might suffer a
localized drought. Because of this, mutual aid groups
outside the village community were extremely important.
Marriage was an important element of social relations
between villages. A married woman could return to her
natal village, help with the harvest, and bring back a
substantial amount of millet for her family. If her
husband's family's land was exhausted, her husband had
access to land provided by his wife's patrilineage in her
natal village. Despite these forms of mutual aid,
families belonging to the same unit of domestic economy
were autosubsistent most of the time.

The rainy season from May to November was conse-
crated almost entirely to farming. The dry season was
devoted to practicing such crafts as pottery, weaving,
leather working, basket and mat weaving, and blacksmith-
ing. Markets, then as now, were held every fourth day.
Women traded raw and processed foods and cloth, while
men traded salt, animals, magic substances, and precious
minerals. Long-distance trade was the prerogative of a
particular lineage, whose members traveled as far as
Mali to exchange village-produced goods for salt.

Even though the villagers depended on long-distance
trade for a few commodities such as salt and in times of
famine were known to travel as far as Niger in search
of grain, they were virtually self-sufficient. All the
foods necessary for their subsistence were provided in
the village.

In the past, social relations and reciprocal forms
of labor gave villagers access to locally produced goods
without cash payments. For example, male relatives supplied women with cotton. Women spun the thread that was
woven by other male relatives, who were allowed to keep
a small percentage of the cloth in exchange for their
labor. The men who had supplied raw cotton to female
relatives could count on these relatives to assist them
in furnishing the cotton bands necessary for brideprice.
Other goods and services were provided for in this
manner.

The Gulma colonial experience differed somewhat from

the Mossi ordeal. Many villagers of the Mossi plateau suffered drastic alterations of their agroeconomic cycle because of forced labor imposed on both sexes by the colonial government. Forced labor, in addition to severe taxation, prompted many to migrate (Skinner, 1960). Some migrated seasonally in order to meet the demands for cash; others migrated permanently in order to escape the repressive colonial government. Even though the population of Northern Gulma was also subject to taxation and forced labor, lack of natural resources as well as low population density kept the colonial power from focusing as much attention on the area as it did in the Mossi region. The young men of Northern Gulma were not exported by the tens of thousands to the plantations of the Ivory Coast, as were the Mossi, which contributed to the development of modern large-scale migrant labor in the Mossi regions. Jean-Marie Kohler, in his report written for Orstom in 1971, shows that in the region in which he conducted his study, 72 percent of the Mossi men between the ages of twenty and twenty-nine were absent during the entire year; most were in the Ivory Coast. In contrast, only about 5 percent of Gulma men migrate to the Ivory Coast or Niger to work.

One of the first steps in the economic transition of Gulma society was precipitated by the imposition of taxes and by the refusal of the colonial administration to accept cowrie shells in payment (Madiega, 1973). Meeting tax obligations compelled the population to produce additional agricultural goods. Originally, taxes were paid through the sale of grain. Later, about 1947, the sale of peanuts as a cash crop was promoted by the chef de canton, formerly head of the kuamba, who had been officially designated as tax collector for the colonial government. Since tax payments were a great burden on the population, the chief felt that the sale of peanuts would provide the revenue needed for it.

When peanuts were introduced as a cash crop, women became the major producers. Men did not cultivate peanuts, for they already had control of the socially more valued millet and cotton crops (Lankoande, 1977, personal communication). In addition, they could easily gain access to women's revenue from the sale of peanuts by selling them cotton (Nadinga, 1977, Lankoande, 1977, interviews).

Women bought raw cotton in order to make thread that they would subsequently weave into bands of cloth. Cotton bands were one of the principal means through which women would accumulate wealth. It is said that in the past, women were often richer than men because they were the only ones who spun thread and thereby had almost exclusive access to cloth. The cloth was exchanged for

cattle and salt, and it was a major requirement for bridewealth. Thus women, particularly in the roles of mother
and paternal aunt, were important contributors to bridewealth. Cotton bands were also necessary as offerings
on a number of other ritual occasions.

Peanut production has increased fourfold since 1947
(Sénéchal, 1973). According to the villagers, the last
ten years show the greatest increase in peanut production.
This is due, in part, to the rise in numbers of men cultivating peanuts. Villagers have stated that men are
cultivating peanuts because of the increasing use of
manufactured cloth and the decline of weaving. The demand for cotton on a local level decreased sharply in
the seven years from 1970 to 1977, which meant that men's
access to money by way of women was limited. In an
effort to offset their losses, men turned to peanut
production (A. Nadinga, M. Nadinga, and others, 1977,
personal communication).

Money from the sale of cash crops was spent primarily in tax payments. Nevertheless, as the economy
gradually became monetarized, the profits from the sale
of peanuts were used for a wider range of purchases.
Because of the rapid integration of other sectors of
Upper Volta into the money economy, by the 1950s almost
all imported goods such as kola nuts, salt, and iron had
to be paid for in cash. Despite revenue from the sale
of peanuts, the Gulmas' access to cash was severely
limited. Thus, their consumption of manufactured and
imported goods remained minimal.


THE DROUGHT AND ITS EFFECTS ON THE ECONOMIC ALTERNATIVES
OF MEN AND WOMEN

The drought occurred at the beginning of the 1970s,
the end of a cycle of prosperity in the highly industrialized countries in the West. There was money available for the countries of the Sahel (Upper Volta, Mauri-
tania, Mali, Senegal, Niger, and Cape Verde) which, unlike Zaire, were not at the top of the priority list of
African countries destined to receive foreign aid (Monde
Diplomatique, 1976).

The Voltan economy had been stagnating if not regres-
sing during the 1960s (Amin, 1971). The sharp change in
consumption patterns that occurred in the 1970s was in
part related to the international response to the drought.
Countries that had never before contributed foreign aid
to Upper Volta were now donating large sums to be utilized in development and drought relief programs. All
over the country the volume of trade increased. The
transportation industry flourished. It grew, in part,

out of money donated for the purchase of trucks to transport grain to severely afflicted regions. Particularly in the Gulma region, new roads were built and old ones repaired, opening up previously inaccessible areas.

Rural areas benefited, to some degree, from drought relief efforts. However, the primary effect of road improvements was to create new sources of surplus grain for speculators supplying grain to urban centers. Grain speculators widened their market, thus increasing their sources of wholesale grain, a factor which enabled them to keep their purchase price low and to maximize their profits. As the villagers' need for cash increased, so did their efforts to produce surplus grain. In times of scarcity, villagers sold "what they didn't have," selling grain they needed to feed their families. Hence, the scarcity was felt severely by rural populations despite the fact that they supplied increasing quantities of grain to urban centers.

Urban areas were the first to be affected by the increase of cash in circulation. More isolated regions were quickly affected for two reasons: (1) the surplus cash in circulation was great enough that some of the excess reached these regions before long; (2) the primary objective of drought relief was to relieve the areas most strongly affected by famine, i.e., the rural areas. In carrying out this objective, drought relief programs became a major force in the full-scale absorption of the population into the national economy.

The pressures of the drought and the state of the Upper Voltan economy at the time encouraged the villagers to choose from a number of economic alternatives. Famine emphasized the importance of paid labor, business investments, and the use of more advanced farming techniques. Careful analysis of the family structure and of the roles of each member of the extended family, the unit of production, is required in order to elucidate the manner in which individuals accommodated to and accepted these changes.

Traditionally, the economic goal of a man has been to head a unit of production made up of his polygynous household and those of his sons, giving him titular control over goods produced and optimum access to labor. In actuality, such heads of households are few. Young men usually seek economic independence as a shortcut to attaining traditional goals. However, the economic opportunities available to young men before the drought were severely limited. Population density has always been low in the area, and income levels were among the lowest in Upper Volta. Sale of cash crops was the principal means of acquiring money. Some young men supplemented their meager earnings from the sale of peanuts by selling such luxury items as kola nuts in small quan-

tities. Even today (1978), in a period of increased
consumption, the most a young man can hope to make on a
given market day from the sale of these items is perhaps
100 CFA frs (250 CFA frs equal $1). Marketing of non-
agricultural goods, another possible economic alternative,
was not viable until quite recently.

Opportunities for participation in the economic
community outside the village were equally limited before the drought. Among the Mossi, a majority of young
men migrate to the Ivory Coast as seasonal laborers.
This was not the case with the Gulmas, for few Gulma
youth worked there. Some young men migrated to Niger for
short periods, but in general migrant workers were few.

In the wake of drought relief programs, male villagers found that economic opportunities were broadening
in Northern Gulma, a relatively isolated area. The national and international response to the drought brought
an influx of strangers: experts supervising relief projects, nomads from the north migrating to less afflicted
regions, and businessmen seeking grain to purchase.

With the increase in population came an inflow of
cash to the region. Drought relief projects had the
greatest impact, for they provided temporary jobs. Projects included road building, dam and well construction,
as well as a number that required unskilled labor. Ex-
patriates moving to the area to manage these projects
contributed to the demand for labor by hiring servants,
translators, research assistants, and so on. Businessmen and expatriate project directors contributed to the
inflow of manufactured goods in the villages, where cash,
because of temporary jobs and increased sale of agricultural goods, became increasingly accessible. The manu-
facture of goods within the village, which began to decline with the growth of the cash economy after World
War II, declined even more because of the influx of cash
and imported goods.

Many young men, though remaining farmers, started
businesses as shopkeepers. Improved roads gave them
easier access to markets where manufactured goods could
be bought. More important, the roads allowed businessmen to bring manufactured goods to the villages with
greater regularity. The increase in demand brought on by
the increase in population with access to money made
selling profitable. Other men chose to open "restaurants"
to feed the growing numbers of strangers at the market,
while older men sought to increase their cereal production.

These new economic alternatives emphasized the role
of the villager as wage earner and profit maker. The
economic transactions focused the villagers' attention
on elements originating outside their community. Urban

centers were seen as sources of goods and cash.  Intra-
village social relations providing access to resources
and goods produced within the village were gradually
undermined.

The social relations of production known to the
villagers began to change as young men sought to take
advantage of the recent economic opportunities.  The
new economic setting required a certain amount of individualization.  Heads of units of production, or compounds,
expected their sons to work with them in the collective
fields.  This expectation was underlined as the pressure
to increase production became greater.  But young men,
perceiving the advantages of converting surplus agricultural produce to all-purpose cash, were now interested
in exploring the economic routes that gave them direct
control over the fruits of their labor.

To show how the sexual division of labor and the
allocation of labor was affected, I shall describe the
traditional social organization of production.  All villagers farm.  They farm two types of fields:  a large
field from which the family is fed, the fruits of which
are controlled by the head of the unit of production or
household head, and small plots of cash crops (peanuts)
or other types of food crops, which are cultivated and
owned by individuals.  Individuals usually sell the
fruits of these fields for cash, which they control per-
sonally.

Because of the decline of the exchange value of
their crops and therefore of their real income, the villagers have had to step up their production of cash crops
for sale in order to keep the purchasing power stable.
Thus, people are farming more now than they did in the
past.  Moreover, they have to farm larger surfaces of land
because, as they told me, the fertility of the land is
constantly declining, a condition aggravated by the
drought.  Their yields are thus substantially lower.

Because of the drought and the declining value of
food crops vis à vis manufactured goods, many men are
taking advantage of any opportunity to engage in wage
labor and to invest their earnings in the purchase and
sale of manufactured goods.  Those who purchase and sell
manufactured goods may do so in a variety of ways.  They
may have permanent shops, stalls in various village markets, and a stall from which they sell within their compound.  In order to sell to as many people as possible,
these merchants visit different village markets, which
are open every three days.  (Each village opens its market
on a different day of the week.)  Thus, if a man tries
to maximize his sales during the rainy season, when
fewer people attend markets, he must visit as many markets as possible.  All of these activities take time away
from agricultural activity.

Because there are two types of farming activity,
private and communal, men's increased efforts to grow
cash crops in their private fields often mean that they
spend less time in the family field.  For the majority
of these men, the only means of earning cash is through
the sale of cash crops; so, in order to launch themselves
in business, they have to concentrate on their production
of cash crops in their private fields.

The role of women in this economic climate has taken
on added importance.  Women have furthered the economic
expansion of men in several ways: (1) they fill the work
gaps created by men engaged in other activities; (2)
they provide men with the material means to start businesses; and (3) as wives, they assist men who want to
establish new units of production.

To explain, I shall examine women's roles within the
traditional village economy.  Each individual works in
the collective family field and in a personal field;
the head of household controls the fruits of labor of
the family field, from which the members of the unit of
production are fed.  The head of the unit of production
must provide for the needs of those working with him and
who are also members of his patrilineage.  Wives who are
not members of the patrilineage are provided with food
but are expected to provide for their personal needs.
They do so with the produce from their private field,
which they market.

Land is still plentiful in Northern Gulma.  Access
to use rights of land is easy.  Women have access to land
from their patrilineages or from their husbands' patrilineages.  If the husband's land for any reason is un-
suitable, the husband may ask a friend for land for his
wife.

A wife is expected to work in her husband's field
until he retires.  This was not the case in the past,
prior to colonization, when agricultural goods were sold
only in small quantities and the pressure to produce was
not as great.  Prior to colonization, a woman was expected to work in her husband's field during the early
years of marriage.  According to elderly informants, a
woman no longer had to work in her husband's fields as
soon as her sons and daughters could help their father,
around the age of ten.  Her principal contribution to
her husband's household was offspring and food preparation. Her private resources were invested in her own
patrilineage.  She provided substantial amounts of the
cloth used to pay bridewealth for her brothers' sons.
(Bear in mind that women controlled most of the cloth
produced in the region.)  She also contributed to her
younger brothers' bridewealth payments. Because of her
active participation in its affairs, a woman not only

maintained strong ties to her patrilineage but played
determinant roles therein. (For example women were often
consulted when their brothers' daughters were to be married. Rarely were their decisions overridden.)

At present, because of recent socioeconomic changes,
a woman spends more time than ever before in her husband's
fields. Not only does she spend more time (70 percent of
total farming time for younger women), but she works in
her husband's fields even when the children are quite
grown.

A woman is nonetheless responsible for providing
for her own economic needs. That is, she must clothe
herself and assist with the children's clothing; she
takes care of her own travel and medical expenses; she
contributes to relatives' funerals; and she pays her own
taxes. A woman's earnings are her own. Thus, the economic goals of each woman have traditionally been tied to
the prosperity of her own patrilineal extended family. A
married woman residing outside of her own lineage must
act as an economically independent being. Although she
takes part in collective farming within her conjugal
household, her economic goals are private, i.e., centered
on herself and her children. Her highest economic goal
is attained when she is old and no longer has to take
part in communal farming but can appropriate all the
fruits of her labor to herself and to her children. That
a woman's economic activity is separate from that of her
husband is clearly illustrated in the rules of inheritance.
If a woman dies leaving no sons, all her property returns
to her father's lineage. Her older brother is in charge
of dispensing her property among her kin.

A woman's position as wife contrasts with her husband's position as a member of his lineage. She is the
stranger; he is the relative. She is concerned with the
immediate family, her children; he is concerned with the
extended family, the lineage segment. Economically, he
functions as a member of a corporate group. His highest
economic status is achieved when he becomes the oldest
and thus head of the compound with control over the
fruits of labor of the unit of production. He stands
to gain from the traditional structure. Women stand to
gain from individual enterprise.

Participation in the modern economy requires a
breaking away from the family. Men have to act outside
of the traditional cooperative structure. Mothers, however, have traditionally benefited from the economic
independence of their sons, for a mother has easier access
to her son's goods than to her husband's. In many cases,
mothers have encouraged their sons to cultivate fields
separate from those of the head of the unit of production. This sometimes implies the institution of a
separate household. This is one reason why women are

such important contributors to their sons' marriages.
A married and economically independent son is a great
asset to his mother.  In all cases, a woman stands to
gain from the economic successes of her son, for whom
the changing economic setting provides added opportunities
for economic independence.  Thus, women's traditional role
as outsider to the families within which they reside
places them in the position of being the most progressive
element of society participating in the economic transformation of the village.  However, the forms that their
participation have taken have laid the basis for their
increasing economic dependence on men.
     Certain conditions created by the drought gave women
added opportunity to aid their sons in their efforts to
be economically independent.  For example, scarcity of
grain became an important element in this process.  One
of the immediate effects of the drought was to place
great strain on the grain reserves controlled by the
head of the household, who is under obligation to feed
his family before he can sell the remaining surplus.
Women, who also grow grain in individual plots, had a
little more surplus than men.  Women, particularly older
women who have a little more time and more access to surplus labor, grow millet for marketing. Since they are
not   obliged to feed their families with their private
stock (their grain is used only in the last resort, if
their children are grown), they were able to take advantage of the great demand for grain from the transient
pastoral groups.  Their sphere of exchange was primarily
in the traditional market, so they bartered rather than
sold much of the grain that was marketed.  As a result,
they were able to build up their livestock holdings by
trading millet for animals.  There seems to be an inverse
relationship between scarcity of grain and the exchange
value of cattle.  During a drought, grain is scarce and
there is less water for cattle.  When cattle begin to die
off because of lack of water, herders are eager to sell
them before they die.  The price of grain is aleady high
because of its scarcity.  Scarcity of grain occurs at
the same time as scarcity of water and grazing land.
Thus, when herders are eager to sell their cattle, farmers
are eager to conserve their grain and the value of grain
is increased in relation to the value of cattle.  In
fact, the grain-to-cattle ratio was so low that many villagers oversold their millet.  I was told by women that
in 1973 they were able to obtain cattle valued at 5,000
CFA frs for a tin of millet worth 350 CFA frs.  A cotton
wrap made of eleven bands of woven cotton worth 300 CFA
frs could be exchanged for a two-year-old calf.  The chef
de canton, concerned that the villagers would be left
without provision for the coming months, ordered the vil-

lagers to stop trading their food and goods for cattle
(Lankoande, 1978).

   This buildup of livestock holdings occurred on a
very small scale.  During the 1970s, there were years in
which there was no surplus to be found anywhere in the
village.  By the time of this field research, no woman
in the village had more than four cows.  Yet many said
that they had bought most of the animals in the early
1970s because of the low purchasing prices.

   The money that came from the eventual sale of these
animals was quickly reinvested in the business activities
of the women's sons.  Many women sold their cattle in
order to assist their sons in the purchase of bicycles
or mobylettes with which to engage in long-distance trade.
Other women financed their sons' business ventures.  Sons
are a major source of economic security for women; it is
not surprising, therefore, that women invest their
material resources in this manner.

   Ester Boserup states that an increase in the population density in rural areas calls for a change of agricultural system towards higher intensity.  Unavoidably,
"this change must affect the balance of work between
the sexes" (1970, p. 35).

   The population density in the Gulma area is still
quite low, but the pressure to increase production,
coupled with the simple level of farming technology, has
resulted in the intensification of farm labor.  The motivation to have direct control over the sale of surplus
produce has prompted young men to break away from the collective farming unit. The result  is a decrease in household size and a decrease in the size of units of production.

   These decreases place an additional burden on the
wife, both in the household and in the fields.  As I have
shown earlier, people have increased their agricultural
activity because of the pressure to produce larger quantities of produce.  In addition, farming for the family was
once shared by a large group of people.  Men did the
bulk of farming destined for consumption by the household.
Now, a smaller group of people has to produce enough to
feed itself and also to sell in order to purchase the
goods necessary to support the household.  Thus, whereas
in the past women farmed in large part for themselves,
they now have to share the responsibility of providing
food for the family by investing more time in the collective field.  This is a result of the fact that men do
not depend as much as they did on their collateral kin
to assist them in farming.  In addition, men are spending more time in their private fields; as a consequence,
women have to spend more time in the collective field.
In addition, the full burden of household duties falls

on her.  She now has less time to devote to her private
field, the source of economic independence.

Men now grow peanuts, a strictly individual crop.
Not only do men invest more time in the production of
this private cash crop, they are also devoting extra time
to building up their businesses.  The result is that women contribute an inordinate amount of time to agricultural production destined for family consumption.

The limiting factor of production in this society is
labor.  Therefore, the time spent in the collective
field has a severely limiting effect on the time a woman
can spend on her private field.  Most of the women's
dry season activity is financed with the cash from the
sale of peanuts grown in her private plot of land.  Her
economic activity for the rest of the year is affected
by the results of the winter crop.  A poor harvest or a
small field can severely limit the volume of business in
which she may engage during the dry season.  I have found
that with increased input of labor in farming, women have
had to modify their expenditure of time in other areas.

Some men have opted to become wage earners.  When
they do so, they lessen their contribution as producers
within the once self-contained village economy.  They have
thus forfeited their control over their own means of production for the chance to earn wages with which to buy
goods and services produced outside the village.  As
wage earners, men form relationships outside their villages and family circles.  Their wives and mothers have
very limited access to these money-making roles. Yet,
they need money to gain access to goods that are no longer
produced in the village.  As a result, the women are
becoming increasingly dependent on men economically.
This has had an effect on the concept of marriage.  In the
past, when access to land was the crucial economic factor,
women welcomed a polygynous household.  More recently,
however, women, especially those married to wage-earning
husbands, prefer monogamous marriages so as not to have
to share their husbands' limited salary.

The growing economic dependency of women on men
mirrors the dependence of village communities on the
national and international economic structure.  Villagers
can participate in the new economic structure only as
suppliers of labor and as consumers of manufactured goods.
By depending on manufactured goods, they are rapidly
losing their traditional means of production.  Although
their level of consumption of manufactured goods has
momentarily increased, villagers are finding that inflation surpasses their earning power, and each year the
purchase value of their money is reduced.

The new economic relations contribute to the fragmentation of traditional socioeconomic structures, with

the result that individuals have greater access to cash
but less access to, and control of, the production of
goods and the appropriation of labor.

As the social relations of production that gave them
access to surplus labor and goods disappear or are modified, women find that they need more and more cash to
buy certain goods and services. However, while money-
making opportunities for men have expanded, women's
alternatives seem to be narrowing. Manufactured goods
have replaced some of the industries that gave women
access to wealth (e.g., weaving). Consequently, women
respond to the mounting economic pressures by trying to
increase their economic productivity along traditional
lines, i.e., farming and marketing. Other avenues are
all but closed to women. They are consumers of manufactured goods, yet they have no opportunity to invest in
them, as their husbands do. The trade of manufactured
goods requires greater contact with urban centers and
foreign language skills that women have not had the chance
to develop. Reforms in farming methods, brought about
by development agencies, still continue to be addressed
to men only. While men engage in some form of techno-
logically advanced farming, their wives continue to cultivate with simple technology.

Women's only form of participation in the new economic system is through the sale of peanuts. But although women are responsible for production of the bulk
of peanuts (80 percent in Kouri), they are not in control
of the crop's distribution or sale, nor do they have control over the prices they can ask for their produce.
Even though women keep the profits from the sale of peanuts, men make the contacts with male buyers and as middlemen receive a small percentage of the money from the
sale.

Because men are the only participants in the new
economic order and as wage earners are the only direct
beneficiaries, it is clear that mothers who operate on
the traditional values of building an independent economic
base by investing in their sons are inadvertently contributing to the dependence of women on men.

CONCLUSION

In summary, the international response to the drought
has stimulated the Upper Voltan economy by (1) improving
transportation and road conditions, thereby opening up
many inaccessible rural areas to full participation in
the national economy; (2) providing jobs in drought-
afflicted regions through the hiring of local labor to
work on drought-related projects; (3) raising the general

level of consumption of manufactured goods even in re-
mote rural areas; (4) increasing the diversification of
the economy by providing alternatives outside of the
traditional economic system.  Although all these appear
to be positive factors, they must be examined in light of
their potential long-range effects.

The amelioration of the problems of the transportation system has brought more merchants in contact with
previously inaccessible areas.  The plethora of buyers
has stimulated peasants to increase their production of
farm products.  However, profits from the sale of produce are barely enough to meet villagers' needs.  In
addition, sale to private merchants fosters a dependence
on a credit system that places producers in debt and
forces them to sell their goods at half the price.  Moreover, villagers do not have the technological means by
which to expand production without increasing their labor
force and the size of their fields.  This limitation on
their agricultural productivity coupled with rising inflation may render small-scale agriculture nonviable,
forcing peasants to seek wage employment.[2]

New sources of income were welcomed by the communities; however, the types of jobs furnished by drought
relief projects are not self-perpetuating.  What will become of dam builders, well diggers, and other laborers
once these projects are terminated?  Pumping money into
the economy without providing the means by which to
perpetuate the prosperity, i.e., the means of production,
the expanded market, and the like, raises the level of
consumption for a while.  However, this state of prosperity is bound to be followed by inflation and subsequent decline in real income.  Production on the village
level should be increased by expanding traditional means
of production in order to reduce the villages' dependency on the national level and on the industrial products.  The market for village-produced goods should be
expanded.  As it now stands, village goods suffer increased competition from manufactured goods that have
invaded local markets while village-produced goods are
sold within a very limited circuit.  Increase in the
use of certain types of manufactured goods stunts the
production of the same type of goods within the village.
Thus, the villagers increasingly depend on the larger
economic community to satisfy their material needs.  As
a result, the level of consumption of manufactured goods
has increased but not the standard of living of the peasant, who is a victim of the increasingly unfavorable
terms of trade.  Franke and  Chasin in Seeds of Famine
(1978) show that in 1947, 100 units of peanuts purchased
100 units of manufactured goods in Niger.  In 1970, 100
units of peanuts purchased 47 units of manufactured goods.

Thus, as mentioned earlier, the superficial prosperity of the region, measured in the amount of manufactured goods consumed by the villagers, masks the increasing marginalization of farmers.

Newly established economic alternatives are more readily available to young men than to any other segment of the population. This inequality of access to wealth fosters the economic dependence of women on men. In addition, participation in new forms of economic activity fosters the breakdown of many positive social relations of production between members of the village community, consequently altering social relations. The villager has less access to communal labor, is not as free to participate in reciprocal relations of production, and must therefore pay for services that he could once depend on his friends and relatives to provide. At the same time that these protective institutions are being dissolved, new economic relations offer few protective structures to replace the old ones.

Integration into the money economy fosters dependence of the village community on the larger economic community. The villagers are obliged to sell their labor and produce in order to procure cash with which to purchase manufactured goods. However, the terms of trade are defined elsewhere. Villagers cannot dictate the value of their produce nor can they modify the prices they must pay for manufactured goods.

The villagers are now searching for the means to expand their earning potential. Farming as a means of access to money is being undermined because of its low profits and constantly diminishing returns. The preponderance of creditors in the village attests to this. As a result, seasonal migration is on the rise in the community, thus increasing the burden of labor for women.


SUMMARY

Ever since 1947, changes in the village economy have occurred at a staggering pace. The extended family is no longer the unit of production and consumption, as it was in the past. At present, single families produce the agricultural products necessary to feed their members and to sell in order to acquire the money with which to purchase household goods. In the village, the standard of living has decreased steadily, and the villagers have had to increase sales of agricultural goods in order to maintain their purchasing power. As the sale of agricultural goods becomes less lucrative, villagers have had to engage in other forms of economic activity in

order to earn cash.  On the surface, it appears that
economic changes have affected only young men, who are
the principal participants in new types of economic
activity.  However, in order to accommodate the loss
of young men's labor within the traditional sphere,
women have systematically increased their contribution
to their conjugal households.  They now shoulder an
increasing part of the responsibility of providing food
for the family.  Economic changes on the national and
village level have resulted in the increase in women's
work in the agricultural and household sphere, paradoxically increasing the economic dependence of women on
men.

NOTES

　　　1.  Northern Gulma is located in the northernmost
part of the Department of the East, between 13° and 11°
north latitude.  The department's administrative center
is located in Fada N'Gourma.  The administrative center
of Northern Gulma is in Bogande, a sous-préfecture within
the Department of the East.  The new, official spelling--
Gulma--has been adopted here; Gourma is the French version and appears on all the maps.
　　　2.  A study conducted by the government of Upper
Volta, Départment de Stabilization des Prix, showed that
in 1977, 80 percent of agricultural goods sold by the
farmers of Upper Volta were sold below the minimum price
set by the government.  This is because farmers are often
short of food during the rainy season and borrow money
in order to purchase grain.  Their debtors are usually
grain merchants, who lend money on condition that the
farmer return double the volume of grain represented by
the loan, at harvest time.  Thus, if the farmer borrows
500 CFA frs during the rainy season, the price of a tin
(18 kilos) of millet at harvest time, he must return two
tins of millet the following harvest.  His loss is worsened by the fact that the price of millet skyrockets
during the rainy season, because of its general scarcity.
Grain speculators usually buy millet during the harvest
season when millet is cheap and resell it at high prices
during the rainy season.  Farmers really do sell their
millet at half the price.  They are perpetual victims of
speculators.

REFERENCES

Amin, Samir. 1971.  "Upper Volta Between the Years 1960
     and 1970."  Dakar:  United Nations African Institute
     for Economic Development and Planning.  May.
Boserup, Ester. 1970.  Woman's Role in Economic Develop-
     ment.  New York: St. Martin's Press.
Franke, R.W., and B.H. Chasin. 1978.  Seeds of Famine:
     Ecological Destruction and the Development Dilemma
     in the West African Sahel.  Landmark Studies.  New
     York: Universe Books.
Kohler, Jean-Marie.  1971.  Activités agricoles et
     changements sociaux dans l'Ouest Mossi (Haute Volta).
     Mémoires de l'ORSTOM, no. 46.  Paris: Publication
     de l'ORSTOM.
Lankoande, C.  1978.  Personal communication.  13 October.
Lankoande, P.  1977.  Personal communication. 21-25
     January.
Madiega, Georges.  1973.  "Rapports entre l'administra-
     tion coloniale francaise et les autorités tradi-
     tionelles du Cercle de Fada N'Gourma (Haute Volta)
     1895-1932."  Master's thesis.
_____. 1978.  "Le Nord Gulma précolonial (Haute
     Volta):  Origine des dynasties, approche de la
     société."  Ph.D. dissertation, University of Paris
     I Panthéon-Sorbonne.
Monde diplomatique.  1976.
Nadinga, A. 1977.  Interviews of 24-28 April.
Nadinga, M. 1977.  Interviews of 25-30 April.
Sénéchal, Jacques.  1973.  Espace et mobilité rurale en
     milieu Sudano-Sahelian:  le changement dans l'isole-
     ment (Gulma du Nord, Haute Volta).  Mémoire Ecole
     Pratique des Hautes Etudes (VIe section) and Centre
     Nationale de la Recherche Scientifique.
Skinner, Eliot P. 1960.  "Labour Migration and Its Re-
     lationship to Socio-cultural Change in Mossi Soci-
     ety."  Africa (London) 30, no. 4 (October): 375-401.

## 9. Women's Work in a Communal Setting: The Tanzanian Policy of *Ujamaa*

*Louise Fortmann*

Julius K. Nyerere, president of Tanzania, has said that "women who live in villages work harder than anybody else in Tanzania" (Nyerere,1968, p. 245). This work falls into three major categories--domestic maintenance activities, food crop production, and cash crop production. Women (and their children) do almost all domestic maintenance tasks--child care, preparation and storage of food, gathering firewood, hauling water, cleaning. Men typically do house construction and repair, although female heads of household may even undertake this task themselves. This paper concentrates on the agricultural part of women's work because it is the most directly connected with ujamaa.

In every area of the country, women are responsible for feeding their family and hence are the major producers of food crops. Among the various ethnic groups, Zaramo women have total responsibility for rice production; Chagga women have main responsibility for farm work, growing bananas and other food crops; Gogo women grow grain; Meru and Iraqw women do most farm work; Haya women have nearly total responsibility for food crops. Some pastoralists have taken to marrying an agriculturalist woman as a second wife in order to procure food crops for their households. (See Swantz, 1970, p. 61; 1975; 1977, p. 56; Rigby, 1969, p. 61; Fortmann, 1977, p. 2.)

Women also work as unpaid laborers on their husband's cash crops. They tend to be assigned the more tedious tasks such as weeding and thinning. Meru women do most of the cultivating, weeding, and harvesting of coffee. Women in Morogoro Region are involved in all phases of cotton production (Mbilinyi, 1972; Bartlett, 1976, unpublished data; Fortmann, 1977, p. 3). Bena, Kinga, and Hehe women are involved in tea production.

The prevailing folk wisdom--particularly male folk wisdom--has it that women are not particularly bright,

191

not capable of learning modern agriculture.  Obviously,
this notion is somewhat startling in a society which
relies on those same women to supply its food.  It also
happens not to be true, as can be seen from the data
presented in Table 9.1.  These data are taken from a
study of the National Maize Project (NMP), a production
program which supplied subsidized inputs.  Participants
are people who purchased inputs from the program;
nonparticipants are those who did not.


TABLE 9.1
Good Maize Practice Scores of Males and Females, by
Region and Participation in the National Maize Project,
1976

|  | Males | Females | t |
| --- | --- | --- | --- |
| Arusha (N=250) | | | |
|   Participants | 9.88 | 9.88 | .00008 |
|   Nonparticipants | 4.09 | 4.17 | .125 |
|   t | 9.38*** | 7.39*** | |
| Morogoro (N=235) | | | |
|   Participants | 6.81 | 5.83 | .856 |
|   Nonparticipants | 4.08 | 3.55 | .896 |
|   t | 4.07*** | 3.34*** | |

Source: Fortmann, 1977, p. 14.

***Significant at .001 level.


     The data show no significant difference between
men and women, although there were highly significant
differences between participants and nonparticipants.
That is, female participants were as modern as male
participants and male nonparticipants were as traditional as their female counterparts.
     Women, then, are competent farmers, absolutely cen-
tral to Tanzanian agricultural production.  However, female agricultural producers are disadvantaged in a
number of ways.  First, they face a series of constraints,
of which some are peculiar to their situation as females
and others are aggravated versions of constraints also
faced by male farmers.  These constraints mainly concern
access to inputs--land, labor capital, and information.

Although in theory women as citizens have the same right to land as men, in practice, traditional rules of land tenure apply. In some places this creates no problem for women. Luguru women have the same right as men to apply to their lineage for land. Zaramo women also have the right to inherit, although chances are great that the land will find its way into the hands of some male relative. Coastal women also retain control of the permanent cash crops they have developed. Haya women, on the other hand, are in a very vulnerable position. They have no rights of inheritance and may be dispossessed by their male heirs. (See Young and Fosbrooke, 1960, p. 61; Swantz, 1970, pp. 96-97; 1977, pp. 6-7.) Women's problems thus begin with difficulties of access to the most essential element of agricultural production--land.

A second constraint on women as producers is the availability of labor. Male- and female-headed households differ in their access to labor. Men have use of their wives' labor and, if they have sufficient resources, can increase available labor by marriage. Women have no such option for obtaining labor solely for the use of their household, although they may be able to join a work-sharing group or have access to festive labor in periods of peak labor demand.

The issue of labor becomes critical if land under cultivation is to be expanded or if labor-intensive technologies are to be used. Female heads of households (roughly 25 percent of the population) are particularly vulnerable in this regard. Unless their brothers or other male relatives help them, they must do all their own work. Further, it is possible that they may be left without the help of their children, since by customary law a man may take his child at the age of seven (approximately the age at which a child can assume some productive functions).

Capital is not readily available to any small farmer, but less so to women. Inputs for cash crops are provided on credit by the cash crop authorities, but, as noted above, cash crops are generally owned by men. Women constituted only 8 percent of the NMP participants and were reportedly actively discriminated against in some villages. Women received 10 percent of the loans granted in a sample of six villages participating in the Tanzanian Rural Development Bank's Small Farmer Food Crop Loan Program (Fortmann, 1978, p.29).

Women also have a more difficult time getting access to information, as can be seen by the significantly lower information contact scores of women presented in Table 9.2. The information contact score primarily reflects contact with the extension service. The reputation of the extension service is not particularly

good  to begin with; its performance with women is dismal.  For example, in Morogoro Region, extension agents
visited 58 percent of the men participating in NMP but
only 20 percent of the women (Fortmann, 1976, p. 30).
Data presented elsewhere (Fortmann, 1977, pp. 14-16)
show that men often do not transmit agricultural information accurately to their wives.  Hence, the lack of
extension contact can result in lack of information.


TABLE 9.2
Information Contact Scores[a] of Males and Females, by
Region and Participation in the National Maize Project,
1976

|  | Males | Females | t |
|---|---|---|---|
| Arusha  (N=250) | | | |
| Participants | 4.08 | 3.54 | 0.68 |
| Nonparticipants | 2.16 | 1.24 | 2.27[*] |
| t | 4.33[***] | 5.73[***] | |
| Morogoro  (N=235) | | | |
| Participants | 5.18 | 2.87 | 2.52[**] |
| Nonparticipants | 2.75 | 1.51 | 2.60[**] |
| t | 4.66[***] | 2.89[***] | |

Source:  Fortmann, 1977, p. 4.

[a]The information contact score consisted of the following
   items:  knows the extension agent's name, visited by
   the extension agent in the past year, attended a farming
   demonstration in the past year, knows there is a demonstration plot in the village, listens to the agricultural radio program, reads the agricultural magazine,
   has seen a film on maize.

[*]Significant at .05 level.

[**]Significant at .01 level.

[***]Significant at .001 level.


Another major disadvantage of women producers is
that they often do not benefit except in a very marginal
fashion from the fruits of their labors.  Men control
the sale of cash crops and are under no particular obligation to share the proceeds with their wives.  Com-

plaints that the men spend their money on home-brewed
beer and other women are prevalent. A man's failure to
provide necessities for the family from his cash income
is a common reason for divorce (Swantz, 1977, p. 22).

One source of these problems is that the government
agricultural policy has been designed as if women were
not the major agricultural producers. Hence, women tend
to fall into the cracks. The extension service is almost exclusively staffed by males, which, given sociocultural constraints on male-female interaction, reduces the likelihood that women will be reached. Credit
and input supply programs are never designed with the
explicit aim of reaching women. The result is that women
are often excluded--sometimes inadvertently, sometimes
deliberately. (While it is clearly against national
interests to deny women access to means of increasing
their production, local decision makers may find the
prospect of economically independent women a compelling
reason for doing so.)

The tenor of agricultural policy to the contrary,
parts of Tanzanian government policy have been very concerned with the advancement of women. Women are being
appointed to high party and government positions.
University entrance procedures have been adjusted to
accommodate women. A recent statement by the vice
president has even initiated the opening of mosques to
women (Daily News, 5 February 1979). The policy of
ujamaa has seemed to provide a vehicle through which
women could both improve their agricultural productivity and control the fruits of their labor.

Ujamaa is a Swahili word meaning "familyhood."
Ujamaa as a policy has two components--the creation of
nucleated settlements of people and the practice of communal agriculture. There are several advantages for
women in this. Women can be registered as members in
their own right rather than merely being an appendage of
the male member. This had been a problem in the early
settlement schemes. Sometimes men left their wives at
home to work the old shamba. Another woman was then acquired more or less as "a necessary piece of equipment."
Although they did the agricultural and domestic maintenance work, such women were excluded from receiving any
of the proceeds. (Brain, 1976, pp. 271-73). As a member
of an ujamaa village, a woman can receive her own share
of the proceeds. Ujamaa guarantees her access to land
in the form of the ujamaa farm. It also offers her
access to capital, inputs, and information. Particularly in the early days of ujamaa, resources were
focused on the ujamaa farm. Extension agents were instructed to work only with ujamaa production, and thus
women in a group could interact with the extension agent.

Credit was available only to cooperatives and ujamaa
villages. Certain crops (tobacco in Iringa Region for
a period) were restricted to ujamaa production. Ujamaa
farms had the service of Ministry of Agriculture tractors[1] and often were provided with free inputs. The
provision of water associated with ujamaa villages would
free women, who traditionally have had to obtain all
water, to engage in other productive activities or even
to rest.

The practical effect of ujamaa on women has de-
viated substantially from the ideal. This has, of
course, varied from place to place. There undoubtedly
are striking exceptions to the situation described below. However, available evidence would indicate that
what is described is, in fact, the rule.

Some of the causes of the deviation from the ideal
lie in the way ujamaa was implemented. In 1967, the
TANU[2] National Executive Committee issued the Arusha
Declaration, setting the country on the road to socialism and self-reliance. This was followed by a series
of articles by President Nyerere describing the rural
part of the policy, ujamaa villages. These writings
were philosophical and utopian in nature. The details
of founding and operating ujamaa villages remained
vague.

This vagueness was a source of difficulty, for
once ujamaa was named as a national policy, bureaucrats
were under pressure to produce something concrete  in
a hurry. The result in many places was a headlong rush
into ujamaa, sometimes accompanied by the use of force
or the threat of force, sometimes using capital goods
(tractors, water systems, agricultural inputs) as incentives. The villages created by these efforts often
bore little relation to President Nyerere's vision.

Ujamaa requires the kind of commitment that is
engendered only by the voluntary decision of the people
to become involved in it. Such a decision may require
a long process that does not fit the bureaucratic need
to get something done fast. When the central government
does not consider "no" to be an acceptable answer, the
decision-making process is not only time consuming, it
is irrelevant. From the bureaucratic point of view,
the flurry of implementation was a necessary step.  Unfortunately, it left behind "ujamaa villages" that
had the form but lacked the substance of ujamaa.  Such
villages were sometimes characterized by dependence,
sometimes by alienation, rarely by ujamaa spirit.  This
is important to remember when the effect of ujamaa on
women is described.  Often what is being discussed is
not ujamaa at all, but a bureaucratic artifact.  Ujamaa
in a real sense was never tried.

Ujamaa's potential for enabling women to gain control over their own lives has sometimes been realized.
In one Iringa village, a man who had beaten his wife
for going to work on the ujamaa farm was jailed, thus
firmly establishing her right to participate in ujamaa
on her own (DeVries and Fortmann, 1974, p. 65).  More
frequently, however, ujamaa has not had this effect.
There are two reasons for this.  One is related to the
mode of implementing ujamaa.  The other is that the
structures for equality have tended to be overwhelmed
by the male-dominated tradition.

Ujamaa, as noted above, often was implemented by
the local bureaucracy in ways that undermined its
credibility as a grass-roots institution.  People often
say of the ujamaa farm, "mali ya umma tu" (just public
property), and refrain from putting much effort into it.
Further, ujamaa exists side by side with private production and must compete with it for land and labor.  The
tendency has been for individuals to concentrate their
resources in the private sector, exactly where women
are disadvantaged.

The results of this situation can be seen in the
quality and quantity of land and labor devoted to
ujamaa and the level of ujamaa production.  Generally,
ujamaa figures are presented on an aggregate basis--e.g.,
350 acres of maize.  However, if these same figures are
looked at on a per-member of per-family basis, as they
are in Table 9.3, a very different picture appears.
Subject to regional variations (in drier regions agriculture requires more land), Tanzanian farms average 2.5
to 4.0 acres in size.  In areas such as Bukoba, an acre
is barely enough to support a family if there is no
source of outside income (Swantz, 1977, p. 17).  Bukoba
agriculture  is generally quite productive.  Thus, it
could be expected that an acre would not be as productive elsewhere.  Yet, out of 99 ujamaa farms in fourteen
regions for which data were compiled, only 23 had more
than one acre per family or member.  That is, on the
average a family could not rely on the production from
the ujamaa farm to meet its subsistence needs.

The situation on the labor front is not much better.
Working days are typically short and few in number, and
absenteeism is a problem.  Work is rarely organized in
a way that takes advantage of economies of scale or
specialization.  Except where work is organized on a
piece-work basis, often one can earn the same points
by a few desultory efforts as by vigorous activity.

TABLE 9.3
Number of Communally Cultivated Acres per Family or
per Member (N=88 villages, 99 ujamaa farms)[a]

| Acres | <0.10 | 0.10-0.50 | 0.51-1.00 | 1.01-2.00 | >2 |
|---|---|---|---|---|---|
| Number of ujamaa farms | 20 | 43 | 13 | 10 | 13 |

Sources: Angwazi and Ndulu, 1973; Bugengo, 1973; Daily
News, 12, 13, 31 Jan., 6 Feb., 20 March, 10, 12 May,
10 June, 10 Oct. 1974; Fortmann, 1976; Guillotte, 1973,
pp. 6-9; Krokfors, 1973, pp. 19-22; Musoke, 1971;
Muzo, 1976; Nyiera, 1978, pp. 15-16; Omari, 1977;
Sender, 1974; Sumra, 1975, p. 13; United Republic of
Tanzania, National Bank of Commerce, 1974.

[a]These data are a bit awkward. There are excellent
political reasons for exaggerating the size of the
ujamaa farm, and this practice is not uncommon. There
were multi-year data available for some villages; hence
there are more farms than villages. Whenever possible,
per member figures were converted to a family basis by
multiplying by five. This technique has probably com-
pounded other inaccuracies.


    The result is that ujamaa production is extremely
low. For example, the communal contribution to Tanzania's Gross Domestic Product (GDP) from agriculture,
veterinary, fish, and forestry in 1974 and the average
per capita income are presented in Table 9.4. Six
shillings a year will not buy a kilo of sugar, let alone
an independent economic base.
    The woman who pins her hopes to ujamaa, then, is not
in a particularly strong position. Ujamaa does indeed
give a woman access to land, but it may not give her
access to very much land or to very good land. Ujamaa
does give her access to labor, but she cannot control
the quality or quantity of that labor. She must rely on
a cooperative spirit, which may have been destroyed by
the bureaucratic methods of implementation, factionalism
within the village, or private interests. Even if production is high, a woman has no guarantee that she will
be rewarded in proportion to her labor. Losses to bad
management, poor bookkeeping, and embezzlement are not
infrequent and are sometimes substantial. In general,

ujamaa production has simply not been reliable enough to provide a firm economic base for a woman and her family.


TABLE 9.4
Communal Production in Four Regions, 1974

| Region | Communal Contribution to GDP per Capita from Agriculture, Veterinary, Fish and Forestry (%) | Annual Average Per Capita Income from Communal Production (T Sh) |
|---|---|---|
| Dodoma | 0.17 | -/30 |
| Iringa | 2.11 | 5/35 |
| Kiguma | 0.09 | -/17 |
| Kilimanjaro | 0.16 | -/66 |

Source:  McHenry, 1977.


    Sometimes ujamaa appears to work to the detriment of women by increasing their work load with little or no reward.  The data on this are mixed.  The sexual division of labor on ujamaa farms is influenced by a number of factors.  Certain crops such as sisal are considered male crops.  When these are the major crop in the village, most of the work will be done by men. Villages which are pioneer settlements have predominantly male settlers and therefore a male work force. Conversely, in areas characterized by large amounts of male outmigration for wage labor, women compose the majority of ujamaa members and, therefore, also laborers.
    Most studies show that women do more ujamaa work than men even when the men comprise a greater proportion of the members.  Field observations in Iringa, Mara, Mwanza, Kilimanjaro, and Ruvuma regions confirm this pattern (Swantz, 1977; Cousins, 1974, p. 34; Bugengo, 1973; Mapolu, 1973; Lewin, n.d.).  Sometimes these women are members in their own right (comprising  up to 90 percent of the membership of the tea-producing villages in Mufindi and Njombe districts) (DeVries and Fortmann, 1974, p. 15); other times, a woman serves as labor for

her husband, who is a member and who receives the proceeds (Swantz, 1977, p. 29). There is some evidence
that women are more dedicated ujamaa members than men
(Cousins, 1974, p. 34). On the other hand, one study
of thirty-nine villages in four regions (Iringa, Dodoma,
Kilimanjaro, and Mwanza) shows that men spend more time
on ujamaa work than women (McHenry, 1977, p. 4).[3] And
in West Lake, Storgard (1975/76, p. 150) found that
according to labor registration books, 40 to 50 percent
of male labor is involved in communal work compared with
29 percent of female labor.

In some villages, women have undertaken to organize
their own economic endeavor through the UWT (Umoja wa
Wanawake wa Tanzania), the national women's organization, which has the blessing of the national government
but not necessarily that of the village men. UWT's
economic activities often take a more traditional form--
brewing beer, handicrafts, tea shops. Women's attempts
to break the male stranglehold on other economic spheres
through collective action tend to be met with fierce
resistance. A UWT in Arumeru was denied land on which
to grow coffee, although it was granted land on which
to grow beans and maize. Permanent crops remain the
property of the person who planted them. Apparently,
the prospect of a group of women in permanent possession
of a source of cash was too much. Women in a Bukoba
UWT had to overcome stiff male resistance, which discouraged several members before they were able to start
selling fish (Swantz, 1977, p. 29). Arumeru women who
wanted to open a communal shop in competition with two
male-owned shops had to fight all the way to the district level to get permission to do so (J. Stanley, 1978,
personal communication).

Nyerere saw "the equality of all members of the community and the members' self-government in all matters
which concern only their own affairs" as the essential
element of ujamaa (1968, p. 353). Village government is
structured to allow such equality. The party is organized in units of roughly ten households each, with an
elected leader. Every village resident over the apparent age of eighteen is a member of the Village Assem-
bly, which elects the Village Council. The Village
Council is responsible for the day-to-day running of
the village. But despite these structures and in some
cases despite female numerical superiority, men continue to dominate the decision-making process.

All ten-cell leaders in an Usambara survey were
male, because "to the Shambalas politics is purely a
business for men" (Mshangama, 1971, p. 25). Most
other studies of ten-cell leaders show them to be male,
generally rich and elderly (Kokwebangira, 1971, p. 46;

Kawago, 1971, p. 58; DeVries and Fortmann, 1974). The
single contrasting example comes from Pare District,
where women were a crucial part of resistance to taxation during the 1940s. In the relative absence of men
who work elsewhere as wage laborers, women have continued their activist tradition and occupy as many as 25
percent of the ten-cell positions in the area (O'Barr,
1975/76, pp. 125, 128).

The ten-cell leader primarily arbitrates and trans-
mits messages from the party and government. Hence, the
tendency to exclude women from this post is less critical except in symbolic terms than it might otherwise
be. Women's exclusion from the decision-making process
of the village is more crucial. They are excluded not
only from leadership positions in village government but
also from more general participation in the political
process.

It is exceedingly rare for a woman to be a village
chairman. I encountered one in the Uluguru Mountains
in 1976. Swantz (1977, p. 30) reports another in Bukoba
in a village, half of the households of which were female headed. There are 7,000 villages in Tanzania. For
a few months, the chairman and secretary of an Iringa
village were women. The men were so outraged by this
state of affairs that the area commissioner engineered
a new election, which was won by a man (DeVries and
Fortmann, 1974, p. 66).

Women are usually excluded from village committees
as well, or relegated to those that are considered
"women's affairs." A 1973 study (Mapolu, pp. 166-67)
of Mwanza villages found that 27.5 percent of the villages had no woman committee members at all, 27.5 percent had 10 percent or fewer, and 22.5 percent had only
11 to 20 percent female committee members. Only 9 percent had 21 to 30 percent women committee members and
13.5 percent had over 30 percent female members. Later
studies in the same region show women to be only on committees concerned with topics such as schools and nutrition. One village had two woman committee members out
of a total of ten (Storgard, 1975/76, p. 152; Swantz,
1977, p. 28). A 1974 Iringa study (DeVries and Fortmann, 1974, p. 66) found that four out of twelve villages
had no woman committee members; only five had more than
one. An Usambara study (Sender, 1974, pp. 34-35) showed
that even where women outnumbered men two to one, there
were no female committee members.

Women do not participate in village meetings,
either. They may have too much work to attend, or may
be too exhausted to participate if they do attend.[4]
Generally, women speak only to support a statement by
their husbands. Women who assert themselves publicly

can often expect to be reprimanded by the other women
and harrassed by the men. The data presented in Table
9.5 show women's participation to be significantly lower
than men's.


TABLE 9.5
Mean Participation by Men and Women in Village Meetings
in Two Bukoba Ujamaa Villages (N=60)

|  | Number of Meetings Attended | Number of Meetings in Which Respondent Spoke | Number of Times Respondent Was Consulted by the Village Development Committee |
|---|---|---|---|
| Men | 4.4 | 2.0 | 2.0 |
| Women | 2.2 | 0.3 | 0.7 |
| t | 4.20* | 3.41* | 4.51* |

Source: Data from Mpesha, 1976, reanalyzed by the
author.
*Significant at the .001 level.


In every case, the participation by women was
significantly lower than that by men. Of the women in
the sample, 21.4 percent had never attended a meeting,
compared with 2.4 percent of the men. Only one woman
had ever spoken in a meeting, although half had been
consulted at least once by the Village Development
Committee. This would indicate that the one hope for
women might well be by more informal influence. How
seriously their advice is taken is not clear. The declaration by students from Kivukoni Ideological College
after a study of Singida villages that "women in villages were highly oppressed, having no say in village
activities" (Daily News, 12 December 1977) does not
leave much room for optimism.
     Ujamaa, then, would appear to have had little
favorable effect on women's work. It has not been implemented in a way that lessens women's workload or
makes them more productive. In some cases, it has increased that workload. It has not, except in a very few

cases, provided women with a reliable alternative to
private production patterns.  It has not increased
women's status and power except on paper.

It is perhaps unfair to be critical of <u>ujamaa</u> at
so early a date.  The policy is barely twelve years old,
and its implementation has been affected by two major
policy initiatives--decentralization of government personnel and villagization (moving eleven million people
into villages in a little over a year).  Nonetheless, it
is clear that if <u>ujamaa</u> is going to affect women positively, the issue must be an explicit part of the policy.
That, to date, has not been the case.


NOTES

    1.  The provision of tractors had contradictory
effects.  It reduced the work involved in cultivating
and planting, but by permitting expanded acerages, it
increased enormously the time required for weeding and
harvesting.

    2.  Tanzania African National Union, at that time
the only legal party in the country.  In 1977, TANU was
merged with the Zanzibar ASP to form CCM, the party of
the revolution.

    3.  There are a number of reasons why the results
of this study run counter to the others.  It includes
sisal-producing villages, where men in fact do more
work, and it appears to be based on workbook records,
which may not reflect reality.  For example, the sample
includes Kilimanjaro, where women are known to work in
their husbands' names.

    4.  Swantz (1977) and Lewin (N.D.) both mention
the problem of exhaustion.  Estimations of working
hours (Bartlett, 1976; Cleave, 1974, pp. 57, 186) indicate the average working day for a woman is roughly
ten hours.  <u>Ujamaa</u> work is typically added to this.

REFERENCES

Angwazi, Joseph, and Benno Ndulu.  1973.  "An Evaluation
    of Ujamaa Villages in the Rufiji Area, 1968-1972."
    Presented at the Annual Social Science Conference
    of the East African Universities, 18-20 December,
    Dar es Salaam.
Bartlett, C.D.S. 1976.  Unpublished tabulated data.
Brain, James L. 1976. "Less than Second Class: Women in
    Rural Settlement Schemes in Tanzania."  In <u>Women
    in Africa</u>, ed. Nancy J. Hafkin and Edna G. Bay.
    Stanford, Ca.: Stanford Univ. Press, Pp. 265-82.

Bugengo, J. 1973. "Ujamaa in Mara Region." Presented at the Annual Social Science Conference of the East African Universities, 18-20 December, Dar es Salaam.

Cleave, John H. 1974. African Farmers: Labor Use in the Development of Smallholder Agriculture. New York: Praeger Publishers.

Cousins, Noel. 1974. "Ujamaa in Iringa." Unpublished paper prepared for UNDP/FAO.

Daily News (Dar es Salaam). Various issues.

DeVries, J., and L. Fortmann. 1974. "A Study of Ujamaa Villages in Iringa Region." Prepared for the UNDP/FAO Planning Team for the Iringa 3rd Five Year Plan. Mimeographed.

Fortmann, Louise. 1976. "An Evaluation of the Progress of the National Maize Project at the End of One Cropping Season in Morogoro and Arusha Regions." Prepared for USAID/Tanzania.

_____. 1977. "Women and Tanzanian Agricultural Development." Economic Research Bureau Paper 77.4, University of Dar es Salaam.

_____. 1978. "Observations on the Mbulu Small Farmer Food Crop Loan Program." Prepared for USAID/Tanzania. Mimeographed.

Guillotte, J.V. 1973. "Attitudes Toward Ujamaa in a Multi-ethnic Rural Community in Northern Tanzania." Paper presented at the 16th Annual Meeting of the African Studies Association.

Kawago, K.S. 1971. "The Operation of TANU Cells in Iringa." In The Cell System of the Tanganyika African National Union, ed. J.H. Proctor. Dar es Salaam: Tanzania Publishing House. Pp. 51-66.

Kokwebangira, R.N. 1971. "Cells in Dar es Salaam and Bukoba." In The Cell System of the Tanganyika African National Union, ed. J.H. Proctor. Dar es Salaam: Tanzania Publishing House. Pp. 42-59.

Krokfors, Christer. 1973. "Agricultural Development in Selected Ujamaa Villages in Sumbawanga District." Bureau of Resource Assessment and Land Use Planning Research Report 41, University of Dar es Salaam.

Lewin, Roger. n.d. "Matetereka." Mbioni 5 (3):21-25.

McHenry, Dean. 1977. "Peasant Participation in Communal Farming: The Tanzanian Experience." African Studies Review, December, pp. 43-59.

Mapolu, Henry. 1973. "The Social and Economic Organization of Ujamaa Villages." M.A. thesis, University of Dar es Salaam.

Mbilinyi, M.J. 1972. "The State of Women in Tanzania." Canadian Journal of African Studies 6 (2):371-77.

Mpesha, M.A.L. 1976. "The Effect of Participation in Decision-Making on Commitment to Ujamaa Work." Special Project, Department of Rural Economy and Extension, Faculty of Agriculture and Forestry, Morogoro, Tanzania. Typescript.

Mshangama, A.H.1971. "TANU Cells: Organs of One-Party
    Democratic Socialism." In The Cell System of the Tan-
    ganyika African National Union, ed. J.H. Proctor.
    Dar es Salaam: Tanzania Publishing House. Pp. 20-31.
Musoke, I.K.S. 1971. "Building Socialism in Bukoba: The
    Establishment of Rugazi (Nyerere) Ujamaa Village."
    In Building Ujamaa Villages in Tanzania, ed. J.H.
    Proctor. Dar es Salaam: Tanzania Publishing House.
    Pp. 1-14.
Muzo, C.R.S. 1976. "Party Leadership and Socialist
    Transformation: A Case Study of Nyakato TANU Branch
    in Bukoba District." In The Party: Essays on TANU,
    by C.R.S. Muzo, et al. Dar es Salaam: Tanzania
    Publishing House. Pp. 1-18.
Nyerere, Julius K. 1968. "Socialism and Rural Develop-
    ment," Freedom and Socialism. London: Oxford Uni-
    versity Press. Pp. 337-66.
Nyiera, M.T. 1978. "Problems of Transforming a Trading
    Center into an Ujamaa Village: A Case Study of
    Misasi." B.A. dissertation, University of Dar es
    Salaam.
O'Barr, Jean. 1975/76. "Pare Women: A Case of Political
    Involvement." Rural Africana 29:121-34.
Omari, Abillah. 1977. "Decentralization and Develop-
    ment: The Case of Madimba Ward--Mtwara District."
    B.A. dissertation, University of Dar es Salaam.
Rigby, Peter. 1969. Cattle and Kinship Among the Gogo.
    Ithaca, N.Y.: Cornell University Press.
Sender, John. 1974. "Some Preliminary Notes on the
    Political Economy of Rural Development in Tanzania
    Based on a Case Study in the Western Usambaras."
    Economic Research Bureau Paper 74.5, University of
    Dar es Salaam.
Stanley, J. 1978. Personal communication.
Storgard, Birgit. 1975/76. "Women in Ujamaa Villages."
    Rural Africana 29:135-55.
Sumra, Suleman. 1975. "Problems of Agricultural Produc-
    tion in Ujamaa Villages in Handeni District." Eco-
    nomic Research Bureau Paper 75.3, University of
    Dar es Salaam.
Swantz, Marja Liisa. 1970. Ritual and Symbol in Transi-
    tional Zaramo Society. Uppsala: Gleerup.
_____. 1975. "Women's Work Is Double." Daily News.
_____. 1977. "Strain and Strength among Peasant
    Women in Tanzania." Bureau of Resource Assessment
    and Land Use Planning Research Paper No. 49, Uni-
    versity of Dar es Salaam.
United Republic of Tanzania, National Bank of Commerce.
    1974. "Our Report on the Visit to Lulanzi Ujamaa
    Village." Mimeographed.

# 10. Women Farmers and Inequities in Agricultural Services

*Kathleen A. Staudt*

Recently, comment on the bias against women farmers that is apparent in agricultural policy throughout much of Africa has become commonplace (for example, see Maud Muntemba and Louise Fortmann's papers, above). Such a bias is paradoxical in the African setting, where women do most of the agricultural labor and indeed even manage entire farm operations. Not only have women assumed heavier workloads in rural agricultural areas, but many observers note an increasing dependency of women on men because of the commercialized economy and the inequitable ways in which the fruits of development have been distributed (for example, see Boserup, 1970; Mbilinyi, 1972; UN/ECA, 1974; Tinker and Bramsen, 1976).

Despite the increased awareness about inequities, we have little empirical data that establishes to what extent discrimination occurs, why it occurs, and the consequences of discrimination both for women's productivity and the general economy. My purpose in this paper is to provide empirical support for the hypothesis that the government gives preference to men in agricultural services. I then explore why such discrimination occurs by examining a number of factors that could possibly account for it. Women are perhaps perceived as traditional, conservative, poverty-stricken, and unwilling or unable to adopt innovations that are promoted by the agricultural administration. From a bureaucratic and economic perspective, discrimination might be seen as the most efficient use of scarce resources if preference is extended to those farmers with the cash, land, and propensity to innovate. Such farmers might have a greater likelihood of adopting innovations promoted by the agricultural administration. As will be evident from the

A version of this paper has been published in Rural Africana 29 (Winter 1975-76):81-94.

analysis, the legitimacy of that bureaucratic perspective
is highly suspect; even wealthy and innovative women
managers with relatively large tracts of land experience
bias in the agricultural services offered to them, compared with those offered to their male counterparts.  The
failure of bureaucrats to extend services to women managers, particularly those women with the material resources and ability to respond to innovative ideas, is a
telling critique of bureaucratic performance and ability
to alter agricultural productivity.  A large part of the
bureaucracy's clientele who are women are, in effect,
ignored.  While women are very much a part of general
development activity, they are not integrated into the
development service network.


RESEARCH SITE

     The data, collected in 1975, consist of a geogra-
phically stratified sample of 212 small-scale farm
households in an administrative location in Kakamega District of western Kenya.[1]  For purposes of the study,
farms were divided into two types:  female management
and joint management, which are farms with a man present.
Joint management includes both husband-wife households
and households where intergenerational management occurs
because land has not yet been parceled out to sons.
Kakamega is a densely populated area where rates of male
out-migration in search of wage employment are among
the highest in Kenya.  A full 40 percent of my sample
consists of women farm managers, and this closely cor-
responds to figures in the 1969 Kenya  Census, which
show a 36 percent female household headship for Kakamega.
A common pattern in Kakamega, as elsewhere in Kenya, is
for men to engage in wage employment away from the farm
and return home upon retirement.
     Research was done among a subgroup of the Luhya
people, whose social organization is both patrilineal
and patrilocal.  Women traditionally have done much of
the agricultural labor; they were responsible for digging in connection with land preparation, planting,
weeding, and harvesting.  Men traditionally cleared the
land, plowed with oxen, and cared for cattle; they also
help with work operations in the women's sphere but are
not totally responsible for them (Wagner, 1949; Sangree,
1966, p. xxxvi).  Men who work outside the district
sometimes "work with money," by sending their wives cash
to hire laborers to plow or to buy seeds, fertilizer,
and tools.  Farms are small in scale, and the average
size for the entire sample is two and one-half acres.
     Women engage in extensive associational activity

including church groups, mutual-aid societies, and communal agricultural groups for planting, weeding, and harvesting crops. More than 90 percent of the women in the sample belonged to some type of organization. A good deal of agricultural information and labor is exchanged among members of these groups. Men, in contrast, attend barazas, weekly meetings in which government announcements and judicial decision making occur. Occasionally at barazas, agricultural information, advice, or demonstrations are given by the extension staff. While women are not prohibited from attending barazas, they rarely do so because of custom and lack of time.[2] These separate gender-based communication patterns have important consequences for the transmission of information between agricultural field staff, who are almost all men, and the female members of their rural clientele.

AGRICULTURAL SERVICES

Agricultural services in Kenya are of several types. The most common is the visit by an agricultural instructor to farmers, all of whom are equally entitled to such visits. Instructors advise farmers about husbandry practices and new crops that are being promoted by the agricultural department, as well as provide information about other services. Visits are most usually initiated by the instructor rather than the farmer and consume the largest proportion of the duties of an agriculture instructor, though only about twenty farms are visited per month, according to a study done in western Kenya (Leonard, 1973a, p. 144).

The instructors with extensive contact with farmers work at the location and sublocation level, the latter being the smallest administrative unit in Kenya. There is generally one instructor for every 1,000 to 2,000 farm households in Kakamega District. Instructors usually have a primary-school education and between one to two years of specialized training in agriculture, depending on their age and the year they entered the agricultural service. Since instructors generally live in or near the area they serve, they know the local people fairly well. Instructors also provide training in the form of demonstration plots in which a group of ten to fifty farmers is lectured on the use of fertilizers or planting in lines. When I carried out my research in the area, this technique was infrequently utilized, with, at best, one demonstration per growing season.

Training centers for farmers are located in every district in Kenya. The training consists of a one- to

two-week course on such topics as cattle husbandry and
the growing of coffee and vegetables. In my research
area, farmers perceive training as "by invitation only"
(from agricultural instructors or local administrators),
though among young farmers there was an increasing
awareness that it is a service to which they are entitled.

In the annual agricultural reports at the district
and national levels, approximately one-third of the
trainees are reported to be women. A closer examination
of courses reveals that they are generally found in home
economics courses in which a primary thrust is domestic
rather than agricultural advice. Lessons include a wide
variety of topics such as cookery, child care, sewing,
health and sanitation, nutrition, home management and
improvement, and vegetable gardening. Although courses
in home economics provide valuable information, the
agricultural aspects are significantly diluted and com-
prise, at best, 30 percent of the course. And while
courses are supposedly for all women, in practice they
tend to be restricted to certain categories, the most predominant being for "chief and assistant chief wives"
and "agricultural staff wives."[3]

Loans are available to farmers in the form of an
advance called a Guaranteed Minimum Return (GMR) for
maize seed and fertilizer, and in cash from the Agricultural Finance Corporation (AFC), a para-statal body.
A land reform program initiated by the colonial government and implemented by the independent government has
created a system of individualized land ownership.
Farmers can use land title deeds or wages as sureties
for acquiring loans.

In recent years, there have been a number of questions raised about the extension model of agricultural
service delivery, whereby instructors visit farmers and
provide them with support services. In the first place,
extension officers appear to concentrate to a large extent on the wealthy and influential farmers (alternatively called "progressive" farmers) to the detriment of
the less wealthy and poor farmers. While wealthy farmers
may be more able to withstand risk and experiment with
new crops, analysts find that an additional large segment of farmers can similarly withstand risk, yet they
are relatively ignored by the administration. It
appears that the least needy farmers receive the most
services (Leonard, 1973b; Ascroft, et al., 1972). A
second problem revolves around the capability of instructors. In a survey administered to extension personnel
in the Western Province of Kenya, Leonard found a 46 to
72 percent range of accuracy on technical points related to particular information which the Ministry of

Agriculture was attempting to convey to farmers (Leonard, 1973a, p. 134). This suggests that it may be unwise for farmers to rely solely on instructors, who may transmit incorrect information or information which contradicts other instructors.

Despite these problems, the extension model is still considered the most viable technique for providing information designed to increase agricultural productivity. Many crop and husbandry innovations have been sucessfully introduced through extension agents, including the use of oxen for plowing, the growing of hybrid maize, and planting in straight lines. Moreover, this study found that there was a high degree of association between farmers who adopted a number of innovations promoted by agricultural agents and the receipt of agricultural services. It is difficult to say, however, whether agricultural instructors were initially responsible for that innovativeness or whether instructors subsequently supported innovative behavior.

The government's orientation toward women has varied since early colonial times. A statement from Kenya's 1929 Annual Report illustrates an underlying assumption about female farmers in the evolution of agriculture. It quotes Lord Lugard, whose words were dogma for many colonial policy makers: "Since men alone tend oxen in Africa, the result, as I have elsewhere said, will be to replace female labor in the fields to a large extent" (Kenya Colony, 1929,p. 57).

Early colonial policies tended to be directed at men through a predominantly male extension service. In the late colonial era, there was some effort to incorporate agricultural services into community development work that concentrated on women. Since independence, however, there has been no explicit recognition of women's role in agriculture, nor any particular orientation to women, with the exception of the home economics program that was initiated in the last decade. Home economics as a department is so recently established and so sparsely staffed that its impact is necessarily diluted. In Kakamega District, there are approximately 300 field workers in agriculture but only three or four assistants in home economics. This means that the extension staff is, for all intents and purposes, male. Even if more home economics assistants were available, agriculture only constitutes a minor part of their activity, and women's agricultural needs would still remain unserved. While community development had a significant agricultural component in its policy during the late colonial era, it has in the last decade concentrated on community self-help activities, sports, and adult literacy classes. Therefore, the extension service is the pri-

mary means by which the government channels information
to farmers in an effort to increase agricultural productivity.

The distinction between cash crops and food crops is
not a useful one in Kakamega. Maize and beans represent
the most significant food and cash crops and are grown
both for family consumption and for sale. Within the
last decade, hybrid maize was introduced to the area and
is now utilized by all but a few farmers. In contrast
to local maize, which provides about six bags per acre,
hybrid maize has the potential to provide more than
thirty-five bags per acre if fertilizer and the proper
husbandry techniques are utilized.[4] In practice, farmers
generally double their output with the use of hybrid
maize. Coffee was also introduced to the area in the
1950s, though it is grown by less than 15 percent of the
farmers in my sample. Other innovative farm products
include passion fruit and "European" vegetables such as
cabbages, onions, and tomatoes, plus the use of grade
cows, which double the daily milk output. Agricultural
instructors are engaged in promoting new crops and productive practices associated with these innovations.


PATTERNS OF SERVICE DELIVERY

In this section, three types of agricultural services will be examined for the extent to which these
services are differentially distributed to women and
men. These three include visits from agricultural instructors, training, and loan acquisition. A visit is
the most common service, while training and loans represent the more valuable services in terms of cost to the
government and benefits to the farm.

Though a small number of farmers ask instructors to
visit their farms, most visits are initiated by the instructor. Since agricultural instructors are men, there
is a problem in transmitting information to a female
clientele, many of whom manage farms alone while husbands are working elsewhere. Conversations between women
and instructors who are not related by kinship could
arouse suspicion, particularly when husbands are absent.

Farmers were asked whether their farms had ever been
visited by an agricultural instructor, and the results
are tabulated in Table 10.1.[5] The data show that female-
managed farms are significantly less well served than are
jointly managed farms. About half the farms managed by
women have never been visited, in contrast to only a
quarter of the jointly managed farms. It appears that
a man's presence has drawing power to agricultural instructors making home visits.

TABLE 10.1
Agricultural Instructor's Visits, Farm Management Type

|                              | Female Managed | Jointly Managed |
|------------------------------|----------------|-----------------|
| Farm Never Visited           | 49% (42)       | 28% (36)        |
| Farm Visited at Least Once   | 51% (43)       | 72% (91)        |

Note:  N=212; Yules Q=.42; degree of significance=.01.


It is also important to consider the situation of
women in jointly managed farms.  There are several distinct husband-wife work patterns in joint management:
some have husbands employed locally who may take a
managerial interest in the farm; others have husbands
who work on the farm; still others have husbands who have
failed in job seeking, dislike farming, and spend most
of the day away from the home.  Due to these variations
in life situations, many women are in fact alone at the
farm during the day when agricultural instructors visit.
For the jointly managed farms, I asked whom the agricultural instructor spoke with, and a common response
was "whoever is there"--and that most frequently is the
woman.  When the husband is present during a visit, a
variety of communication patterns occur, depending on
the personalities of the couple and the agricultural instructor.  While the norm is for the husband to speak
and to represent the household, this does not necessarily
mean that the woman leaves the discussion or maintains
silence.  Women in jointly managed farms may have more
frequent and direct contact with agricultural instructors
than their husbands do.  It is difficult to determine,
however, whether or not the quality, intensity, and
duration of the communication between an instructor and
a lone woman, one whose husband is away for the day,
compares favorably with that between an instructor and
husband.  I suspect that it varies as well with the personal style of the people talking.  It is important to
bear in mind that many middle-aged and older women have
a strong sense of personal efficacy and considerable
prestige, derived from their reputation as hard-working
farmers and mothers of many children.  Thus, with in-

creasing age, the potentially problematic nature of
communication between women and instructors becomes less
important.
    Another indicator of services is attendance at a
farmer training center.  Sessions vary in length,
usually lasting one to two weeks.  Though highly subsidized by the government, a fee of Shs. 10/50 (approximately $1.50) is required, a sizeable sum for farmers
without a regular cash income.  Training represents a
direct and intensive service for farmers, as its duration is long compared to other services and it makes
available highly qualified teachers.  Agricultural instructors or local administrators generally invite
farmers to these training sessions, though it is possible for farmers to request training.  Courses are not
well publicized, which means that many farmers are un-
aware of the availability of training.
    Typically, the nearest training center is five to
fifteen miles away from most farms in the sample and
has been open since 1923.  Table 10.2 shows the results
from the sample on training by type of farm management.
(By training, I mean a person has completed a course at
the farmer training center.)  The most striking finding
is the overall low level of training, given the proximity of the center to farmers.  Aside from that, great
disparities exist between female and joint management,
with a fourfold greater likelihood of training for the
latter.  Clearly, as a vehicle for training in agriculture, centers are not serving women.


TABLE 10.2
Farmer Training, Farm Management Type

|  | Female Managed | Jointly Managed |
|---|---|---|
| None in Household Trained | 95% (80) | 80% (102) |
| One or More Household Members Trained | 5% (4) | 20% (25) |

Note: N=211; Yules Q=.66; degree of significance=.01.

Husbands are often wary about wives' being away for
extended periods of time, and, in some cases, the chief
or assistant chief must persuade husbands to allow
their wives to attend. For women managing farms alone,
a one- to two-week training period presents special
problems. They must arrange that day-to-day household
responsibilities and cultivation be provided for while
they are away. In the eighty-four female-managed farms
in the sample, only four women had ever had any training.
Of the twenty-five jointly managed farms where some member had attended a training course, six of those trained
were women, and the remainder, husbands or sons. In a
number of cases where sons were trained, they have since
moved away from the farm and found employment as cooks
and watchmen. In several cases where husbands were
trained, it was evident that the men were old and, for
all practical purposes, retired from active farm work.
The invitation to be trained appears to be a status-
conferring mechanism for some farmers. Nonetheless, it
is still an activity that requires motivation on the
farmer's part because it requires a good deal of time
and financial commitment. Such examples illustrate the
waste involved in extending training to a precious few.
There is more likelihood that trained women will remain
on the farm and engage in farm work than trained men.
Most women are full-time farmers, both in the sense of
the number of hours they work daily and of the continuity
of farm work throughout their life. Men, in contrast,
tend to seek outside employment during youth and middle
age and retire to the farm when old.

The ability to acquire a loan is a crucial indicator
in any assessment of agricultural services. Information
about loans and contacts with knowledgeable people are
important resources in learning how to obtain a loan.
Information about the loan procedures comes from associ-
ating with agricultural instructors and local administrators, attending barazas, and participating on committees. These contacts, knowledge, and experience de-
note a kind of sophistication and an ability to argue
persuasively one's case, be it for a loan or something
else. Contacts and influence are solidified by blood
and clan ties; women, who are relatives only by marriage
(the practice of exogamy), do not have access to those
kinds of ties. Moreover, women are informally discouraged from publicly participating in barazas and fre-
quenting bars and beer clubs.[6] They participate on
development committees as token representatives but have
only minimal access to situations where influence and
assertiveness are acquired. Additionally, as previously
documented, women have less intensive contacts than men
with agricultural personnel.

To acquire a loan, one must have either a title deed
to land or a regular salary to serve as sureties.[7]  Title
deeds are for the most part held in the husband's name,
and wage employment is more readily available to men,
who are more educated and have a wider array of employment options than women.  Therefore, if a woman wants a
loan, she must persuade her husband, who then puts up a
guarantee in the form of a title deed or salary.  If
husbands are not regularly at home, or are not interested in the farm, this may be difficult to arrange.  The
only genuinely independent women for loan purposes are
widows, who can arrange legally to have the title deed
transferred to their names (a process much more complicated and costly than for the male).  The few women who
do purchase land are usually employed in the government
or the schools, but they are few indeed, given the population density and the high cost of land in that area.
Putting title deeds in male names, a result of land reform, has solidified male control over a powerful resource, and this has obvious implications for acquiring
other resources as well.

Table 10.3 shows whether the respondents knew anything about loans, about loan procedures, or had actually
received a loan, by type of farm management.  What is
very evident is the extremely few loans--only three--
acquired by the 211 households, and these loans went to
jointly managed farms.  I inquired from farmers whether
or not they had ever applied for a loan or if they knew
how to do so, and an additional small proportion could
correctly relate the application procedure.[8]  Quite
significantly, only one of the nineteen households that
had either received a loan or been aware of the application processes was female-managed.  That particular
woman was not only wealthy but was linked to the local
power structure by membership on the development committee, by marriage to another committee member (though
absent), and by an in-law relationship with the local
politician.

Clearly, loans are not part of the repertoire of
services that ordinary farmers either expect or desire.
This is in great contrast to local elite farmers (not
included in this study), who have access to other resources that make the risks of borrowing less onerous.
Nevertheless, the contrast in access to loans between
men and women is quite striking, and these figures represent a sample of farmers that had had access to AFC loans
for three years.  Such grave disparities in the initial
stages of dispensing loans may grow wider; the long-term
consequences of women's not gaining access to this
highly valued resource are significant.

TABLE 10.3
Loan Information Acquisition, Farm Management Type

|  | Female Managed | Jointly Managed |
|---|---|---|
| Knew Nothing About | 99% (83) | 86% (109) |
| Knew Application Process or Had Applied for Loan | 1% (1) | 12% (15) |
| Acquired Loan | -- | 2% (3) |

Note: N=211; Gamma=.86; degree of significance=.01.


ECONOMIC FACTORS AND WILLINGNESS TO INNOVATE

     All farmers are entitled to extension services and,
ideally, their sex should have no impact on who gets
what services.  In reality, however, it appears to have
a substantial impact, as has been demonstrated.  Perhaps
extension personnel perceive women as unwilling or unable to adopt innovations and therefore avoid visiting
female managers.  The data collected make it possible
to test whether or not such an assumption has any base
in reality.  In this section, I will examine the effect
of economic standing, size of farm, and the early adoption of innovations on patterns of service delivery.
     Access to cash is essential if many innovations are
to be adopted.  For instance, money is required to purchase new brands of seed and chemical fertilizers or to
hire laborers.  Women acquire money from a number of
sources--the sale of produce, the brewing of beer, and
from husbands who work for wages and send money home.
I developed a five-point scale to measure access to
cash.[9]  The mean score was identical for both female and
jointly managed farms.  For purposes of simplicity, the
income scale was dichotomized into low and high, with
low representing a near-subsistence living style with
little access to cash.  Only slightly more female-
managed farms were in the low category (58 percent) than
were jointly managed farms (54 percent).
     Table 10.4 examines how economic standing and type
of farm management affects visits by agricultural in-

structors.  The data support other studies, which show
a tendency for access to services to increase with
wealth.  What is striking about the table, however, is
not so much that poor women receive the fewest visits,
which is fairly predictable, but that this bias is maintained even at higher economic levels.  In fact, the
proportion of women farm managers receiving services at
higher economic levels is exactly the same as that of
jointly managed farms in the lower economic category.
Thus, the argument that women are justifiably ignored
because they lack cash and hence the means by which to
experiment with new crops does not hold.

TABLE 10.4
Agricultural Instructor's Visits, Farm Management Type,
Controlled for Economic Standing

|  | Low | | High | |
|  | Female | Joint | Female | Joint |
| --- | --- | --- | --- | --- |
| No Visit | 57% (28) | 39% (27) | 39% (14) | 16% (9) |
| Visited 1[+] Times | 43% (21) | 61% (42) | 61% (22) | 84% (49) |
|  | N=118 | | N=94 | |

Similar reasoning on the part of extension officers
might occur with respect to land.  They might perceive
women as holding such small parcels of land that they
had no land on which to experiment with new crops.  The
minimal size considered an "economic" holding by the
divisional land board is four acres, though in practice
the mean and median measures of farms are well below that
minimum.  There is a slight tendency for women managers
to inflate low acreage categories because approximately
a quarter of them are widows whose sons and daughters-in-
law utilize the major portion of their husbands' land.
Widows are, in fact, somewhat more likely to receive
services because of their age and long residence in the
community.
    Table 10.5 presents only those farms which are over

five acres. Women, as 40 percent of the entire sample, are only slightly underrepresented in the large-farm category. Though the numerical size of this group demands cautious interpretation, it is evident that even women managers with extensive acreage are discriminated against in access to services. Farmers with large acreages tend also to have higher economic status, and thus both the required money and needed land on which to try new crop and husbandry practices. Explaining away the disparity in visits on the basis of lack of land simply cannot be done.

TABLE 10.5
Agricultural Instructor's Visits, Farm Management Type
(Farm Over 5 Acres)

|                            | Female Managed | Jointly Managed |
|----------------------------|----------------|-----------------|
| No Visit                   | 38% (3)        | 7%  (1)         |
| Visited 1+ Times           | 62% (5)        | 93% (14)        |

Note:  N=23; Yules Q=.79.

Another assumption that might lead agricultural instructors to neglect certain categories of their clientele might be a perception that women managers are unwilling to try new ideas. An examination of the mean numbers of cash or food crops adopted by farm management type reveals only very slight differences, despite the additional labor available to jointly managed farms because of the presence of two or more adults. [10]
Another way to examine responsiveness is to compare the earliness with which farmers adopt new crops. The most significant innovation in recent years is the introduction of hybrid maize. Both female and joint farm managers averaged a three and one-half year period from the time they had begun using hybrid maize. In an examination of early adopters--that is, farmers who grew hybrid maize as early as five or more years ago--it was found that a significant proportion of the women managers have never been visited by extension officers. Table 10.6 illustrates this finding. Almost a third of

the women who were early adopters had no administrative
support or advice for such a move, while only 3 percent
of farms with a man present were so neglected.  This
might suggest an even greater innovativeness on the part
of female managers compared to jointly managed farms,
since to make such a decision without expert advice
probably required autonomy, self-reliance, and a willingness to take a risk, qualities fostered by these women's
independent lifestyles. Yet, despite their responsiveness, innovative women farmers tend to be ignored, compared with their male counterparts.


TABLE 10.6
Agricultural Instructor's Visits, Farm Management Type
(Early Adopters of Hybrid Maize)

|                           | Female Managed | Jointly Managed |
|---------------------------|----------------|-----------------|
| No Visit                  | 31% (5)        | 3% (1)          |
| Visited $1^+$ Times       | 69% (11)       | 97% (33)        |

Note: N=50.


CONCLUSION

   Women managers experience a persistent and pervasive
bias in the delivery of agricultural services, services
to which they are entitled.  Indeed, the bias increases
in intensity as the value of the service increases and
it makes no difference whether the women have high
economic status, large farms, or have shown a willingness to adopt agricultural innovations.  Yet, despite
these inequities women managers appear to be as productive and as adaptive as male farmers.
   This discrimination appears to be the result of prejudice against women.  Early policy pronouncements were
directed primarily to men, and the agricultural extension service is largely composed of men.  Present communication patterns, at least in rural Kenya, tend to
occur among members of one sex, rather than between the
sexes.  Although administrative attitudes were not a

prime focus of my research, I spoke with a number of agricultural instructors and found that a third expressed somewhat prejudicial attitudes toward women.[11] Thus, the majority did not express overtly prejudicial attitudes.  Women were apparently avoided because of customary patterns whereby men spoke to men and women to women.  This practice is evident in the following quotations from agricultural personnel:  "In the African way, we speak to the man who is the head of the house and assume he will pass on the information to other household members."  "Being men, of course it is easier for us to persuade men."[12]

In farms where there is a man present, women farmers may benefit from agricultural services because the presence of a man places the farm within the communication network of the extension service.  But farms managed by women, and those represent a sizeable portion of farm households, are not in those networks and are thus ignored.

Women have managed to maintain farm productivity largely without the aid or encouragement of the agricultural service.  Though not discussed in this paper, the diffusion of agricultural information was found to occur among women's networks, particularly among the numerous women's communal agricultural and mutual-aid associations.  In the short run this strategy is effective, but in the long run, women's associational activity may not be able to compensate for the increasingly valuable services being provided to farmers.  Unless this discrimination is eradicated, the future appears grim both for women's productivity and the economy as a whole.


NOTES

1.  A geographically purposive sample of 212 farm households was obtained in the Idakho location research site between December 1974 and June 1975.  It represents 10 percent of the total number of households in the geographic areas targeted.  My initial concern was to assure that varying distances from the road and main paths, and thus from agricultural instructors and services, would be covered.  These geographic areas coincide with clan and subclan identities.  Once spatial areas were designated in order to obtain geographic and clan representativeness,  I attempted to select farms that would be representative of varying economic standings and age groupings.  Numbers were based on my approximations of their proportion of the population.  I did not know in advance, however, about who managed the farm until the interview had begun.  The close correspondence

of women managers to the proportion of female heads in
Kakamega reported in the 1969 Census supports the notion
that my choice of farmers was "chancelike" in method.
The sample is not, however, a random one, and the uni-
verse of this sample is restricted to one location. The
sample does not purport to generalize to all of Kenya
or Africa, but rather to illustrate sex differences
within a sample, which may be suggestive for other parts
of Kenya or Africa with agriculturally based economies
in areas of high population density and rates of male
out-migration. Though scientific sampling techniques
were not utilized, I am confident that the sample
judiciously represents a reasonable cross-section of
farmers in western Kenya. The basis of this confidence
is my six-month residence in one of the sublocations
studied with a family who graciously welcomed me as an
additional member. Through my residence there and my
participation in community life, I gained in-depth knowledge of that subclan and that geographic area. A female research assistant from the area and I conducted
the interviews, and she translated questions and responses from Luhya to English. We asked a systematic
set of questions from each farmer about crops, husbandry
practices, sources of information about farm practices,
agricultural services, and demographic information. A
typical interview took forty minutes.

2. I attended a number of barazas and never were
there more than 10 percent women in attendance.

3. The national figures of one-third women remain
relatively constant from the late colonial era until
the late 1960s and are reported in the Ministry of
Agriculture Annual Reports. Figures about the portion
of classes devoted to vegetable gardening and the restriction of courses to the wives of administrative personnel were found in Kakamega District Annual Reports in
agriculture, 1970-1973.

4. One bag is 200 pounds, or 90 kilos.

5. See the sample technique utilized, n.1. Because
this is not a random sample and thus does not purport a
normal distribution, the chi-square tests of significance are technically not appropriate. The size of the
sample may mean it approximates a normal distribution,
and thus tests of significance have been included for
exploratory purposes. Table sizes of less than 212
indicate missing data or are subsamples, as specified
in the table title. Numbers have been rounded off to
the nearest percentage.

6. See n.2 on women's baraza attendance. While
some women do drink, it is frowned upon for the majority
of ordinary women and prohibited by the Protestant and
African Independent churches in the area, many devout

members of which are women.

7. These sureties are for the most common type of loan in the area, one from the Agricultural Finance Corporation (AFC), which has made loans available since 1973 when the sublocations studied had completed the land-reform process and were declared adjudicated areas.

8. Given the short time period (three years) in which AFC loans have been available, farmers who may have their loan application denied have not been formally notified but merely experience delay in response to their loan request. Therefore, that category of farmers who knew about loan applications includes both those who knew the procedure and those who applied, regardless of whether it has been informally denied by the delay, or may be formally denied in the distant future.

9. The income scale was based on the value of the house and included such characteristics as the type of roof and the construction of the floor and walls and the possession of material goods such as the type and quantity of furniture.

10. For analytic purposes, these are divided into food and cash crops, though hybrid maize is included in both categories. The cash crops include the hybrid maize-beans combination, coffee, European vegetables, passion fruit, and sugar cane. The food crops include the hybrid maize-beans combination, European vegetables, root crops (sweet potato or cassava), millet crops (finger millet or sorghum), and nut crops (groundnuts or monkey nuts). Mean adoption rates are as follows:

|  | Female Managed | Jointly Managed |
| --- | --- | --- |
| Cash Crops | 1.5 | 1.5 |
| Food Crops | 1.9 | 2.0 |

11. I interviewed a dozen male agricultural instructors, several of whom were interviewed a number of times, at various levels in the administrative hierarchy in Kakamega.

12. First interview at Bukura, Dec. 1974; second, in Idakho, Feb. 1975.

REFERENCES

Ascroft, Joseph, et al. 1972. "Does Extension Create Poverty in Kenya?" East African Journal (March).
Boserup, Ester. 1970. Woman's Role in Economic Development. London: Allen and Unwin.

Kenya Colony and Protectorate.1929.  Annual Report.
    London: HMSO.
Kenya, Republic of. 1963-68.  Ministry of Agriculture.
    Annual Reports.  Nairobi: Government Printer.
    _____. 1969-73.  Ministry of Agriculture.  Kakamega
    District.  Annual Reports.  Mimeographed.
Leonard, David K. 1973a.  "Organizational Structures for
    Productivity in Agricultural Extension." In Rural
    Administration in Kenya, ed. David K. Leonard.
    Nairobi: East African Literature Bureau.
    _____. 1973b.  "Why Do Kenya's Agricultural Exten-
    sion Services Favor the Rich Farmer?"  Paper pre-
    sented to the 16th Annual Meeting of the African
    Studies Association, Syracuse, N.Y., Oct.-Nov.
Mbilinyi, Marjorie. 1972.  "The 'New Woman' and Tradi-
    tional Norms in Tanzania."  Journal of Modern
    African Studies 10:57-72.
Sangree, Walter. 1966. Age, Prayer, and Politics in
    Tiriki, Kenya.  London: Oxford University Press.
Tinker, Irene, and Michele B. Bramsen, eds. 1976.  Women
    and World Development.  Washington: Overseas Develop-
    ment Council.
UN/ECA. 1974.  "The Changing and Contemporary Role of
    Women in African Development."
Wagner, Gunter. 1949.  The Bantu of North Kavirondo,
    vol. 1.  London: Oxford University Press.

## 11. Women's Employment and Development: A Conceptual Framework Applied to Ghana

*William F. Steel*
*Claudia Campbell*

INTRODUCTION

Employment of women in less developed countries bears on both the sources and the impacts of development. Growth of incomes in the commercial economy requires a shift of labor from subsistence production (i.e., for direct household consumption) into production for the market, and full productive use of available labor resources is critical for sustained socioeconomic development. The actual and potential contributions made by women to development have, however, been too frequently ignored and underutilized. At the same time, increasing concern for dependent relationships (between individuals as well as between nations) associated with development and for the status of women has focused attention on the way development affects women's socioeconomic position. Much of the literature on these issues uses women's employment as an index both of their contribution to development and of their socioeconomic independence (Boserup, 1970; Boulding, 1976; Chapman and Gates, 1976; Giele and Smock, 1977; Tinker, 1976; Youssef, 1974).

This paper seeks to provide a conceptual framework for analyzing the interrelationship between development and women's employment, focusing on variables that determine the impact of development on employment and labor force participation. Women's three-way choice between market employment, home production, and leisure is introduced, and the importance of attitudinal variables is discussed. Supply and demand interactions are analyzed,

The views expressed in this paper are those of the authors and not necessarily those of their institutions. We are grateful for comments and suggestions from Karamat Ali, David Dunlop, Sam Morley, Yasmeen Mohiuddin, and Claire Robertson.

with particular emphasis on the role of labor market
discrimination. Different patterns of market employment are related to the concept of female economic independence. A distinction is drawn between the effects of
industrialization and of development for women's employment opportunities and labor force participation.

The second section of the paper utilizes this conceptual framework to analyze the possible explanations
for the dramatic increases in female labor force participation (FLFP) and employment in Ghana over 1960-70. It
is argued that sociocultural obstacles to female market
activity are minimal, although women's opportunities are
limited somewhat by biases in education and occupational
structure. Increased demand and decreased discrimination
are found to be inadequate explanations for the observed
changes. The increase in FLFP is explained principally
as an effort to maintain the level and growth of real
family income, in response to the stagnation of income
per capita during the 1960s. The paper concludes by
pointing out that female employment growth is not necessarily a sign that development has benefited women.


CONCEPTUAL FRAMEWORK

Labor Force Participation and Sexism

Mainstream labor economics focuses on the choice
between wage employment and "leisure." This framework
is, however, inapplicable to women's decisions about
economic participation in most societies because it ignores the economic value of goods and services produced
within the household, the major cost of being employed
(i.e., the opportunity cost of market employment) experienced by women charged with responsibility for food
preparation, child care, and housekeeping. A growing
literature on female and household employment decisions
is based on a tripartite labor-supply model, including
home production as well as market work and leisure.[1]  In
this model, female labor supply depends not only on the
available wage but also on other family income, which
affects the demand for household production and can also
buy goods that substitute for it. A rising market wage
stimulates increased female labor supply by raising the
opportunity cost of home production ("substitution
effect"). Increased income from the husband or family
(including from higher female wages) is generally found
to have a negative effect on female labor supply ("income
effect") (Bowen and Finegan, 1969; McCabe and Rosenzweig,
1976; Mincer, 1962; Smith, 1972). Conversely, a decrease
in male or family income tends to increase FLFP, to make

up the lost income ("additional worker effect").

These improvements in modeling the determinants of female employment have been primarily static and oriented toward economic variables influencing supply.  Less attention has been paid to sexism as it affects supply through sociocultural traditions and demand through discrimination.  These issues are important because differences in social attitudes can explain supply differences both between countries or regions and over time within a country, and because failure to distinguish between the operation of sexism on supply and on demand can lead to misinterpretation of results.

Attention to cultural determinants of labor supply has focused mainly on the restrictive effect of Islamic traditions on female labor force participation (e.g., Boulding, 1976).  Islamic prohibitions against female contact with men outside the family impose a heavy social cost on women who nevertheless decide to seek market employment, and their choice of occupations is sharply restricted.[2]  Less formalized social norms regarding women's "proper" place (e.g., in the home) exert similar if less apparent pressures.  Differences in women's attitudes toward the acceptability of market employment is a potentially significant determinant of differences in female labor force participation in static comparisons across countries or even regions within a country.[3]  Dynamic studies over time in a single country are particularly subject to bias resulting from the omission of this attitudinal variable, if a movement away from cultural inhibitions against women seeking employment reduces the noneconomic costs of FLFP.  At the least, the possibility that such a change explains observed increases in FLFP must be examined.

Only a few studies of women's employment analyze the demand as well as the supply side (Blitz and Ow, 1973; Kreps, 1971; Oppenheimer, 1970).  It is particularly important to know whether observed employment and wage changes are due to shifts in demand, supply, or (more likely) both.  Figure 11.1 illustrates that a demand-induced employment increase is accompanied by an increase in the average wage (and hence in total income), whereas an increase originating solely in supply involves a lower wage (and possibly lower total income).  If both supply and demand shift, the wage could remain the same, rise, or fall.  In dynamic terms, the question is whether demand (at a given wage) is growing faster than, slower than, or at the same rate as supply.  In comparing FLFP in different countries or for two points in time, the analyst must take account of differences or changes in discrimination that affect demand for female workers.

228

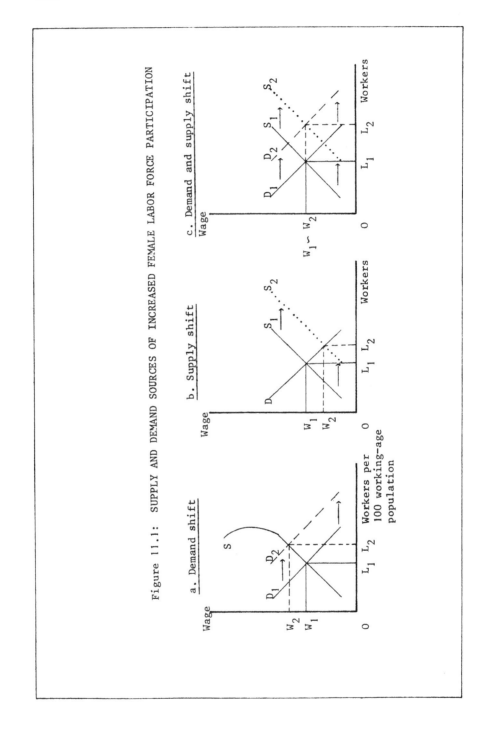

Figure 11.1:  SUPPLY AND DEMAND SOURCES OF INCREASED FEMALE LABOR FORCE PARTICIPATION

Labor market discrimination against women may be manifested in a higher unemployment rate, exclusion from certain occupations, and lower wages for equivalent work compared to men.[4] Static and dynamic considerations must be clearly separated. In static analysis, the question is the difference between actual female employment, occupational choice, and wages and what would obtain without discrimination. Over time, changes in discrimination must be taken into account as possible explanations for changes in female employment and incomes. Even when discrimination is constant, it can affect the relationship between development and female employment if growth is centered on occupations from which women are excluded. Two questions must be asked: (1) are employment changes biased for or against women? and (2) has the degree of bias changed?

Socioeconomic development can affect both supply of and demand for female employment through its effects on attitudes and discrimination. Separation of the supply and demand sides is important because changes can move in opposite directions. Historically, industrialization has been associated both with increased demand for wage labor based on productivity rather than personal characteristics such as sex, and with a tendency to relegate women to homemaking roles as production moves out of the home and men take on a role as principal income earners. Conversely, women in many African countries are expected to earn cash income outside the home but are restricted from certain occupations. Labor market discrimination may be high in a country that nevertheless has no tradition against women's working outside the home, while another country where FLFP is discouraged may treat on an equal basis those women who do enter. Thus, attitudes that raise the psychological cost of women's supplying their labor to the market must be distinguished from labor market discrimination that restricts the demand for their services.

## Economic Dependence

"Dependence" in its most general sense means reliance of one entity on another for support and maintenance. In terms of international political economy, dependent nations are those whose trade, investment, and decision making are dominated by more powerful nations or by external forces. In demographic terms, the proportion of the population presumed too young or too old to support themselves determines the dependency ratio. We use the term "female economic dependence" to refer to reliance of adult married women on their husbands for the cash income necessary to buy goods and services sold on the market.

Different patterns of female economic dependence and independence are represented in Table 11.1 in terms of participation by husband and wife in household and market production.[5]  Our emphasis on the process by which women choose to move from home production to wage employment leads us to exclude from the discussion non-market economies (line A) and the "leisure class," in which women are not substantially engaged even in home production (line D).  We classify the remaining female economic relationships as follows:

Dependence:  the woman has access to market goods only through her husband's income (lines B and C, column 2);

Semidependence: most household market goods are pur-chased out of the husband's income, but the woman earns some income over which she has direct control (line B, column 1);

Independence:  the woman earns enough income directly to provide substantially all her basic needs (and those of her children, if she is responsible for them) beyond what is met through household production (line C, column 1, and also line B, column 1, when the woman's income is above the poverty level).

Since our definition is based heavily on income, it is possible for a woman (or a man) to be working full time in the market and not be considered independent.[6] The degree of dependence also depends on the relative size of the man's and woman's income and their arrange-ments (if any) for sharing their joint income.  It is therefore possible for women to become more dependent even when their labor force participation increases, if the increase is accompanied by a decline in their real wage or a greater increase in male employment and earnings.  Hence, development must be analyzed in terms of its impact on women's incomes, not just employment, to understand its implications for women's economic position.  We must also examine relative changes, com-pared to men, not just absolute changes.

Since a state of dependence implies that one is to some extent subordinated to and controlled by another, the latter has an incentive to try to create and maintain that state (whether for social, political, or economic power).  Whether intentional or not, subordination is the consequence of cultural norms inhibiting women from seeking wage employment and of labor market discrimina-tion, as discussed earlier in relation to determinants of female labor supply and demand.  Thus, in order to understand the implications of development for women's socioeconomic status (as indicated by dependence), we must also examine its effect on attitudes toward women's role and on sex discrimination.

TABLE 11.1
Patterns of Female Economic Dependence and Independence

| Household economic orientation | 1. Economic independence[a] | | 2. Female dependence[b] | |
|---|---|---|---|---|
| | Household production (1a) | Market production (1b) | Household production (2a) | Market production (2b) |
| A. Nonmarket (subsistence) | (F,M)[c] | | | |
| B. Market oriented | (F,M)[c] | (M,F)[c] | F,M | M |
| C. Fully specialized | | (M,F)[c] | F | M |
| D. Leisure class[d] | | | | M |

Note: F denotes activity by female, M by male.

[a] For single-person households (with or without children), delete either M or F.

[b] For male dependence, switch F and M.

[c] The amount of time spent (or income earned) may be equal for both or greater for one. If the female works only part time in the market while the male works full time or earns only a relatively small portion of family income, she may be considered in a status of semi-independence.

[d] Income may be derived from assets rather than earnings, in which case the household might be classified as "idle rich."

Development and Female Employment

Economic development may be defined as a shift toward a more monetized economy with increased access to
goods and services through rising personal incomes and/or
provision of public services.  Development is generally
accompanied by industrialization, but we find it important to distinguish the effects of industrialization from
those of development in general.  The extent to which
women have access to increased opportunities for income-earning employment and to public services such as
education determines the extent to which development im-
proves their status.  Industrialization tends to be
biased against female employment in that it requires
full-time work away from home and therefore is not
readily compatible with the child rearing and homemaking
responsibilities that most societies continue to assign
to women.  In addition, production in large-scale industries employing a predominantly male work force competes
directly with simple manufactures produced in cottage
industries, often an important source of income for women
in early developing economies (Boserup, 1970, p. 111;
Galbraith, 1973, p. 31).  Industrialization of economies
in which women are active in agricultural or small-scale
production is therefore likely to reduce their economic
independence.[7]  Hence, we must analyze the extent to which
the jobs created by industrialization are accessible to
women.
    Development as a whole, on the other hand, exerts
some indirect pressures that are likely to increase
women's income-earning opportunities.  Urbanization
tends to break up the extended family structure and,
therefore, the customs regarding women's role that may be
perpetuated by it.  Increasing emphasis on money also may
help overcome any inhibitions against women's supplying
their labor for cash income.  On the demand side, urbanization creates many income-earning opportunities that are
compatible with domestic duties, especially trading and
preparing food for sale.  An emphasis on growth of production and profit motivation helps break down any labor
market discrimination that may have existed.  Public
investment in education can improve women's access to
a wider range of employment, although a bias of education toward men can also serve as a discriminatory tool
to limit women's opportunities and wages.  To the extent
that public health expenditures reduce fertility, the
cost of women's entering the labor market or the duration
of their withdrawal is reduced.[8]  Comparisons of FLFP
between countries or over time must therefore take into
account the differences in urbanization, education,
fertility, and other determinants of female labor supply
and demand that may be associated with development.

## Summary of the Conceptual Framework

Our discussion implies that analysis of the inter-relationship between development and women's employment must begin with an understanding of the sociocultural influences on women's attitudes toward market employment and on sex-related discrimination in the labor market. Indicators of the extent to which women are free to enter the labor market include familial systems, marriage and divorce patterns, the role of women as providers of family income, legal status, and religion. The responsiveness of women to the economic determinants normally included in labor force participation models is conditioned by these sociocultural attitudes and by changes in them. That is, female labor supply is affected by social norms, education, fertility, etc., as well as by the market wage and family income. The importance of these variables should be assessed qualitatively even if they cannot be measured quantitatively.

Women's employment provides a useful indicator of the effect of development on women's status only if both supply and demand sides are taken into account. A supply shift in the face of inelastic demand can actually reduce the total absolute (as well as relative) economic power of women. Demand-stimulated employment increases, on the other hand, are more likely to improve women's economic position. Here again, there is simultaneous interaction, as demand pressure may reduce sexist discrimination in employment, wages, and occupation, while an autonomous decrease in discrimination itself stimulates demand. The existence of sex-related biases in these variables must first be determined, for new employment as well as for the existing structure. The continuing existence of bias must be distinguished from the trend over time in such biases. Development may appear to improve women's economic position from one point of view, while from another it may only be reducing their relative disadvantage. The remainder of the paper applies this framework to an analysis of the meaning of trends in women's employment in Ghana over 1960-70.

## APPLICATION TO GHANA

### Trends in Aggregate Female and Male Employment

Aggregate measures of Ghana's employment experience over 1960-70 mask a major shift toward increased female market activity. Total labor force participation (Table 11.2, section A) remained steady at 73 percent, reflecting labor force growth at the same 2.2 percent

TABLE 11.2
Labor Force Participation and Growth by Sex, 1960-70 (percentage)

| | Total | | Women | | Men | |
|---|---|---|---|---|---|---|
| | 1960 | 1970 | 1960 | 1970 | 1960 | 1970 |
| | (1) | (2) | (3) | (4) | (5) | (6) |
| A. Labor Force Participation Rates | | | | | | |
| 1. Total, ages 15 and over | 73.0 | 73.3 | 56.7 | 63.6 | 89.0 | 83.5 |
| 2. Age-specific[a] | | | | | | |
| a. 15-19 | 57.2 | 40.8 | 53.3 | 39.2 | 61.0 | 42.3 |
| b. 20 and over | 75.7 | 80.0 | 57.2 | 68.3 | 93.8 | 92.5 |
| B. Employment Growth (average percent per annum) | 1960-70 | | 1960-70 | | 1960-70 | |
| 1. Labor force, total ages 15 and over | 2.2 | | 4.1 | | 1.1 | |
| 2. Employment, all sectors | | | | | | |
| a. Total | 2.2 | | 4.3 | | 1.0 | |
| b. Modern[b] | 3.5 | | 15.6 | | 2.9 | |
| 3. Nonagricultural employment | | | | | | |
| a. Total | 3.7 | | 5.6 | | 2.4 | |
| b. Modern | 4.5 | | 15.2 | | 4.0 | |

C. Shares of Additional Employment

1. Female & male shares of
   additional employment

   | | | |
   |---|---|---|
   | a. Total employment increase | 100.0 | 73.9 | 26.1 |
   | b. Nonagricultural | 100.0 | 63.0 | 37.0 |
   | c. Modern, total | 100.0 | 34.1 | 65.9 |
   | d. Modern, nonagricultural | 100.0 | 24.3 | 75.7 |

2. Modern sector share of employment increase

   | | |
   |---|---|
   | a. Total employment increase | 20.3 | 6.2 | 61.2 |
   | b. Nonagricultural employment increase | 34.1 | 9.4 | 72.3 |

Source: Ghana: 1960 Population Census, Vol. IV, Tables 1,3, and 10, and 1970, Vol. II, Table 1 (worksheets), and Vol. IV, Tables 3 and 18 (worksheets); Labour Statistics, 1960, Table 3 and 1970, Table 3.

aFor further details, see Table 11.3.

b"Modern" denotes employment recorded in Labour Statistics (approximates all establishments with 10 or more employees), with the following adjustment: the figure reported
for public administration in the 1970 Census has been taken as representing the
modern sector, rather than the Labour Statistics figure (which would drastically
underestimate the growth of the government sector from 1960 to 1970. This adjustment
raises the growth rate of modern sector employment by half and doubles the rate for
men, but it has relatively little effect on the rate for women.

average annual rate as population age fifteen and over
(but slower than the approximately 2.9 percent overall
population growth rate). Female labor force participation, however, jumped from 57 percent to 68 percent among
women age twenty and over, while the male rate fell in-
significantly from 94 percent to 93 percent. The rapid
4.1 percent annual growth of the female labor force age
fifteen and over was almost four times the male growth
rate. Women accounted for almost three-quarters of the
aggregate increase in employment between the 1960 and
1970 censuses.[9]

Employment growth data show that nonagricultural
activities, especially in the modern sector,[10] led the
increase. Nonagricultural employment grew at an average
annual rate of 3.7 percent, while the modern sector grew
at 3.5 percent, absorbing 20 percent of the total employment increase and 34 percent of additional nonagricultural jobs (Table 11.2, sections B and C.2). The impact
of modernization on female employment appears to be
especially strong, with a 15.6 percent average annual
growth of female modern sector employment.

Before concluding that the rapid rise of female
employment was the result of increased demand generated
by modernization, one must remember that the high female modern sector growth rate was from a very low base:
women constituted less than 5 percent of recorded employment in 1960 (Ghana, Labour Statistics, 1960, Table 3).
Modern sector employment remained strongly biased against
women in the 1960s, even though the bias was less than
previously: women filled only one-quarter of the net
addition to modern nonagricultural jobs from 1960 to
1970 and men three-quarters, the opposite of their shares
of the total employment increase (Table 11.2, section C).
The notion that modern sector expansion stimulated increased female employment and labor force participation
is called into question by the small proportion of additional female employment absorbed into the modern sector: less than 10 percent even for nonagricultural
activities, whereas the modern sector accounted for 72
percent of the net increase in male nonagricultural employment over 1960-70. The reduction in degree of bias,
represented by the near doubling of women's share of
modern sector employment, masks the strong bias of the
modern employment increase toward male workers.

In order to interpret this conflicting evidence regarding the impact of modernization on female employment
behavior, we will examine some variables that can indicate the relative importance of demand and supply shifts.
The relatively rapid rise of female employment and participation may be chiefly a response[11] to rapidly rising
demand for female labor as a result of: (1) reduced wage

and occupational discrimination in the labor market, leading to improved wage opportunities; (2) reduced employment discrimination, leading to lower unemployment and a higher probability of finding a job (especially in the modern, high-wage sector); and/or (3) a faster rise in demand for goods and services produced in female-dominated industries and occupations. On the other hand, the dominant source of increased participation could be a shift in supply due to: (1) stagnant real family income, drawing inactive workers into the market in an attempt to maintain income;[12] (2) reduced sociocultural pressure against women's entering the labor force; and/or (3) demographic changes resulting in an increased share of women in age groups or areas with high participation in the labor market. The first step in the analysis is to examine the determinants of women's economic role in Ghana and the extent of discrimination in the labor market.

## Women's Status and Economic Independence in Ghana

Women have a high degree of socioeconomic independence under both the matrilineal and patrilineal family systems prevalent in different parts of Ghana. Transfer of wealth occurs primarily between blood relations rather than between husband and wife, and children retain strong obligations to their parents and blood relatives (North, et al., 1975, pp. 4-5). Perhaps because family bonds remain so strong, marriages tend to be rather unstable, so that women often are the primary family income earner.[13] In addition, husbands and wives not infrequently live apart, due to local custom or temporary male migration. Although actual practice of polygamy is on the wane, this tradition adds to women's concern to find an independent source of income for themselves and their children.

Even in a stable, monogamous marriage, women are generally expected to provide income for certain basic household expenses and often for additional expenses such as their own clothing. Although women are also responsible for child care, food preparation, and other housework, the extended family system enables working-age women to leave many of these chores to younger and older relatives while working outside the home. Nevertheless, many women "equate financial dependence on a husband with high-status marriage" (Robertson, 1976, p. 125).

Ghanaian law does not restrict female economic activity--even though illiteracy and social customs often prevent full and equal application of the law in practice (North, et al., 1975, p. 4). Ghanaian women have the right to own and purchase property, enter into business

contracts, borrow money from banks, and receive equal
treatment in employment and education.  The only major
sociocultural tradition tending to restrict women's
economic activity is Islam, which is especially prevalent
in the north.  Restrictions against women's interacting
with men and the generally protective attitude toward
women on the one hand, and the security afforded by strong
prohibitions against divorce on the other, reduce the responsiveness of Muslim women to incentives to work outside
the home.
     These sociocultural patterns imply relatively little
constraint in Ghana on women's seeking income outside
the home, except among the Islamic community, and indeed
some pressure to do so.  Hence, we may expect the supply
of female labor to be responsive to economic incentives
and conditions.  The effectiveness of these incentives
may be seen in the high FLFP rate in Ghana relative to
other developing countries, rising from 56.7 percent in
1960 to 63.6 percent in 1970 and accounting for 38.7 percent and 45.2 percent of total employment in those
years.[14]

## Labor Market Biases

     The fact that women are expected to participate in
earning incomes does not signify an absence of biases
regarding appropriate male and female roles.  Many occupations are identified with one sex or the other, and
the range of activities considered appropriate for women
is particularly limited.  No women are found in 14 of
the 75 occupations recorded in the 1970 Labour Statistics,
whereas men are in all.[15]  Of 72 detailed industries
identified in census statistics for 1960, females constitute over 80 percent of employment in only 4, all of them
with more than 90 percent of employment in small-scale
enterprises, whereas 26 industries (over a third) are
more than 95 percent male dominated, at least 13 of them
with more than 10 percent of employment in the modern
sector.  Little change in this sex-typing is evident
over 1960-70: the female-dominated industries still had
over 90 percent female employment in 1970, while 18 of
the male-dominated industries remained over 95 percent
male in 1970 and only three of them fell below 90 percent male.
     Male dominance of the modern sector, which generally
imposes educational barriers in hiring, and of occupations
requiring training reflects the sex bias in education.
In 1960, females represented 34.9 percent of enrollment
in primary schools, 28.2 percent in middle schools, 18.1
percent in secondary schools, and 4.4 percent in universities (UNESCO Statistical Yearbook, 1969 and 1974).
These shares, however, are not as low as female shares

of modern sector employment and most predominantly
male industries. Furthermore, women constitute a higher
share of professional and technical occupations (23.5
percent in 1960) than of administrative (3.1 percent)
and clerical (7.4 percent) occupations, which have lower
educational qualifications (Ghana, 1960 Population Census
Vol. IV, Tables 1 and 10). This evidence suggests that
occupational discrimination exists within the labor
market, in addition to differences resulting from the
greater number of males with educational qualifications.

Data on wages in Ghana are not sufficient to determine whether outright wage discrimination exists. Within
the modern sector, the average male wage exceeded the
average female wage for 1958-60 by over 90 percent in
construction, agriculture, and manufacturing, and by
over 20 percent in mining and commerce (Ghana, Labour
Statistics, 1959 and 1960). This does not necessarily
mean that the legal requirement of equal wages in the
same job was violated, since the differences may have
resulted from aggregation of occupations with different
wages and sex compositions. At the very least, however,
there must be a close association between wage levels
and occupational sex-typing, such that women tend to be
concentrated in relatively low-wage occupations.

Open unemployment is not a relevant measure of employment discrimination when a large proportion of the
population is self-employed and no unemployment compen-
sation is available. Surplus labor is more likely to
engage in part-time or low-income activities. In 1970,
for example, recorded census unemployment was only 6.0
percent, while the total share of the labor force not
working full time was 29.4 percent. Although female
open unemployment is consistently lower than male unemployment in Ghana, a much higher proportion of the female
labor force works only part time, so that the total share
working full time is slightly lower than for men (69
percent as against 73 percent in 1970). Since part-time
work reflects supply-side choices as well as demand-side
exclusion from full-time work, no firm conclusions regarding discrimination in hiring can be drawn from the data.

The evidence suggests that women face some handicaps
in the labor market: on the whole, women have relatively
little of the higher-level education necessary for higher-
paying jobs, and (perhaps partly as a consequence) a
disproportionate share of such jobs are considered the
province of men. It is difficult to prove outright discrimination on the demand side, however, since occupational patterns can result from worker preferences as
well as employer bias. Although sociocultural attitudes
place some restrictions on opportunities available to
women and/or on their willingness and ability to take

advantage of them, there is no evidence of pervasive discrimination against women who do enter particular occupations.

## Shifts in Demand, Wages, Unemployment, and Discrimination

The evidence does not support demand-induced expansion as an explanation for the dramatic increases in female employment and labor force participation. Real Gross Domestic Product (GDP) barely kept up with the increase in population of 1960-70. The aggregate increase in employment attributable to increased production can be roughly estimated by multiplying the increase in GDP by the economy-wide ratio of employment to output growth. If the employment-output "elasticity" for the period 1955-62 of 0.66 (Uphoff, 1972) had held during the 1960s, the 30 percent increase in real GDP would have generated an employment increase of 20 percent. This estimate is close to the actual 23 percent increase in the number of women age twenty and over, so that aggregate demand and supply increases were approximately in balance, in the absence of exogenous changes. The labor supply of women in this age group, however, increased by 46 percent over 1960-70, double the population increase.[16]

The demand increase might, of course, have been strongly biased in favor of activities dominated by women. The evidence, however, suggests the contrary. The rapid expansion of government services and of investments in industry and infrastructure during the 1960s favored the large-scale modern sector. Nonagricultural employment in the modern sector grew twice as fast as the overall rate of increase, and the modern sector accounted for 34 percent of the increase in nonagricultural employment and 20 percent of total additional employment (Table 11.2, Section C). Less than 5 percent of modern sector workers in 1960, however, were female, and the modern sector accounted for only 9 percent of the increase in nonagricultural female employment and 6 percent of the total increase. The most rapid growth of real output over 1960-70 was in utilities, transport, and manufacturing (World Bank, 1976, pp. 104-5). The first two are the sectors with the lowest proportions of female employment (under 3 percent in both 1960 and 1970 censuses); although women are heavily engaged in small-scale manufacturing, they remained no more than 7 percent of large-scale manufacturing in 1970 and thus cannot have gained significantly from its rapid expansion in the 1960s.

A demand-induced employment increase should be accompanied by higher wages and decreased unemployment. Unfortunately, wage data are limited to the modern sec-

tor, and open unemployment figures do not adequately
capture labor underutilization in a developing economy
such as Ghana's in which virtually everyone can (and
must) find some means of gaining income.  The fact that
the average modern sector real wage fell slightly over
the 1960s indicates that demand for labor was not growing
faster than supply.  On the other hand, the gap between
male and female modern sector wages did close over the
1960s overall and in manufacturing, construction, and
agriculture,[17] suggesting some improvements in either
discrimination or women's qualifications.  Open unemployment remained at 6 percent in the 1970 as well as the
1960 census, although female unemployment fell while male
unemployment rose (due to a sharp rise in the fifteen to
twenty-four age group).  Since comparative data are not
available for part-time work, which is several times
the unemployment rate, we cannot say conclusively whether
the female  unemployment decrease represents increased
demand of a "discouraged worker" shift into part-time
work or home production.
     The relatively low level of outright restrictions
in Ghana against women's working means that reduction of
discrimination is an unlikely explanation for the observed
strong increase in FLFP.  In any case, there is no evidence that occupational structure biases resulting from
attitudes and customs were in fact eliminated.

Income Changes

     The lack of evidence that increased demand or wages
explains the rise in FLFP leads us to examine supply-side
explanations.  A shift away from attitudes barring female
market activity is an implausible explanation, given
Ghana's long-standing tradition of women's earning income
for certain family expenses.  Another possible explanation is the increase in urbanization, from 23 percent of
the population in 1960 to 32 percent in 1970 (World Bank,
1976, p. 511).  This demographic change has, however,
little bearing on the observed labor market changes,
since  FLFP is actually little different in rural areas
(64 percent of women age fifteen and over in 1970) than
urban (63 percent).
     Ghana's real income per capita stagnated over the
1960s, falling in each of the years 1964-67.  Given a declining share of population in working ages and a sharp
fall in labor force participation among fifteen- to
nineteen-year olds (from 57 percent to 41 percent) associated with expanded education, real income per capita
would have fallen if labor force participation of women
in older age groups had not risen as rapidly as it did
(Table 11.3).  A response to decreased family real in-

come had to come primarily from increased participation
of female rather than male members, given the latter's
already high participation rate of 95 percent or better
for ages twenty-five to sixty-four combined and in all
age groups from twenty-five to fifty-four in 1960.[18]  We
conclude therefore that increased female participation
was principally an attempt to maintain the level and
growth of living standards--that is, a supply shift representing the income effect of declining real family income from other sources in the mid-1960s.

TABLE 11.3
Age-Specific Labor Force Participation Rates by Sex, 1960
and 1970   (percentage of population in age group)

| Age Group | Female Rates | | Male Rates | |
|---|---|---|---|---|
| | 1960 | 1970 | 1960 | 1970 |
| | (1) | (2) | (3) | (4) |
| 15-24 | 53.0 | 50.3 | 75.7 | 59.8 |
| 25-44 | 57.2 | 70.9 | 97.2 | 97.1 |
| 45-64 | 67.9 | 76.5 | 94.7 | 95.8 |
| 65 and over | 42.6 | 47.5 | 71.3 | 75.4 |
| Total:  15 and over | 56.7 | 63.6 | 89.0 | 83.5 |

Source:  Ghana, 1960 Population Census, Vol. IV, Table 1;
and 1970, Vol. III, Table C1, and Vol. IV, Tables 12A
and 12B (worksheets).

CONCLUSION:   IMPLICATIONS FOR WOMEN'S STATUS

Under our interpretation, the rapid growth of female
employment in Ghana during the 1960s is best represented
as a supply shift in response to stagnant real income
(see Figure 11.1b).  The implication is that women's real
wages must have fallen, which is consistent with the wage
and income data presented.  Hence, the employment increase does not necessarily represent expanded purchasing
power, but rather a means of maintaining it.
We have shown that although women's employment and
share in the modern sector grew rapidly, it nevertheless

absorbed only a minimal share of the new female job-seekers while employing the bulk of the additional male workers.  Policies aimed at large-scale industrialization and modernization therefore did not work to the general benefit of women and even tended to displace them from traditional sources of income.[19]

Our conclusion is that the increase in female employment and labor force participation in Ghana cannot be taken as a sign that development has increased women's economic independence.  It is more a reflection of an already relatively high degree of independence, in that women have been self-reliant in seeking to maintain their real incomes.  It does not mean, however, that women command more purchasing power, either in real terms or relative to men.  The analysis shows that employment changes are not necessarily good indicators of changes in income and status when direct measures are unavailable. A conceptual framework taking into account the complex interrelationships between development, employment, and economic independence is essential to analyze and interpret the meaning of changes in women's employment.


NOTES

1.   Seminal articles are Mincer (1962) and Becker (1965).  For a review of concepts, theories, and empicical studies in a development context, see Standing (1978).  With the integration of human capital theory into this framework,  the relevant income for maximization becomes lifetime family (or individual) earnings. Education, experience, and number of children (actual and desired), as well as the cost of market-purchased substitutes for home production are therefore relevant variables for estimation of the determinants of decisions by members of a household concerning labor force participation.

2.   Ironically, the restrictions may be less in Islamic nations, where separate institutions (especially education and medical) for women offer greater professional opportunities, than in non-Islamic nations, where most occupations would necessarily involve contact with men. (We are indebted to Yasmeen Mohiuddin for this point.)

3.   This variable should be measured by additional studies, or by dummy variables for the presence of religious or other practices that inhibit women from participating.  Female labor force participation is a tempting measure but an inappropriate one in statistical analysis to represent the independent variables that determine FLFP.

4. The source may be monopsonistic restrictions as well as sexism. Differences may be partly explainable by differences in education, but then the existence of discriminatory limitations on female education must be investivated.

5. The discussion is in terms of one couple and dependents (which could include members of an extended family). The analysis can be extended to more complex situations by examining whether each person has access to income or goods directly or only through someone else. Single heads of household would be classified as dependent only if they receive income at the discretion of others rather than through their own efforts.

6. Line C, column 1 would be classified as "semi-independent" in this case.

7. Standing (1978) notes, however, that growth and urbanization tend to raise female participation rates in those "countries where women have played an insignificant role in agriculture," resulting in a general convergence among developing countries as they industrialize.

8. McCabe and Rosenzweig (1976) argue for joint determination of fertility and labor force participation by a common set of exogenous variables (wage, income, and education of husband and wife), and find evidence that "female potential wages rising pari passu with each other will be positively associated with both labor force participation and fertility . . . even though the simple correlation between the latter two variables is negative" (pp. 141-42).

9. Increases in employment referred to in this paper are net, i.e., over and above replacement of employment turnover resulting from death, retirement, and other sources of withdrawal from the labor force.

10. "Modern sector" refers conceptually to large-scale and public establishments subject to minimum wage laws and other government policies. In terms of statistics cited, it refers to employment recorded in Ghana's annual Labour Statistics (approximately covering all establishments with ten or more employees).

11. I.e., a movement along the supply curve, attributable to the substitution effect of higher market income opportunities relative to the value of home production and leisure.

12. This income effect could conceivably occur even with rising real family income, if aspirations that depend on cash income are rising faster or if the increase falls below the long-run expected trend and is viewed as a temporary income reduction. The effect could also occur if less family income (especially income earned by the husband) is made available to the

wife, forcing her to seek her own sources of income.

13. Bleek's study (1974; in North, et al., 1975) of matrilineage in Ghana found that 56 percent of marriages ended in divorce and that after divorce fathers often failed to meet minimal financial obligations toward their children's upkeep. Dutta-Roy (1969) found that about a third of both urban and rural households in the Eastern Region were headed by women, most supporting themselves.

14. Calculated from Ghana, 1960 Population Census, Vol. IV, Tables 1 and 3, and 1970, Vol. IV, Tables 3 and 12 (worksheets). For comparison, see World Bank (1976), Series IV, Table 3; Boserup (1970); and Standing (1978).

15. In general, women tend to be concentrated in tertiary activities in which training is relatively important, men in secondary activities in which tools and machinery are important. Women represent over 40 percent of 1970 recorded employment in the following detailed occupations (which are among the top ten employers of women): nurses and midwives (70 percent); housekeepers, stewards, and matrons (47 percent); telephone and telegraph operators (45 percent); and stenographers and typists. Men account for over 97 percent of modern sector employment in the following (which are among the top ten employers of men): carpenters, joiners, etc. (100 percent); road transport drivers (100 percent); tool makers, machinists, plumbers, etc. (99 percent); miners, quarrymen, and mineral treaters (98 percent); and fire fighters, policemen, and guards(97 percent). The overall shares of women and men in 1970 recorded employment are 9.7 percent and 90.3 percent, respectively (Ghana, Labour Statistics, 1970, Table 6).

16. Population and employment figures in this and the succeeding paragraphs are calculated from Ghana, 1960 Population Census, Vol. IV, Table 1, and 1970, Vol. III, Table C1, and Vol. IV, Table 12 (worksheets).

17. Nevertheless, the female wage remained less than 75 percent of the average male wage in these sectors and mining over 1968-70 (calculated from Ghana, Labour Statistics).

18. Actually, economic activity could increase even though participation is 100 percent if people take on second jobs. This is what has happened under the worsening economic conditions of the 1970s, suggesting that Ghanaians do respond to decreased income by increasing their income-earning efforts.

19. In addition to the indirect effect of promoting and subsidizing large-scale manufacturers of substitutes for goods produced by women in cottage industries, direct policies have been aimed at women in trade. Traders

have been prohibited from trading in certain commodities, forced to buy kiosks and then to move them, and arrested for selling above the control price even when they had to pay that price for the goods.

REFERENCES

Becker, G.S. 1965. "A Theory of the Allocation of Time." Economic Journal 75, 299 (Sept.): 493-517.
Blitz, R.C., and C.H. Ow. 1973. "A Cross-Sectional Analysis of Women's Participation in the Professions." Journal of Political Economy 81, 1 (Jan./Feb.)
Boserup, E. 1970. Woman's Role in Economic Development. New York: St. Martin's Press.
Boulding, E. 1976. Women in the Twentieth Century World. Beverly Hills, Cal.: Sage.
Bowen, W.G., and T.A. Finegan. 1969. The Economics of Labor Force Participation. Princeton: Princeton University Press.
Campbell, C. 1977. "Women's Employment and Incomes Under Industrialization: A Case Study of Ghana." M.A. thesis, Vanderbilt University.
Chapman, J.R. and M. Gates, eds. 1976. Economic Independence for Women: The Foundation for Equal Rights. Beverly Hills, Cal.: Sage.
Dutta-Roy, D.K. 1969. "The Eastern Region Household Budget Survey." Technical Publication Series No. 6. Legon: Institute of Statistical, Social and Economic Research. University of Ghana.
Galbraith, J.K. 1973. Economics and the Public Purpose. Boston: Houghton Mifflin.
Galenson, M. 1973. Women and Work: An International Comparison. Ithaca: New York State School of Industrial and Labor Relations, Cornell University.
Ghana, Republic of. Labour Statistics. Annual. Accra: Central Bureau of Statistics.
_____ . 1960 Population Census of Ghana, Vols. I-IV. Accra: Central Bureau of Statistics.
_____ . 1970 Population Census of Ghana, Vols. I-IV and worksheets. Accra: Central Bureau of Statistics.
Giele, J.Z. and A.C. Smock, eds. 1977. Women: Role and Status in Eight Countries. New York: Wiley and Sons.
de Graft Johnson, K.T. 1978. "Factors Affecting Labour Force Participation Rates in Ghana, 1970." In Labour Force Participation in Low-Income Countries, ed. G. Standing and G. Sheehan. Geneva: International Labour Office.

Kreps, J. 1971. Sex in the Marketplace: American Women at Work. Baltimore: The Johns Hopkins University Press.

Leibowitz, Arleen. 1974. "Education and Home Production." American Economic Review 64 (May): 243-50.

McCabe, J.L., and M.R. Rosenzweig, 1976. "Female Labor Force Participation, Occupational Choice and Fertility in Developing Countries." Journal of Development Economics 3, 2: 141-60.

Mincer, J. 1962. "Labor Force Participation of Married Women: A Study of Labor Supply." In Aspects of Labor Economics, ed. H.G. Lewis. Princeton: Princeton University Press (for National Bureau of Economic Research).

Mullings, L. 1976. "Women and Economic Change in Africa. In Women in Africa: Studies in Social and Economic Change, ed. N.J. Hafkin and E.G. Bay. Stanford: Stanford University Press.

North, J., M. Fuchs-Carsch, J. Bryson, and S. Blumenfeld. 1975. Women in National Development in Ghana: Study and Annotated Bibliography. Washington, D.C.: U.S. Agency for International Development.

Robertson, C. 1976. "Ga Women and Socio-economic Change in Accra, Ghana." In Women in Africa: Studies in Social and Economic Change, ed. N.J. Hafkin and E.G. Bay. Stanford: Stanford University Press.

Schultz, T. Paul. 1975. Estimating Labor Supply Functions for Married Women. Santa Monica: Rand Corporation.

Smith, J.P. 1972. "The Life Cycle Allocation of Time in a Family Context." Ph.D. dissertation, University of Chicago.

Standing, G. 1978. Labour Force Participation and Development. Geneva: International Labour Office.

Standing, G. and G. Sheehan, eds. 1978. Labour Force Participation in Low-Income Countries. Geneva: International Labour Office.

Tinker, I. 1976. "The Adverse Impact of Development on Women." In Women and World Development, eds. I. Tinker, M.B. Bramsen, and M. Buvinic. New York: Praeger Special Studies.

UNESCO. 1969 and 1974. Statistical Yearbook. New York: UNESCO.

Uphoff, N. 1972. "The Expansion of Employment Associated with Growth of G.N.P." Economic Bulletin of Ghana 2nd ser. 2, 4: 3-16.

Vyas, N., and J.C. Leith. 1974. "Labour Force Participation of Women in Ghana." The Economic Bulletin of Ghana 2nd ser. 4:53-60.

World Bank. 1976. World Tables 1976. Baltimore: The Johns Hopkins University Press.

Youssef, N. 1974. <u>Women and Work in Developing Societies</u>.
    Population Monograph Series No. 15.  Berkeley:
    University of California Institute of International
    Studies.

## 12. Fertility and Employment: An Assessment of Role Incompatibility among African Urban Women

*Barbara Lewis*

Students of population change, moved perhaps more by malthusianism than by feminism, have been interested in female employment largely as a variable affecting fertility. Feminists are bent on freedom of choice. They wish to be free to control their fertility but will not accept any mutual exclusivity between productive and reproductive roles.

Women's productive and reproductive roles clearly interact. Our purpose here is to study that interaction among women in Abidjan, the large and growing capital of the Ivory Coast--a setting which imposed new conditions on a population with largely rural roots. Altered women's roles and the availability of Western means of avoiding pregnancy are among these new conditions.[1] But in focusing on the interaction of employment and fertility, we must not overlook all the other factors which may affect fertility levels. Thus, the introduction situates employment among other variables potentially altering fertility and then states the central hypothesis regarding women's fertility levels and work status. Following a brief description of the study's method and sample, we present data on employment and fertility, desired family size, household help, and respondents' explanations of their work status. In conclusion, the theoretical basis of the hypothesis is re-evaluated.

Differences in fertility levels are the <u>intended</u> and <u>unintended</u> consequences of behaviors dependent on a variety of factors.[2] One hypothesis associated with

_____
This study was conducted in 1974 under the auspices of the Ministry of Planning of the Ivory Coast. I am grateful to the Ministry of Planning, the Population Council, and the African-American Scholars' Council, whose support made this research possible.

modernization is that the delayed age of marriage and thus a later start bearing children will reduce the total number of childbearing years and thus reduce family size. Another familiar example suggests that the failure to respect traditional norms dictating sexual abstinence from the birth of a child until weaning (or, in other societies, until the child walks) will reduce spacing between children and thus increase fertility. Of course, infant mortality may be decreased by modern medical care, particularly vaccinations, which will increase the proportion of children born who live to adulthood. Medical care and health conditions will also affect the number of miscarriages and the number of infertile women, while marital instability is likely to decrease the frequency and regularity of sexual relations and thus decrease the total number of pregnancies.

The list of factors could be lengthened considerably, but these examples (all apropos of contemporary West Africa) draw our attention to the complexity of change in fertility levels. First, this complexity reminds us that fertility levels may decline for reasons other than access to and use of modern contraceptives, or even reasons other than behaviors intended to limit family size. But contraception or abstinence, if used to avoid early pregnancy by students, will reduce completed family size if all other factors are equal. If, for example, advanced schooling results in better access to and more effective use of modern medicine, and if women no longer respect norms of postpartum abstinence, a greater number of surviving children may well result. Thus, in a modernizing society, a number of fertility-related behaviors are likely to be changing simultaneously, some with an unintended positive--or negative--impact on fertility. Also, hypotheses regarding such complex interacting processes are extremely difficult to verify empirically.

Changing attitudes toward fertility is another relevant area of research. One major hypothesis links the changing economic value of children to changed attitudes toward desired family size. Thus, the move from farm to city renders each additional child an economic drain rather than an asset as farm labor. Urban residence is presumed to alter the number of children desired. In the long run, this rationalistic response to the cost of children may well occur, but the short-run response to urbanization may be quite different. Lowered fertility is favored not only by changed attitudes among childbearing women, but also by a decline in pronatalism on the part of women's kinsmen and spouses. Further, behavior limiting births appears to require unprecedented kinds of communications between spouses. Alternatively, the

woman must assume the considerable social risk of acting
autonomously to limit her fertility in the face of
others' pronatalist values.  Thus, we may assume at
least a two-step process in value change--the first, in
which some awareness of the advantages of alternative behaviors develops, and the second, in which a significant
number of conditions favoring changed behavior make possible new behaviors effectively achieving these new
goals.  Similarly, high infant mortality may favor pronatalism because parents want to be sure there will be
"enough children."  Decreases in infant mortality are
initially welcomed by parents without altering their pronatalist views.  Only eventually, with increased family
size and increased certainty that children will survive,
will pronatalist attitudes be moderated.

These examples should suggest how complex are the
models one can construct to explain fertility levels in
a population.  Also, elaborate models including the
physiological, behavioral, and attitudinal variables all
logically impinging on fertility change can rarely be empirically tested because of the related problems of adequate sample size and data availability.  The optimal
strategy for research on fertility change is, I think, to
select some variables which--given the context of re-
search--appear promising and to explore them with explicit awareness of the assumptions and preferences underlying the choice of model.


ROLE INCOMPATIBILITY:  PRODUCTIVE AND REPRODUCTIVE ROLES

Western women social scientists often find the com-
patibility/incompatibility of motherhood and labor force
participation to be an immediately appealing focus for
empirical inquiry.  Most of us are keenly aware of the
conflict between these two roles in our own lives and
many of us have elected to limit, more or less, our
family size to permit continued labor force participation (hereafter LFP).  And as we worry about babysitters,
we yearn to be in a context in which mothering is more
compatible with labor force participation.  Peasant women
or women in cottage industries of the past or of contemporary Africa come readily to mind, for those women can
and do integrate their reproductive and productive roles
with little apparent strain.

What about women in West Africa's urban areas?
Visitors to West Africa remark on the economic visibility
and vigor of these women and the aplomb with which they
fill their maternal roles while participating in the
labor force.  Yet, urban living means significant changes
in the work conditions of West African women, whether

they are traders or salaried workers.  They are also exposed to Western education and Western values, resulting
in new personal aspirations and knowledge of Western
medicine, including Western contraceptive methods.  They
face huge increases in the cost of living.  Do these
diverse pressures introduce a conflict for West African
women between traditional expectations of high fertility
and their traditional economic productivity?  What evidence is there that these women alter their attitudes
and behaviors related to fertility?  Furthermore, does
the evidence link women's LFP to their fertility attitudes and behavior?

Boserup's now classic book offers two hypotheses
that provide a useful focus.[3]  First, she states that
urban residence entails pressures of a primarily economic
nature which tend to limit fertility.  The cost of food,
clothing, fuel, and education are all constraints on
high fertility, which should influence the fertility
attitudes of men and women.  Boserup also observes that
the transition from rural to urban residence is associated with a decrease in female LFP.  In African agriculture, women constitute an estimated 80 percent of the
total numer of "man hours" expended.  The rural woman
is a member of the productive labor force, and her work
is easily combined with her maternal role.  Infants
can nurse at her workplace, children can be scolded while
she works, and older children are free to assist their
mothers.

Among urban West African women, research shows LFP
to be markedly lower than among rural women (Boserup,
1970).[4]  A survey in Sierra Leone showed less than 50
percent of the urban female population to be economically
active, for the most part in petty trade (Dow, 1971a,
1971b).  In Abidjan, my sample also showed that, among
those women with fewer than nine years of schooling, less
than half worked, when "work" was broadly defined to mean
any form of cash-generating employment.  Less-educated
women such as these constitute the great majority of the
female population of Abidjan.

Boserup's two propositions lead us to focus on the
link between fertility and LFP.  Do urban women have
lower LFP rates than their rural counterparts?  Is it
because urban women can less easily combine their work
roles and their maternal roles?  Who are the urban women
who work?  Are they distinguished from those who do not
work by differential fertility?  If there is a differential, is it because women who work limit their fertility--
presumably to permit continued LFP?  Or does involuntary
infertility lead to LFP?

We can summarize Stycos and Weller's formulation of

these questions in a succinct proposition: if an
acceptable means of contraception is not available, then
low fertility leads to employment and not the reverse
(1967, p. 216). Presumably, by "acceptable means of contraception," Stycos and Weller mean some pharmaceutical
barrier to conception rather than abstinence. Their
proposition further implies that in the absence of such
contraceptive products, women are unlikely to avoid
pregnancy in order to work. The maternal role thus is
primary and independent, and employment activity secondary and dependent. As a result, women who are invol-
untarily subfecund will be more likely to work than women
who have normal fertility levels.

There are other aspects of this proposition to be
noted. "Acceptable means" suggests that the problem with
contraceptive acceptance is one of means (aesthetics,
comfort, convenience) rather than ends (whether persons
really want to limit the number of children they have).
I suggest that perhaps both the ends and the means must
be acceptable before fertility behavior will be inten-
tionally changed in a pronatalist society.

The underlying assumption of incompatibility between
maternal and LFP roles does not specify the nature of a
viable solution. Is one child as conflict-producing as
eight (or more so, if older siblings can care for younger
ones)? Nor does it specify that children's ages are ger-
mane (that is, preschoolers cause insoluble conflict
which school-age children do not). When this role conflict centers on the mother's primary role as caretaker
of the children, a viable solution is finding some other
person to care for the children. This caretaker may be
an older child who does not go to school, a co-wife,
or a relative (depending upon household space, the husband's willingness to house that relative, and the costs
versus benefits of maintaining such a person). Alternatively, a woman may use paid help, again, depending
upon cost relative either to total household income or
to the wife's income, if the husband insists child care
is her responsibility.

A crucial ambiguity of Stycos and Weller's hypothesis lies in the meaning of role compatibility. Does
role incompatibility mean roles which can be combined
only with significant stress, such as dissatisfaction regarding available mother substitutes, or that mothering
undermines job success because mothering means periodic
absence from the job or inflexibility regarding work
hours? Or does role incompatibility mean roles that are
mutually exclusive?[5] In the area of child care, compatibility is relative to cultural values. Clearly, if
work requires separation from children, then a mother
cannot fill both roles at once. But if child care sub-

stitutes are acceptable, then an acceptable solution to
the conflict would be determined by cash flow factors,
combined with the woman's views regarding the adequacy
of available child care arrangements.  The more stringent definition of mutual exclusivity is in the spirit of
Stycos and Weller's hypothesis:  role incompatibility
means roles which cannot possibly be filled simultaneously.  This does not exclude an element of subjectivity.
For example, nineteenth-century English factory women
gave their babies opium to silence them while the mothers
were at work; this was a solution to the incompatibility
of their roles.  The definition of mutual exclusiveness
poses directly the question of alternative solutions.

    How, in the population under investigation, do
womens' jobs differ regarding the conflict between productive and reproductive roles?  Can women with children
fill both roles at once?  If no role conflict is present
or if alternative solutions that resolve the role conflict
are available, then whether or not a woman works may depend on factors other than fertility levels.

    In Abidjan, "salaried employment" always means work
outside the home. Given the low level of industrialization in West Africa, salaried female labor typically
means clerical or professional white collar work.  Less
educated women have very little opportunity to find regular work; thus, they are largely relegated to self-
employed petty trade involving food preparation or sale,
or the resale of imported toiletries, foodstuffs,kitchen-
ware, and the like.  Some of these women sell for a few
hours a day in front of their homes.  Others rent space
and sell daily at one of the city's big markets.  Although the latter clearly cannot bring their household
to their workplace, they can bring infants on their backs
and they can alter their hours or miss a day if family
responsibilities require their presence.  Thus, petty
trade is clearly not as incompatible with mothering as
is salaried work, although most types of petty trade in
Abidjan also require some assistance to meet family responsibilities.  The survey data on household help--in
cluding (1) paid help or (2) informally paid family
members--will help us to understand the relationship
between LFP and household obligations.


CONCEPTS AND MEASURES USED IN THIS STUDY

    We turn now to the empirical relationships between
employment and fertility found among Abidjan women.  Respondents have been grouped to distinguish women who are
inactive (have no money-earning activity), petty traders
(including all self-employed home manufacturers and mar-

ket sellers), and salaried workers (including all regularly paid salaried workers). This categorization most accurately distinguishes the conditions of work relevant to incompatibility to maternal roles.

Data on respondents' household help is presented with salaried help distinguished from relatives who receive room, board, and some pocket money. These two categories certainly do not cover all possible child care solutions. Indeed, in the stereotypic African household (a less than accurate picture for Abidjan) co-wives, kin not brought to serve as household help, and older children are all sources of child care. Furthermore, while we can show whether or not persons who have what they call "household help" are more likely to work, we cannot verify the causal link, that is, whether an individual sought work because she had child care available or whether she sought child care in order to work.

Another source of data on role compatibility is an open-ended question: "Why do you work?" or "not work?" In an open-ended question, respondents are not guided or limited in their responses, as they are in a multiple choice or agree/disagree item. The detailed codes, derived from content analysis of a 10 percent sample of the completed questionnaires, include all responses given, ranging from "Because I have no one to care for the children" (indicating role conflict), to "Because I am ashamed to be a street seller/market woman" (with no apparent role conflict).

The data on fertility include desired number of children, knowledge and use of African and Western contraceptive methods, and actual family size (including children born alive and children surviving at the time of the interview). The desired number of children shows whether the extremely pronatalist rural tradition is undergoing modification, presumably due to the many pressures of urban life and economic change on Abidjan women. Contraceptive knowledge and use we have shown elsewhere to be positively related to formal education (Dow, 1971a; Lewis, 1975, pp. 80, 89; see also Olusanya, n.d.). To collect our data on contraceptive use, we asked if the respondent had ever used some means of limiting or delaying pregnancy and, if so, what. Thus, those respondents tabulated as "users" of contraception could be persons who have used contraception during a specific period with no desire to limit overall births, or persons seeking a particular number of children.

THE DATA BASE

The sample of 880 respondents interviewed in 1973-
74 was drawn from three neighborhoods of Abidjan selected
for their differing socioeconomic characteristics.  It is
a purposive stratified sample aimed at overrepresenting
the upper- and middle-status minorities in the city's
population rather than representing the entire population in accurate proportions.  The three neighborhoods
were selected on the basis of known rent and value of
housing, type of housing, and approximate income of inhabitants.  The upper-status quarter, Cocody, is the
elite neighborhood of the city, housing largely Ivoirians
in white-collar jobs, members of the diplomatic corps,
and Europeans.  Housing, either apartment buildings or
single family dwellings, was (in 1973) valued at a monthly
rate of 18,000 CFA frs or more.  The second neighborhood,
Nouveau Koumassi, is a partly state-owned housing estate
of one-story row houses ranging in rent from 7,000 to
15,000 CFA frs.  These two neighborhoods contrast with
the third in that all homes have running water, flush
toilets, and electricity, and all are designed in the
European manner as single-family dwellings or apartments.
The third neighborhood, Treichville, is the old African
quarter of the city.  Its dwellings are the traditional
courtyard usually lodging several families, and 85 percent of all rents are less than 8,000 CFA frs.  While its
inhabitants' lifestyles are more traditional, and their
standard of living clearly lower (66 percent have electricity, 18 percent flush toilets, 36 percent running
water), Treichville cannot be characterized as typically
lower class.  It is centrally located and its sanitation
facilities and health services are far superior to most
of the city's peripheral areas.  Thus, the sample must be
assumed to exclude the lowest status group of the population.  Furthermore, by drawing approximately the same
number of respondents in each of the three neighborhoods,
the sample is skewed to overrepresent the higher socioeconomic strata.  Thus, meaningful statistical comparisons of women with different socioeconomic characteristics is gained at the expense of an accurate profile of
the city's entire population.
Within each neighborhood, maximum care was taken to
draw a representative sample of eligible respondents.
Eligible women are of the Bete, Baule, or Dyula ethnic
groups.  The ethnic groups selected represent major cultural types in the Ivory Coast.  The Bete are patrilineal forest dwellers, the Baule matrilineal forest
dwellers, and the Dyula are Mande-speaking, patrilineal
Muslims from the savanna regions of the Ivory Coast,
Guinea, and Mali.  The three groups constitute nearly

one-half of the Ivoirian population.  A complete census
of randomly selected clusters yielded a list of eligible
women.  Each woman was then interviewed by an interviewer
of her ethnic group in her maternal language, unless she
wanted to respond in French.  Thus, every effort was
made to assure a positive rapport, comprehension of questions, and reliability of responses.

EMPLOYMENT STATUS AND FERTILITY

     Before exploring the relationship between employment
and fertility behavior in detail, we must note the distribution of salaried employment among Abidjan women.
Table 12.1 shows the very strong positive relationship
between salaried employment and education.

TABLE 12.1
Education[a] by Employment Status

|  | No education | Some primary | Some secondary | University or professional | Total[c] |
|---|---|---|---|---|---|
|  |  |  | (percent) |  |  |
| Inactive | 44 | 55 | 23 | 2 | 36 |
| Commercial[b] | 53 | 20 | 4 | 5 | 32 |
| Salaried | 2 | 21 | 57 | 71 | 25 |
| Student, apprentice | 1 | 4 | 16 | 22 | 7 |
| Total | 100 | 100 | 100 | 100 | 100 |

[a]Refers to French education only.

[b]Refers to self-employed petty traders.

[c]N=873.

Among the women at university and professional school
levels, nearly all of those not currently students or
apprentices are salaried workers.  Only 2 percent are inactive and 5 percent are self-employed in commerce.
Among women with little or no education, about half are

inactive. The compelling attraction of LFP among the better educated is clear. It is due to the access of this strata to better jobs, the great demand for educated Ivoirian workers in the Ivory Coast, and the social pressures on women to avoid financial dependency on spouse or family.[6] For the purposes of our inquiry, we cannot compare the fertility of active and inactive women among the educated elite because the inactive group is too small to be measured statistically. Thus, we cannot fully test the impact of employment upon fertility by using a control group of educated but inactive women because women able to get good jobs in Abidjan rarely stay at home. However, we can look at the fertility of these women in comparison with other groups. We turn now to those data.

Table 12.2 shows the mean number of children ever born per respondent grouped by LFP (salaried, commercial, or inactive) and by age. Comparisons of the means for the same age groups shows whether work as a petty trader or as a salaried employee is related to lower fertility. Age controls are particularly necessary in fertility studies. First, the older the woman, the greater the number of children she is likely to have. Second, we cannot assume that the age distribution of all salaried women is equal to that among all housewives. Indeed, the unemployed tend to be younger than the others, and petty traders tend to be older. Thus, the mean number of children by employment status alone could be misleading.

The other data in Table 12.2 show no evidence that children are an insurmountable barrier to LFP. The market women 20 to 35 years old have higher fertility levels than either the inactives or the salaried women. The salaried women have the fewest children, except within the oldest age cohort (35 to 50), where they have the most.

This jump in fertility among salaried women (relative to market women and inactives) under 35 compared to salaried women 35 and older is intriguing. A possible interpretation is that salaried women who, in the Ivory Coast, constitute the vast majority of the more educated women, have lower fertility levels initially because they delay marriage for schooling but that they "catch up" to the other women in their later years. However, we cannot be certain that the fertility history of younger salaried women will, in a decade or two, look like the fertility history of older salaried women currently at the end of their childbearing years.[7]

TABLE 12.2
Mean Number of Children Born Alive, by Age and Employment
Status of Respondent

|  | Mean | N |
|---|---|---|
| Age 20-24 | 1.7 | 264 |
| Inactive | 1.7 | 141 |
| Commercial[a] | 1.9 | 46 |
| Salaried | 1.5 | 77 |
| Age 25-29 | 2.9 | 272 |
| Inactive | 3.0 | 90 |
| Commercial[a] | 3.3 | 99 |
| Salaried | 2.4 | 83 |
| Age 30-34 | 4.3 | 183 |
| Inactive | 4.6 | 54 |
| Commercial[a] | 4.8 | 69 |
| Salaried | 3.4 | 60 |
| Age 35-50 | 5.5 | 154 |
| Inactive | 5.5 | 36 |
| Commercial[a] | 5.4 | 81 |
| Salaried | 5.7 | 37 |
| Total |  | 873 |

[a]Refers to self-employed petty traders.


     Our statistics show that the older, more educated
women had lower than average fertility when they were 20
to 35, thus supporting our interpretation regarding
salaried women.  Of course, only when the younger women
have themselves completed their childbearing will we be
certain.  It is possible that the younger cohort will
stop bearing children, perhaps through use of contraception, with a smaller number of children than their
older salaried counterparts.  (See the data on desired
family size below.)
     Table 12.3 presents the respondents' total number
of surviving children to complement the data above on
the number of children ever born at the time of interview.
These means are also grouped by age and employment status.
As long as women lose a number of children in childhood,
they will continue to want many children to insure that

"enough" reach adulthood. Thus, a low rate of infant mortality may be a prerequisite to voluntary limitation of family size.

TABLE 12.3
Mean Number of Children Surviving at Date of Interview, by Age and Employment Status of Respondent, and Difference Between Number Ever Born and Number Surviving

|  | Mean | Difference | N |
|---|---|---|---|
| Age 20-24 | 1.4 | | 264 |
| Inactive | 1.5 | .24 | 141 |
| Commercial[a] | 1.5 | .4 | 46 |
| Salaried | 1.3 | .13 | 77 |
| Age 25-29 | 2.6 | | 272 |
| Inactive | 2.8 | .3 | 90 |
| Commercial[a] | 2.7 | .4 | 99 |
| Salaried | 2.2 | .2 | 83 |
| Age 30-34 | 3.7 | | 183 |
| Inactive | 3.9 | .7 | 54 |
| Commercial[a] | 4.1 | .7 | 69 |
| Salaried | 3.1 | .3 | 60 |
| Age 35-50 | 4.8 | | 154 |
| Inactive | 4.9 | .58 | 36 |
| Commercial[a] | 4.5 | .9 | 81 |
| Salaried | 5.1 | .6 | 37 |
| Total | | | 873 |

[a]Refers to self-employed petty traders.

The more educated, whose attitudes are more open toward Western medicine and whose financial means enable them to benefit far more fully from available Western medical care, may be expected to have lower infant mortality. Thus, in our sample, we would expect the infant mortality to be somewhat lower among the salaried than among the petty traders. If so, this would narrow the gap between petty traders' and salaried women's fertility levels observed above in the 20 to 35 age cohorts.

Table 12.3 shows differences between children born and those surviving are lowest among salaried women and highest among traders. This difference is a partial explanation of the greater number of surviving children among salaried women in the oldest (35+) age cohort, with traders lowest and inactive women falling between the two.

The data do not, on balance, show the negative relationship between fertility and LFP predicted in the presence of incompatibility between maternal and employment roles. There is a low level of fertility among younger salaried women, apparently due to prolonged education and later onset of childbearing. But this disappears when salaried women are over 35 and becomes reversed when infant mortality is taken into account: in the oldest cohort, salaried women have the largest number of surviving children! It is, of course, doubtful that salaried work per se increases family size, for education and medical care are the more probable explanations. But the incompatibility proposition finds little support.

What about attitudes toward family size? Are there differences in attitudes regarding the number of children respondents say they would like to have which are consistent with a role stress hypothesis, if not a role incompatibility hypothesis?


WORK STATUS AND DESIRED FAMILY SIZE

In a sequence of changes leading to the intentional reduction of family size, new attitudes favoring smaller families are expected to precede actual behaviors limiting family size. Data on desired family size is of particular interest because many women in Abidjan may well be at that transitional point between attitudinal and behavioral change. Abidjan is a very new and rapidly growing city in which the full range of pressures to limit family size is surely not a generation old. Women are experiencing the impossibility of growing any food for consumption at home, great housing scarcity and cost, and nearly universal primary school attendance with its attendant fees and consequent loss of household help from older children. Access to Western contraception is recent and family planning is not publicized. Although the legality of contraception is ambiguous, contraceptives can be obtained through private and some public doctors.

There are many reasons we may expect women not to act effectively to limit family size. However, the data on desired family size will suggest whether working mothers, despite having found some form of child care,

want fewer children because of the strain and cross-
pressures of their dual roles.  Perhaps also, as cash
earners as well as consumers, they appreciate more fully
the cost of urban living than do their inactive counterparts.


TABLE 12.4
Mean Number of Children Desired, By Work Status of
Respondent

| Employment Status | Mean | Total N | N Pronatalist Respondents[b] |
|---|---|---|---|
| Inactive | 6.7 | 268 | 48 |
| Commercial[a] | 7.0 | 231 | 54 |
| Salaried | 5.0 | 246 | 11 |
| Total | 6.2 | 745 | 113 |

[a]Refers to self-employed petty traders.

[b]Not calculated in the means, because these respondents
said "as many as possible," "as many as God gives," etc.
These responses cannot be assigned a numerical value, but
they are unquestionably pronatalist.


        Tables 12.4 and 12.5 show the mean number of child-
ren desired.  The response to the question "How many
children would you like in all, if you could choose?" is
grouped by work status only in Table 12.4 and then by
education and work status in Table 12.5.  Most women
answered with a number, but some (113 women) refused to
adopt other than a wholly passive stance; guided perhaps
by tradition, perhaps by religious piety, these women
said only "As many as God gives" or "As God wishes."
These responses cannot be included in the numerical
averages.  However, these women were certainly adverse to
contraception or any other means of limiting family size.
Rather than altering the averages to reflect these pronatalist respondents,[8] I have excluded them from the
calculation of means but listed the number of respondents
saying "as many as God gives" next to each category.
Thus, Table 12.5 shows that most of these 113 women are

those with no Western education.  Such a passive acceptance of traditional pronatalist values regarding family
size nearly disappears with increasing education.


TABLE 12.5
Mean Number of Children Desired, By Work Status and
Education of Respondent

|  | Mean | Total N | N Pronatalist Respondents[b] |
|---|---|---|---|
| Inactive | 6.7 | 268 | 48 |
| No education | 7.5 | 160 | 43 |
| Primary-secondary (1-9) | 5.7 | 100 | 5 |
| High (10+) | 4.2 | 8 | 0 |
| Commercial[a] | 7.0 | 231 | 54 |
| No education | 7.2 | 194 | 50 |
| Primary-secondary (1-9) | 6.0 | 28 | 4 |
| High (10+) | 4.6 | 9 | 0 |
| Salaried | 5.0 | 246 | 11 |
| No education | 7.5 | 12 | 4 |
| Primary-secondary (1-9) | 5.7 | 82 | 4 |
| High (10+) | 4.5 | 152 | 3 |
| Total | | $\overline{745}$ | $\overline{113}$ |

[a]Refers to self-employed petty traders.

[b]Not calculated in the means, because respondent said
"as many as possible," "as many as God gives," etc.
These responses cannot be assigned a numerical value,
but they are unquestionably pronatalist.


    Although in all groups the mean number of children
desired is very high from a European perspective, respondents' aspirations differ by work status.  The salaried

workers have the lowest mean number of children desired
(5), while the petty traders are highest (7) and the inactive women only slightly lower than the petty traders
(6.8). Since salaried work is far more inflexible regarding separation of mother and child than petty trade,
role incompatibility may explain these differences in
aspiration. However, we must examine a competing explanation that increases in education are related to the decline of traditional, rural pronatalist attitudes.

Table 12.5 shows that education has a far greater
impact on desired family size than employment status.
Among the salaried, the inactive, and the petty traders,
the desired number of children drops from over 7.5 among
those with no Western education to 4.6 or less among
those who have reached at least the upper level of
secondary school. The very skewed nature of the distri-
butions within work status groups makes clear that the
relationship between work status and pronatalist attitudes is spurious. Note, for example, the great concentration of salaried workers in the highest educational
category, and also that the tiny number of uneducated
salaried women are as pronatalist as any group. The
data also show that the most educated among the inactive
(also a tiny number: 8 out of 268) want the smallest
family of any group.

We are still not certain what the completed fertility
of younger educated women will look like. They live in
a changing society and they may not follow the path of
the older educated women. However, while they are less
pronatalist than the less educated, the number of children they say they want is about what they appear likely
to achieve! Salaried women 35 to 50 average 5.2 living
children, which is very close to the 5.1 that all salaried women say they want. Similarly, women 35 to 50
with at least nine years of education average 4.9 living
children; all of these more educated women said they
wanted 4.5. The data suggest that the more pronatalist
and less educated women are unlikely to reach their
ideal family size, while those wanting fewer children
may well have about their desired number.


LFP AND HOUSEHOLD HELP

In a further effort to explore how working women
solve their child care needs, we asked respondents
whether they had someone to help them at home, apart
from their co-wives. The household help category was
further separated into salaried help or nonsalaried residents. The latter are very often family members or
needy villagers who do housework in return for room,

board, and pocket money. It may seem inappropriate to categorize such persons as "unsalaried help," because a woman often assists relatives by assuming responsibility for the upkeep of family members who may, in turn, help the woman with household tasks. Thus, unsalaried help need not be primarily or solely a benefit to the receiving household. However, from the perspective of role compatibility, such help does constitute substitute child care. Last, in cases where a respondent had both paid employment and resident kin assisting with child care, she was categorized as having "paid help."

By correlating work status and the presence of household help (paid or unpaid), we can see to what extent women in the labor force appear more likely to pay someone to meet their household obligations. The presence or absence of unpaid relatives suggests to what degree extended family institutions provide the solution to women's conflict between productive and reproductive roles.

TABLE 12.6
Respondents' Work Status, By Household Help (No Children Living with Respondent)

|  | Salaried | Commercial[a] | Inactive | Total |
|---|---|---|---|---|
|  |  | (N) |  |  |
| No household help | (25) 36% | (34) 71% | (58) 74% | (117) 60% |
| Unsalaried household help | (14) 20% | (10) 21% | (12) 16% | (36) 18% |
| Salaried household help | (31) 44% | (4) 8% | (8) 10% | (43) 22% |
| Total | (70) 36% | (48) 26% | (78) 40% | (196) 100% |

[a]Refers to self-employed petty traders.

Tables 12.6 and 12.7 show the relationship of LFP and household help among respondents with none of their children living with them (Table 12.6) and those with one or more living with them (Table 12.7). The tables do

not reveal whether respondents have sent one or more
children to live with kinsmen, perhaps precisely because
they themselves are in school or working.  Comparing the
number of respondents with no help, salaried help, or
unpaid help among women with and without child care responsibilities will suggest the extent to which help is
brought in to care for children of working mothers.

TABLE 12.7
Respondents' Work Status, By Household Help (One or More
Children)

|  | Salaried | Commercial[a] | Inactive | Total |
|---|---|---|---|---|
|  |  | (N) |  |  |
| No household help | (27) 14% | (180) 73% | (155) 64% | (362) 53% |
| Unsalaried house- hold help | (40) 21% | (34) 14% | (47) 19% | (121) 18% |
| Salaried house- hold help | (121) 65% | (33) 13% | (42) 17% | (196) 29% |
| Total | (188) 100% | (247) 100% | (244) 100% | (679) 100% |

[a]Refers to self-employed petty traders.

It is rather surprising that 40 percent of the women
without children at home have help, paid or unpaid.
Seventy-one percent of the petty traders without children
at home (Table 12.6) and 73 percent of those with children
at home (Table 12.7) say they have no help, while only
36 percent of the salaried women without children at home
say they have no help.  There is clearly no positive relationship between household help and the ability to
conduct petty trade.  In contrast, salaried women with
children are more likely to have assistance, paid or unpaid, than their salaried counterparts without children
at home (86 to 64 percent).  Does this mean that women
in trade have no problem working and caring for children,
but that the salaried employees experience great conflict
between their roles?  Or is the difference between the
groups explained by their income levels more than by role

conflict, by the fact that salaried women's greater incomes permit them the relative luxury of household help?

The difference regarding household help is greater
between salaried women and traders than it is between
women with and without children.  Though some inactive
women with children and some traders with children have
salaried help, salaried women with children are nearly
four times as likely as traders to have regular paid
help.  Indeed, salaried women often pay their household
help solely from their salaries, for household maintenance is, their husbands say, the wife's responsibility.
Traders' incomes vary greatly, but the majority, earning
a few dollars a day, would be hard pressed to purchase
their replacement in the home.

The greater income of salaried women compared to
most petty traders appears to explain the salaried women's greater frequency of household help.  But is there
support for a competing hypothesis that salaried work,
because of longer and inflexible hours, requires formal
salaried child care?  For example, women trading in the
city's main markets return home by two in the afternoon,
while salaried women must work until five-thirty or six.
Does this mean that there is less role conflict among
traders than salaried workers?  This argument can be
greatly overstated.  Market women must leave their homes
early to get wholesale goods.  They can take an infant on
their backs at the market and thus avoid missing feed-
ings, but in Abidjan, market sellers very rarely take
more than one child to market.  Of course, other aspects
of their work, such as food preparation, cloth dyeing,
and sewing, are compatible with child care.  Nonetheless,
most petty traders certainly need some regular and
reliable assistance in order to fulfill their mothering
roles.  Thus, the 73 percent of traders with children
who cited no household help appear to rely heavily upon
the more traditional family structure; the presence of
an adult relative, a co-wife, or an older child not
attending school is essential.

To what extent does child care appear to be a problem to respondents?  Is it a common determinant of employment status or is it a matter for which solutions
are fairly easily available?

At the end of the survey, respondents were asked
"why do you/do you not work"?  The question is totally
open ended and interviewers were instructed to note
everything the respondents said.  Then, based on a 20
percent sample of the questionnaires, comprehensive cod-
ing categories were established.  Because this particular questionnaire was primarily devoted to fertility
attitudes and history, respondents were surely cued to
cite "children" or child care if they felt such a re-

sponse was at all relevant. Furthermore, if a respondent's answer coincided with more than one coded response, both (or all) responses were included in the analysis. This inclusion of up to three responses per respondent explains why the total number of responses exceeds the total number of respondents: there are 831 responses for 482 respondents.

Given the high fertility levels and high LFP we have seen thus far, it is not surprising to see that only two individuals (0.2 percent of responses) give the one response suggesting a tradeoff between work and children; that is, they say they work because they have no children. This response, corresponding directly to Stycos and Weller's hypothesis, receives negligible support. The most frequent response is the conventional "help out with household/children's costs." Another widespread response is "my own little needs," a response far more common among petty traders than salaried women. This rather self-effacing expression reflects the husbands' view that women should look after their own needs (including clothing and social obligations requiring cash) and women's oft-stated view that "It makes one ashamed to hold out one's hand to one's husband." This is evidence that the new dependence of urban women is not easily accepted by men or women. The greater frequency of the response among traders is, I think, an accurate reflection of the meager possibilities afforded by the small earnings of many petty traders. The response that "I work in order to aid my family" (i.e. her own kinsmen, not her relatives by marriage) is also more frequent among salaried women than traders. This is perhaps surprising to those assuming that because the salaried are more educated, more "modern," they are also less traditional in their maintenance of family ties and their resistance to the limitation of the nuclear family. This is surely not the case; indeed, educated women often felt particular responsibility to help out their own family because, they say "my parents sacrificed to get me through school, so also now I must thank them." Work as a source of pleasure and self-esteem is a notion made current by the Western press and particularly by the women's movement; it is not surprising that this is primarily a response of the more educated salaried workers.

The question "Why don't you work?" seems to a contemporary American an invitation to extol women's role as mother, or at least to note her responsibility for child care. Tables 12.8 and 12.9 present the response frequencies. Those who responded that they were students or apprentices are excluded from these percentages, because students over twenty, like apprentices, all said they would work when their studies were ended. Among the

TABLE 12.8
Reasons Why Respondents Work, By Work Status[a]

| | Commerce[a] | Salaried | Total[b] |
|---|---|---|---|
| To support the household (aid husband, buy for children, house) | 49% | 40% | 45% |
| My own little needs | 27 | 12 | 21 |
| Aid my family ("mes parents") | 12 | 19 | 16 |
| To not hold out hand to husband, to be independent | 5 | 7 | 6 |
| Pleasure of working, contacts, to get out, develop myself | 2 | 11 | 6 |
| Insurance for old age, to prepare for my future | 0 | 2 | 1 |
| Because I have no children | 0.2 | 0.3 | 0.2 |
| Necessity, obligation to work | 0.4 | 2 | 1 |
| Need for money | 0.4 | 1 | 1 |
| To attain a higher standard of living, move up | 0.4 | 0.5 | 0.4 |
| To build a house | 0.5 | 0.5 | 0.5 |
| For anything that might happen (deaths, etc) | 0.5 | 0 | 0.3 |
| Parents sent me to school; am educated, must work | 0.8 | 3 | 1 |
| Nothing else to do | 0.4 | 2 | 1 |
| For the country | 0.2 | 0.5 | 0.3 |
| | 56% | 44% | 100% |

[a]Refers to self-employed petty traders

[b]Table 12.8 has 831 responses but only 552 respondents. Response codes were derived from respondents' verbatim responses. Thus two codes were used for a single respondent when that best captured the reasons she had given.

TABLE 12.9
Reasons Why Respondent Does Not Work (all inactive)[a]

| | |
|---|---|
| Husband opposed | 28% |
| No money to begin; no place in market | 22 |
| No one to care for children | 8 |
| No occupation; illiterate | 16 |
| No time, visits to village; obliged to leave home | 9 |
| Prefer caring for children | 11 |
| Don't like petty trade, ashamed to do it | 7 |
| Just gave birth or pregnant | 4 |
| Life is too expensive or lost credit | 7 |
| | 100%[b] |

[a]Apprentices, students all excluded because they say that they will work  and they are very likely to find employment.

[b]Table 12.9 has 346 responses, but 281 respondents.  Response codes were derived from respondents' verbatim responses.  Thus two codes were used for a single respondent when that best captured the reasons she had given.

271 inactive respondents remaining, the most common response (28 percent) was that their spouses forbade them to work.  This tension between spouses regarding women's working outside the home appears to be fairly common in West Africa.  Men complain about women's flirtatious nature and the devious nature of other men as well as women's tendency to become headstrong when they have their own incomes (DeLancey, 1978).  The tension is exacerbated by the common separation of earnings by spouses and husbands' insistence that women do not contribute enough to household upkeep, spending on themselves and their kinsmen (Oppong, 1974).  Women in turn note men's expenditures on their mistresses and on their kinsmen.

Another major response category groups women who cast themselves as eligible only for petty trade; 22 percent of the responses concern the absence of conditions to start trading:  "Not enough capital or no selling place on the market."  The last response (.7 percent), "lost my working capital," is similar.

The 16 percent who said that they had no occupation or were illiterate either misunderstood the question as referring to salaried work only or they are indicating their preference for salaried jobs, to which they have no access.  In the same vein, 6 women (only 0.7 percent) said that they did not like petty trade or were ashamed to do it.  Such responses reflect the greater earning and status of salaried work, which is, given Abidjan's low level of industrialization, largely white collar. I have shown elsewhere that the less educated, for whom salaried work is inaccessible, are nearly four times as likely to be inactive, because their only option is petty commerce, a saturated sector in which earnings are slight and risks great.

Three response categories indicate role conflict between mothering and work.  Eight percent of the re-sponses were "I have no one to care for the children," which meets the definition of role conflict directly. Eleven percent said they prefer caring for their child-ren, which also underlies the necessity of choice, but not a forced choice.  Another 4 percent of the responses indicated that they are inactive because they have re-cently or are about to give birth, again indicating role incompatibility for the moment.  These three explana-tions total 23 percent of all responses, a significant percentage ranking just below husband's opposition to wives' LFP and just above the absence of capital or a place on the market to sell.  Another 9 percent of re-sponses concern role conflict in a broader sense:  house-work, visits to village or trips home are obligations or desires which are part of the respondents' role in the extended family.  Like "husband's opposition," "visits to village" does not indicate role conflict in the narrow sense employed here:  when no solution is available per-mitting respondents to fill their maternal and work role simultaneously.  "Husband's opposition" and familial role obligations constitute conflict between respondents' roles as spouse or kinsperson and employment, but not between roles as mother and worker.

What, then, is our conclusion regarding the comple-mentarity or conflict between the roles of mother and of labor force participant?  We have looked at the average number of children by mothers' age and employment status and seen little evidence that employment correlated with fertility levels.  The data suggest that an apparent re-lationship between salaried work and fertility up to 35 years old is really due to the postponement of childbear-ing while in school.  LFP among the more educated, who hold jobs the most incompatible with child care, is strik-ingly high, dramatically disproving our hypothesis.

CONCLUSION

In summary, we have shown that:

(1) Fertility does not keep women from working. The fertility data give us no reason to believe that women are voluntarily limiting their family size in order to work. Even the highly educated with an initially lower number of children due to delayed childbearing appear to "catch up" to their cohort because of lower infant mortality.

(2) How women who work meet their child care needs varies. Clearly, for the foreseeable future, salaried women will be able to benefit from the very cheap household help available. Only when unskilled salaried women's work approaches domestic help in pay level will salaried women be unable to hire outside help. The family network also serves as a backup. However, this resource may be limited by universal education and by more well-paying jobs that compare favorably to living and working with kin.

(3) The profits of most petty traders are small enough that these women are generally unable to hire or maintain outside help. Thus, the less educated who do work are more likely to depend on relatives or cohabitants than outside help. The free child care essential to many of these petty traders will diminish as older daughters continue longer in school, as housing becomes more costly and more crowded, and as extended families disperse or lose the cohesion necessary for regular and reliable assistance.

(4) Although social change will probably decrease the availability of familial child care, one wonders if this will be the cause of women's withdrawal from the labor force. The responses of the inactive women in this study suggest that insufficient employment opportunities rather than unavailable child care lead to women's declining LFP.

The concept of role compatibility is perhaps deceptively attractive and finally of limited usefulness. Vast numbers of women fill urban work roles and have large families. A focus on the availability and cost of child care substitutes offers a better analytic tool entailing the calculation of costs and earnings to find the breakeven point between the two.

Our failure to demonstrate any impact of maternal and employment role incompatibility is supported by other African data. Research from Ibadan and from a state tea plantation in Cameroon replicate the finding that high fertility is not negatively related to employment (Arowolo, 1978; DeLancey, 1978). The absence of incompatibility is partially explained by legal and social struc-

tures.  At independence, most West African states inherited elements of social legislation from the European
colonial powers, which were far more generous to working
women than contemporary practice in the United States.
Maternity leaves, assurance that jobs would be saved and
seniority retained, maternity allowances, and, in the
francophone countries, family allowances paid regularly
for each child to the head of household have reinforced
pronatalism or reduced conflict between work and maternity for the few women with jobs in the modern sector.
African family structure offers considerable opportunity
to locate unpaid or informally paid sources of child care
via co-wives or kin.

Yet, the extended family is not the universal panacea
it may appear to be.  In Abidjan and elsewhere, women re-
count their dissatisfaction with their country kinswomen
who serve as child care substitutes.  Their reasons suggest their changing awareness and values.  Some mention
basic health care and worry about correct preparation of
infant formulas.  Others are concerned about the quality
of the French or English the children are learning, saying that proper grammar is essential to success in school.
European-style housing and changing expectations between
spouses produce increasing dissatisfaction with resident
kinsmen from the spouse's family.  When Abidjan women
were asked by the new ministre de la condition féminine
what they wanted, women listed crèches (nurseries) second only to more employment opportunities.  In Lagos,
commercial nurseries are a widespread and growing phenomenon (see Fapohunda's article, below).  Research on
nurses and teachers in Ghana bears ample witness to the
strains of running the household and working long hours.

If role incompatibility is not present, role stress
certainly is (Oppong, 1977).  But the result has not
been withdrawal from LFP; rather, there appears to be
considerable innovation regarding new child care solutions.  Clearly, we observe a social process rather than
a mechanical balancing between two roles.  Understanding
the path that process takes involves understanding the
values supporting both LFP and continued high fertility.

There is room for research and analysis on both.
The West African woman has always assumed a major role
in the productive economy of the household.  She desires
to avoid dependency on her spouse and to be a vital
participant in the support of her children and her parents.  Attachment to LFP seems deep rooted and central
to her well-being (Lewis, 1977).  High fertility, some
argue, remains the rational economic choice of most West
Africans (Caldwell, 1976, 1978).  Pronatalist attitudes,
based on an agricultural economy with intense seasonal
labor shortages, is only a partial cause.  Even when the

costs of living, schooling, and getting ahead move a
person to limit family size, one will find oneself obligated to assume care of several children of a kinsman
because a person, having but a few, should share the extended family's burden (Caldwell, 1976, 1978; Ware, 1977).
Thus, the argument goes, until the extended family is
replaced by the nuclear family, that is, until the reproductive unit of husband and wife coincides with the
productive and consuming unit, lowered fertility will
not be economically rational.

It may be argued that Stycos and Weller's role
compatibility hypothesis has not been fully tested until
longitudinal data on women's share of jobs has been
collected. It is possible that while some women are
innovating to resolve role stress, another larger group
is withdrawing from LFP, accepting the growing "incompatibility" of roles.

These trends need to be explored, as does the economic rationality thesis regarding lowered family size
and paid child care to permit mothers to work. Further,
rationality in both instances needs refinement to determine the benefits of different options to husband, wife,
and the family taken collectively. Indeed, this may be
the most important contribution, for it will shed light
on the dynamics of women's options and their responses
to changing familial and economic conditions. But any
analysis must explore the interplay of maternal and
employment roles.

NOTES

1. The analysis of contraceptive use among women
interviewed distinguished African methods (purges, traditional charms, cited by 1.2 percent) from Western
methods (rhythm, cited by 6 percent, and IUD, foam, the
pill, cited by 10 percent). We did not include those
who cited abstention or the use of some inappropriate
Western medicine, such as anti-malarial pills. In reading these figures, one must recall that our sample was
deliberately biased to overrepresent women of high economic and educational status. Thus 16 percent of the
sample has at some time used some Western method to avoid
pregnancy. But 75 percent of these "users" lived in the
elite neighborhood of Cocody; the rate of use among the
other women in the sample, in the neighborhoods far more
typical of the city, was thus negligible.

Contraceptive use is heavily concentrated among
the students and salaried workers (76 percent of all
users), who are, of course, the most educated. Fifty-
two percent of the users had attended technical school or

university, although such educated women are a tiny
group in the entire urban population.  Users who have at
least some secondary schooling compose 76 percent of all
users.  As noted below, the number of educated inactive
women is too small to permit statistically reliable conclusions regarding the causal role of education versus
employment regarding the adoption of contraception.

2.  Davis and Blake (1955) note eleven factors
(voluntary and involuntary) affecting fertility levels,
emphasizing that these "intermediate variables" must
always be assessed and explained by social structure.

3.  Boserup (1970):  re fertility, see p. 208;
re labor force participation, see pp. 98, 100, and 80ff.

4.  On the basis of available data, Boserup finds
Southeast Asia has much higher rates of employment among
urban women, and the Middle East, low rates of employment among both rural and urban women.  In Africa, the
intense competition for urban employment and the colonial
pattern of male education and vocational training have
resulted in a particularly sharp difference in the productive activities of rural and of urban women.  But
Boserup's data are scattered and include East and Southern Africa.  Data from West Africa suggest a somewhat
greater proportion of urban females in economically productive activities.

5.  DeLancey (1978, p. 17) discusses the meanings of
compatibility; I have used the standard DeLancey adopted.

6.  I explore the relationship between education and
LFP fully and discuss the peak of inactivity among those
with "some" primary school education (which I see as related to their unrealistic aspirations of finding work
in the modern sector) in Lewis (1977).

7.  See the age specific fertility rates in Lewis
(1975, pp. 42, 50).  Also, note that the data are here
presented in the simplest possible tables (for example,
means without standard deviations), and that our interpretation seeks overall patterns rather than cell-by-
cell analysis.  Less impressionistic, more rigorous
interpretation would be permitted by the statistical results of the analysis of co-variance, but such findings
would be less accessible to our audience.

8.  For example, one could perhaps defend assigning
a numerical value such as 10 to such verbal responses
and then including them in the averages.


REFERENCES

Arowolo, O.O. 1978.   "Female Labor Force Participation
     and Fertility:  The Case of Ibadan City."  In
     Christine Oppong, et al., eds., Marriage, Fertility,

and Parenthood in West Africa. Canberra, Australia: Australian National University. Pp. 533-65.

Boserup, Ester. 1970. Woman's Role in Economic Development. London: George Allen and Unwin.

Caldwell, John C. 1976. "Toward a Restatement of Demographic Transition Theory." Population and Development Review 2, nos. 3 and 4 (Sept., Dec.): 321-66.

————. 1978. "A Theory of Fertility: From High Plateau to Destabilitization." Population and Development Review 4, no. 4 (Dec.): 553-77.

Davis, Kingsley, and Judith Blake. 1955. "Social Structure and Fertility: An Analytical Framework." Economic Development and Cultural Change 4, no. 3: 111-35.

DeLancey, Virginia. 1978. "The Relationship between Female Labor Force Participation and Fertility: Compatibility of Roles on a Cameroon Plantation." Paper presented at the Annual Meeting of the African Studies Association, Baltimore, 1-4 Nov.

Dow, Thomas. 1971a. "Fertility and Family Planning in Sierra Leone." Studies in Family Planning 2, no. 8: 153-68.

————. 1971b. "Family Planning Patterns in Sierra Leone." Studies in Family Planning 2, no. 10: 211-22.

Lewis, Barbara. 1975. "Etude sur la Fécondité, L'emploi, et le Statut de la Femme en Ville." Abidjan, Ivory Coast: Ministry of Planning, multicopied.

————. 1977. "Economic Activity and Marriage among Ivoirian Urban Women." In Alice Schlegel, ed., Sexual Stratification: A Cross Cultural View. New York: Columbia University Press. Pp. 161-92.

Olusanya, P.O. n.d. (data 1966). "A Study of the Beginnings of Demographic Modernization." University of Ibadan: Nigerian Institute of Social and Economic Research, multicopied.

Oppong, Christine. 1974. Marriage Among a Matrilineal Elite. Cambridge: Cambridge University Press.

————. 1977. "The Crumbling of High Fertility Support: Data from a Study of Ghanaian Primary School Teachers." In The Persistence of High Fertility, ed. John C. Caldwell. Canberra, Australia: Australian National University. Pp. 331-61.

Stycos, J. Mayonne, and Robert Weller. 1967. "Female Roles and Fertility." Demography 4, no. 4: 210-17.

Ware, Helen. 1977. "Economic Strategy and the Number of Children." In The Persistence of High Fertility, ed. John C. Caldwell. Canberra, Australia: Australian National University. Pp. 469-595.

## 13. The Child-Care Dilemma of Working Mothers in African Cities: The Case of Lagos, Nigeria

*Eleanor R. Fapohunda*

Women in southern Nigeria, like women in many other parts of West Africa, are not only responsible for the care of the home and children but are also expected to contribute to their families' incomes by engaging in farming, trading, or crafts. Today in urban industrial centers such as Lagos, mothers are confronted with a dilemma not experienced by women in the past or by their contemporaries in agricultural communities. Away from home for a significant portion of each day, working mothers are faced with the difficulty of finding dependable parental surrogates at nonprohibitive expense to care for their children. Moreover, urban educated mothers are finding that the time requirements of child care are increasing. Because they believe that a good education will help insure their children's future, educated mothers feel they should spend time coaching their children with their studies or arranging educational activities (E.R. Fapohunda, 1978, p. 231).

In agricultural communities, the care of young children presents no serious problem for there is either no separation of the home and workplace for the mothers, or the nature of their work permits mothers to bring their babies to their workplaces. Women can undertake child rearing and nondomestic activities, with one not adversely affecting the other. In addition, the duties and responsibilities associated with child raising are not considered to be the exclusive responsibility of the conjugal pair, but rather are thought to be a matter of concern for the whole extended family. Female members of the extended family, particularly grandmothers, play a supportive role in sharing child-rearing responsibilities when mothers cannot take their young children to their places of work. In a congenial family compound, all members feel it is their responsibility to generally supervise and discipline the family's children. At times, children are sent to live in the homes

of other members of the extended family.     This practice
of voluntary fostering is viewed as an educational experience that may prevent parental spoiling or teach children
certain skills.

The child-rearing functions of the extended family
should be understood within the general socioeconomic
functioning of the extended family system.    In a world
of poverty and great uncertainty, the extended family
system encourages cooperative efforts among kin to improve the standard of living of all members and provides
some measure of social security.    For example, cooperative child-care assistance can lead to increased family
production.    In the modern sector, an extended family
can provide its members with important contacts and information to promote upward mobility.    The power and
prestige of an extended family varies with its size and
solidarity.    Such a family system, therefore, not only
encourages high fertility but also tries to build group
solidarity by deliberately depreciating strong emotional
attachments between children and parents (Caldwell, 1976,
pp. 98-99).    For example, the practice of exchanging
children among family members encourages them to identify
with the family group.

Child-care arrangements within agrarian polygynous
families should also be viewed in terms of the functioning of the institution.    In antagonistic polygynous
homes, wives, vying for scarce resources including the
husband's favors, rarely cooperate.    The lack of cooperation strengthens the relative power of the husband
(Clignet, 1970, p. 350).    In congenial polygynous homes,
co-wives cooperate with each other in child-rearing
activities and therefore are able to increase their own
economic activities.    The relative power of each wife
in relation to the husband's power increases with her
economic independence and her cooperative efforts with
her co-wives (Clignet, 1970, p. 47).

Although in all parts of the country in the past,
and in agricultural communities at present, a woman
could harmoniously be both a worker and a mother, nowadays West African working mothers living in urban industrial centers find that their child-care responsibilities
conflict with their employment activities.    Quantitative
information concerning child-care problems of working
mothers in West Africa is generally scarce, although
some studies have been done in Ghana and Nigeria (Oppong,
1975, 1977; Fapohunda and Fapohunda, 1976).    Christine
Oppong, using small surveys, has studied the child-care
problems of educated Ghanaian women in two modern sector
occupations--nursing and teaching.    She found that the
women were experiencing fatigue, stress, and anxiety in
trying to cope with their child-care responsibilities,

for they were trying to produce and rear many children without adequate support from their kin or husbands. In a 1975 Lagos study, E.R. and O.J. Fapohunda investigated the problems women experience in trying simultaneously to be a worker in different segments of the urban economy and to be a mother. To understand the problems associated with different occupations, the study used a sample of 824 women stratified by the 1963 census occupational distribution for Lagos. As a control group, 100 nonworking wives were included in the survey. This paper will draw on some of the findings of that study.

Living in a society whose contours are changing, the working mothers of Lagos find that traditional child-care institutions are withering and that there are few replacements. These women's child-care problems have been further complicated by fast-changing economic conditions and marginally changing, if not dormant, social and demographic expectations. Women are offered better educational opportunities, greater wage employment, and higher wages, while traditional sex role expectations and the desire for large families remain relatively static.

In Lagos, the main industrial and administrative center of Nigeria, industrialization has altered the nature and requirements of market work. In the modern sector, women rigidly follow patterns of fixed work days and must leave their children at home for long periods of time. Poor urban transportation facilities have combined with a lack of part-time jobs to accentuate the problems associated with a separation of home and workplace.

Since Lagos is a city primarily composed of migrants seeking improved economic opportunities, conjugal units are physically separated from their extended families in other parts of the country or in different parts of the city. Significantly, only 10 percent of the 824 working mothers interviewed were born in Lagos. About 70 percent of the women migrated to Lagos either to improve their income-earning capacities or to better their previous level of income. Similar findings have been documented in other studies of the population of Lagos (see O.J. Fapohunda, 1977).

Because of this physical separation of conjugal units, the duties and responsibilities of child rearing are becoming more restricted to the nuclear family. Aged parents, finding living accommodations in Lagos cramped and urban life very strange, are unwilling to come to or remain in Lagos for long periods of time to take care of their grandchildren. Still, until recently, some of the child-rearing activities of the extended family continued, as poorer rural relatives' children were often sent to live and work in the homes of their

Lagos kin. These working children helped with the care
of their relatives' children while perhaps receiving
some educational or vocational training. To a rural parent, the placement of a child in a kinsman's house in an
urban industrial center was an opportunity to improve
the child's future life prospects.

But rural parents have become reluctant to follow
this course, for the federal government now provides
free primary education. As far back as 1955, the old
Western Region instituted a free primary education
scheme, a program also later undertaken in the Federal
Territory of Lagos and the former Eastern Region. The
Eastern Region, finding this educational policy too expensive, subsequently reinstituted payment of school
fees from class three. But in Lagos and the Western
Region, free primary education continued. Many of the
maids who came to work in Lagos during the 1960s and
early 1970s were primary school or secondary modern
school leavers. Since then, the situation has changed.

In September 1976, the federal government initiated
a Universal Free Primary Education Scheme throughout
the country and substantially reduced fees in high
schools. Using these educational programs, from the
viewpoint of the rural parents, provides a better alternative path for the future of their children than sending
them to Lagos as household helpers. At the same time,
the Nigerian oil boom has made possible larger investments in both the public and private sectors. These
investments have generated better-paying jobs which offer
more freedom to the youths who otherwise would have
sought employment as household helpers. Thus, government
education policy and economic growth have tended to reduce the supply of domestic labor.

In Lagos, as in other West African cities, the formal institution of polygyny has been affected by urbanization and imported marriage practices. For the lower
income classes, high urban living expenses tend to dis-
courage polygyny, while limited physical space forces
co-wives to live in separate house, thereby limiting
any cooperative child-care arrangements. Meanwhile, a
new form of de facto polygyny has developed among the
educated, professional men. These men, exposed to
Western ideas in school, have married under church or
civil ordinances that permit only monogamous relationships. However, they enter into relatively permanent
extramarital relationships, which lead to the establishment of an "outside wife" in a separate household and
the birth of "outside children" (Kisekka, 1976-77, p. 34).
Although these relationships do not involve traditional
marriage ceremonies, the man assumes financial and
social responsibilities for his extra-marital family.
This practice of de facto polygyny provides few of the

domestic work-sharing benefits of formal polygynous arrangements, while at the same time, as will be suggested later, it contributes to the maintenance of traditional sex-segregated roles in the household.

Although the requirements of women's nondomestic work have been changing in the cities, the traditional family division of labor, with the wife assuming responsibility for the daily care of home and children, has not been altered significantly. In fact, 23 percent of the 824 surveyed Lagos working mothers claimed that their husbands did nothing in the house. Only 16 percent of these women said that their husbands supervised servants and children, while a mere 5.8 percent claimed that their spouses cooked food (Fapohunda and Fapohunda, 1976, p. 125).

A significant redefinition of conjugal roles with increased sharing of domestic duties may require, as a precondition, the development of stronger nuclear families with closer emotional ties between spouses. John Caldwell has argued that the Nigerian extended family deliberately depreciated emotional relationships between spouses because it was important for family solidarity that the husband give primary consideration to the wishes of his kin rather than of his spouse (Caldwell, 1976, p. 92). If a husband attempted to assist his spouse with "female" domestic tasks, his mother or kin would intervene and would warn him of the unnatural influence of his spouse (E.R. Fapohunda, 1978, p. 232).

Caldwell further argues that the emotional relationship between the spouses may become stronger as a result of the importation of Western ideas through the communications media. A stronger emotional relationship between spouses would help to weaken the extended family system (Caldwell, 1976, p. 107). It may be hypothesized that as the husband's extended family obligations shrink, wives may become more willing to make larger financial contributions to support their conjugal family. Furthermore, as the wife increases her financial contribution, the husband, feeling a further strengthening of the conjugal bond, may reciprocate by sharing more domestic tasks (E.R. Fapohunda, 1978, p. 232).

However, two alternative developments may prevent a greater sharing of daily child-care and other domestic responsibilities among the urban elite. First, some elite men, adopting the Western view that a close mother-child relationship is essential for a child's intellectual development, may insist that their spouses adopt the foreign "housewife" role, thereby abandoning market activities and becoming economically dependent. Second, monogamously married women may fear that their husbands will become involved in de facto polygamous rela-

tionships and may be reluctant to substantially commit
their funds to family finances.  These women may worry
that their money will be used for outside women and
children.  Or, men involved in such relationships will
not have the time or inclination to become deeply involved
in each household's daily domestic tasks.  Thus, it
seems unlikely that in the immediate future, even among
the urban elite, there will be a substantial reformula-
tion of conjugal roles, particularly in regard to shared
child-care responsibilities.

At the same time, daily child-care responsibilities
will continue to remain primarily the concern of the
working mothers. The time requirements of this responsibility have increased for many in recent times.  As
Kenneth Little emphasizes, elite men expect their wives
to follow modern practices of child welfare and to be
capable of checking their children's homework (1972,
p. 277).  In Lagos, working mothers feel that they
should set aside an appreciable time to play with or
teach their children.  Of the 824 working mothers interviewed, 30.2 percent said that they set aside one or two
hours a day to play with or teach their children, while
59 percent claimed that they devoted more than two hours
to this purpose (Fapohunda and Fapohunda, 1976, p. 144).
Given the scope of the responsibilities of these women,
it is likely these latter responses are exaggerations.
But what is significant is that even if the answers were
a little exaggerated, they do show that these women felt
an obligation to devote much of their limited time to
their children's intellectual development.

The care of the sick child poses additional problems
of both time and energy for the Lagos working mother.
A mother of several small children in particular may
spend substantial periods of time away from her work
waiting in overcrowded public hospitals and clinics.
Twenty-six percent of the interviewed Lagos mothers
reported that they did not go to work when they were
ill and 22 percent claimed that they took time off from
work when their children were sick.  Several were so
worried about the time lost in public clinics that they
felt that their child-care arrangements could be improved
if they could get a private doctor for their children
(Table 13.1).

The child-care problems of urban Nigerian women are
further complicated by their continuing desire to have
large numbers of children.  Less than 4 percent of the
interviewed Lagos working mothers wanted three children
or less, while 60 percent wanted four or five children.
Working mothers wanted five children, on the average, a
result consistent with earlier Lagos studies (The exact
mean was 5.2 children.  Mott and Fapohunda, 1975, pp.
84-86).

TABLE 13.1
Improvement in Child-Care Arrangements Desired by
Working Mothers

| Improvement Desired | N | Percent |
|---|---|---|
| Nothing | 282 | 34.2 |
| Government should establish nursery schools | 38 | 4.6 |
| Responsible person to care for children | 88 | 10.7 |
| The children should be better supervised so that the house is in better order | 10 | 1.2 |
| The children should be properly cared for | 20 | 2.4 |
| Private doctor should care for children | 6 | 0.7 |
| Working mothers should be allowed time off for some days or to close earlier from work | 11 | 1.3 |
| Don't know | 369 | 44.8 |
| Total | 824 | 99.9 |

Source: Fapohunda and Fapohunda (1976, p. 144).

With relatives providing less child-care assistance
and spouses refusing to assume more responsibilities,
Lagos working mothers are forced to compete in the labor
market for paid domestic help. In 1975, three out of
every ten working mothers covered in the survey had
household help, which included 209 housemaids and 26
nannies. Typically, housemaids are young girls with
some primary or modern school education who help with the
housework and child care. They are often quite young
and inexperienced. About 38 percent of the housemaids
in the survey were less than fourteen years of age, while
54 percent were fifteen to nineteen years old. Nannies
are responsible only for the care of children and are
usually much older (50 percent of the reported nannies
were over thirty-five years of age).
The child-care dilemma of Lagos working mothers is
becoming more acute. The number of women with some educa-

tion who want to enter the urban labor market and who
need household help is growing rapidly, while the number
of people willing to work as housemaids or nannies on a
long-term basis is increasing slowly if not declining.
The resultant rising wage trend is accentuated by the
availability of more school opportunities and alternative
job prospects that offer more freedom if not higher real
wages.  This has led to a high turnover of household
help.  Not surprisingly, the working mothers covered in
the survey overwhelmingly claimed (65 percent) that their
main problem in hiring household helpers was that their
employees stayed only for a short time (Fapohunda and
Fapohunda, 1976, p. 153).

By 1978-79, the working women of Lagos were beginning to turn to new commercial businesses to take care
of their children. These businesses, proliferating rapidly in local neighborhoods, vary widely in physical
facilities, personnel, and costs.  Some are simply
single rooms located in low-income housing with minimum
toilet facilities, while others are modern, specially
constructed concrete structures with metal playground
furniture in high-income communities.  Similarly, the
backgrounds of the owner-operators and staff vary from
minimal primary or modern school education to training
in recognized nursery institutions abroad.  Children
as young as one year old are being sent to boarding
nursery schools, which are largely unregulated by
government.  This is a significant departure from the
past, for in the 1975 Lagos survey, only 54 of the 824
mothers said that they would send their children aged
six months to two and a half years to day-care centers.
The new trend suggests that within the past four years,
child-care problems have appreciably worsened in Lagos.

The growing urban child-care dilemma affects the
individual working mother and her family on one level
but also has wider implications for the nature of
national economic development.  On the family level, the
working mother, burdened with the conflicting responsibilities of work and motherhood, experiences fatigue,
stress, and even anxiety that can adversely affect her
behavior with spouse and children, perhaps leading to
problems of marital stress and family instability.  Significantly, 45 percent of the Lagos working mothers
claimed that their main problem in trying to combine
work and home responsibilities was that they had no
rest or leisure time.  Their children, left alone for
long periods of time without proper supervision, are
not only exposed to health and physical safety risks
but also are deprived of adequate parental training.

Child-care problems affect women's work performance
or productivity by causing losses of time and energy that

may result in loss of income and job opportunities.
More than half of the working mothers interviewed in
Lagos, both self-employed and salaried, claimed that
being a mother affected their progress at work.  The
reasons they gave ranged from a loss of concentration due
to worrying about children to absences from work.

On the national level, the utilization of women's
productive capabilities and the distribution of the benefits of economic development will be affected by the
growing child-care dilemma.  For example, during the
1980s women will compete increasingly with men for modern
sector junior-grade level jobs.  The Third National
Development Plan, 1975-80, will generate only a limited
number of such positions, while the number of applicants
will rise because of the impact of the Universal Free
Primary Education Scheme (E.R. Fapohunda, 1978, p. 235).
At the same time, the child-care problems of urban working mothers will intensify, causing women to take more
casual or sick leave from work.  From the viewpoint of
modern sector employers, these additional costs will
make female labor more expensive.  Thus, women's employment gains are likely to be modest and the benefits of
development unevenly distributed between the sexes.

The Nigerian urban working mother, confronted with
mounting child-care worries, may respond in different
ways.  Initially, some may simply recognize the existence
of the growing child-care dilemma without thinking about
alternatives or taking positive steps to deal with the
problem. For example, 369 of the mothers dissatisfied
with their present child-care arrangements had no idea
how they could be improved (Table 13.1).  Some may try
to deal with the problem by modifying their own behavior.
Although traditionally, southern Nigerian women breast
fed their babies for up to two years, 63 percent of the
Lagos working mothers, faced with work problems, breast
fed the last baby only up to six months (Fapohunda and
Fapohunda, 1976, p. 140).  With the greater availability
of substitutes for mother's milk, this practice will
become more widespread.  Eventually, as more women become better educated, young women, faced with the growing problems of role conflict, may decide to opt for
smaller families.

Urban working mothers may begin to leave the labor
market for a period of time.  This would not be a viable
option for many Lagos working mothers because they value
their economic independence in a predominantly male-
oriented society and because they spend their earnings
on themselves and their children rather than on the
families of their birth. Even though the most frequently
given reason for working by the women interviewed in
Lagos was to contribute to the maintenance of the

family (21 percent), other reasons which amounted to
taking care of themselves and their children were given
by 62 percent of the women.  Only 16 percent of the respondents said that they were working to use their education or to avoid boredom.  Moreover, when asked if they
thought it was wise for a woman to stop working for five
to ten years to take care of her children, 503 of the
824 women disagreed.  The women who felt it was a good
idea reasoned that the children would be properly cared
for and, significantly, that the mother would have time
to rest and to take care of herself.

Finally, some urban working mothers may seek new
ways to handle their child-care responsibilities with
the cooperation of other women.  The Nigerian Council of
Women's Societies, originally in conjunction with a
Danish women's group, has been running a day nursery in
the Ebute-Ero market of Lagos  for the past fourteen
years (Olaniyan, 1979).  At times, the suggestion of an
outsider may mobilize a group of women to petition the
government for the establishment of a child-care facility.
At the  time  of the survey, for example, plans for a
new model market at Tejuoso were being drawn up by the
Lagos State government.  Individuals from the University
of Lagos and the state suggested to the market women's
association that the inclusion of a child-care facility
in the plans would greatly benefit them.  Hence, all of
the surveyed working mothers (38) who said that their
child-care arrangements could be improved if the government establishes children's playgrounds were market
women from Tejuoso market (Table 13.1).  Such facilities,
run on a cooperative basis or with the economic support
of private sector employers or government subsidies,
would probably provide better, more reasonably priced
child care than those offered by the unregulated commercial establishments springing up in Lagos.

In drawing up its manpower and national development
plans, the Nigerian government has not specifically
considered women's employment problems and the child-
care issue.  In national documents, women are not regarded as a distinct category of human resources separate
from men.  Rather, it is implicitly assumed that the work
behavior patterns of the two sexes are the same.  For
example, youth employment projects envisaged under
Nigeria's Third National Development Plan include training programs in wood and metal work, masonry, electronics
(E.R. Fapohunda, 1978, p. 236).  Certainly, if Nigerian
planners were cognizant of the problems of women school
leavers and women workers, they would consider programs
to train nursery school assistants.

If there is to be significant success of manpower
planning in Nigeria, it must be recognized that women

contribute to economic development directly by producing goods and services and indirectly by affecting
the quality of the future labor force through child-care
practices. The requirements of these two contributions
increasingly conflict as development proceeds. If the
contributions of both activities are to be maximized,
then the Nigerian government must adopt policies to increase their complementarity. As yet, the Federal Government of Nigeria has only recognized the value of pre-
primary education and has announced its plans to review
the educational laws relating to the establishment of
nursery schools (Federal Republic of Nigeria, 1977, p. 6).
In order to have a meaningful national manpower planning
program, the Nigerian government must develop a national
child-care policy.

In conclusion, the further breakdown of the extended
family system and the continuation of traditional conjugal roles in Nigeria seems likely. Thus, in the
immediate future, working mothers in Lagos will be increasingly forced to turn to commercial ventures or to
voluntary women's associations to deal with their
child-care problems. Eventually, the Nigerian government will become more concerned with this problem and
its implications, both for the family and for the
nation's economic development. But the growth of this
concern and the implementation of new public policies
will probably require a strengthening of women's collective public voice through their various voluntary associations and by means of political activism.

REFERENCES

Caldwell, John C. 1976. The Socio-economic Explanation
    of High Fertility. Canberra: Australian National
    University.
Clignet, Remi. 1970. Many Wives, Many Powers: Authority
    and Power in Polygynous Families. Evanston, Ill.:
    Northwestern University Press.
Fapohunda, Eleanor R. 1978. "Women at Work in Nigeria:
    Factors Affecting Modern Sector Employment." In
    Human Resources and African Development, ed. U.G.
    Damachi and V.P. Diejomaoh. New York: Praeger.
    Pp. 220-41.
Fapohunda, Olanrewaju J. 1977. Employment and Unemploy-
    ment in Lagos. Institute of Social Studies, ISS
    Occasional Papers No. 6. The Hague.
Fapohunda, Olanrewaju J., and Eleanor R. Fapohunda.
    1976. The Working Mothers of Lagos. Report of a
    study submitted to the Interdisciplinary Communi-
    cations Committee of the Smithsonian Institution,
    Washington, D.C.

Federal Republic of Nigeria. 1977. National Policy on
    Education. Lagos, Nigeria: Federal Ministry of
    Information.
Kisekka, Mere Nakateregga. 1976-77. "Polygyny and the
    Status of African Women." African Urban Notes 2,
    no. 3 (Fall-Winter, pt. 2): 21-42.
Little, Kenneth. 1972. "Voluntary Association and
    Social Mobility among West African Women." Canadian
    Journal of African Studies 6, no. II: 275-88.
Mott, Frank L., and O.J. Fapohunda. 1975. The Popula-
    tion of Nigeria. Lagos, Nigeria: Human Resources
    Research Unit, University of Lagos.
Olaniyan Bassey (Senior Librarian, University of Lagos).
    January 1979. Personal letter to author.
Oppong, Christine. 1975. "Nursing Mothers: Aspects of
    the Conjugal and Maternal Roles of Nurses in
    Accra." Paper presented to the Canadian African
    Studies Association Meeting, Toronto. February.
_____. 1977. "The Crumbling of High Fertility Sup-
    ports: Data from A Study of Ghanaian Primary
    School Teachers." In The Persistence of High
    Fertility, ed. John C. Caldwell. Canberra: Aus-
    trailian National University. Part I, pp. 331-59.

## 14. Women's Cooperative Thrift and Credit Societies: An Element of Women's Programs in the Gambia

*Coumba Ceesay-Marenah*

The Gambia covers an area of over 400 square miles with a population of 493,000 (1973 census). The majority of its people live in rural areas and are engaged in agriculture, the core of the Gambia's economy. Gambian women, 85 percent of whom live in the countryside, have always played an important part in the socioeconomic development of the country. Even though they are mostly illiterate, women through agriculture are to a great extent responsible for the physical welfare and the economic strength of the family. Gambian women need to be exposed to innovations and to learn better practices in family planning, farming, nutrition, child care, and in all other areas that would make them better mothers, wives, and food and cash crop producers. They need to participate equally with the men in all areas of national development.

The traditional occupation of the women in the Gambia, in addition to the care of the children, is the growing of rice, vegetables, and other foodstuffs for family consumption. In some areas, women are engaged in the production of cash crops, and particularly in the growing of groundnuts, Gambia's main export crop. More recently, women have begun the production of handicrafts, including tie-dye, batik, and weaving, as an extra source of income. Some of these activities have been encouraged and supported through various women's programs.

But women's activities go far beyond child care and economic production. What little free time women have after they complete their agricultural tasks is often used up in organizing and participating in various social functions. Events like weddings and christening ceremonies, and even political campaigns, may owe their success to women's work.

The government of the Gambia recognizes the role of women in national development and has encouraged the creation of institutions to assist them. Rural women

have been a particular target of government concern.  To
date (1981), the following programs for women have been
introduced:  (1) the National Women's Bureau; (2) Women's
Programmes Unit of the Department of Community Development; (3) Women's Programmes of the Rural Development
Projects (RDP); (4) cooperative thrift and credit societies; (5) training for women and girls under the National
Vocational Training Programme.

The Women's Bureau is a new institution recently
established under the president's office.  Charged with
the coordination of all institutions with women's activities in the country, it will work both with governmental
and nongovernmental organizations.  The Women's Bureau
will also seek funds for the financing of projects for
women.  Although at the time of this writing the bureau
has not yet started activity in full, the unit is being
organized and staffed with an executive secretary
(the bureau head), a deputy head, a public relations
officer, clerks, and typists.  The bureau has also set
up a Women's Council of rural women who are illiterate.
The purpose is to encourage women from the rural areas
to define and present their local problems for a common
solution.  I am of the opinion that once the National
Women's Bureau begins to function, most of the problems
of rural women in the Gambia will have a point of focus.

The Women's Programmes Unit of the Department of
Community Development, a branch of the Ministry of Economic Planning and Industrial Development, deals directly
with rural women.  It coordinates the women-directed
activities of the Ministries of Agriculture and Health
and other government agencies. The World Bank is helping
to set up programs under the Rural Development Projects
to deal with family questions and cooperatives.  The
RDP generally assists women farmers with agricultural
inputs and gives farming advice.  The cooperative thrift
and credit societies were first among the institutions
that sought to work with women in rural areas; they will
be considered in detail below.  The National Vocational
Training Programme plans a center for women and girls
in the rural areas.  Such a center will train women in
productive skills and help set up marketing cooperatives.
The latter in turn will be organized and assisted by the
IBAC, the Indigenous Business Advisory Committee.  These,
then, are the five institutions so far established by
the government to help the women of the Gambia participate more fully in national development.

These institutions are designed to assist rural
women in particular by providing the knowledge and
skills they need to increase income and improve family
condition.  Activities include classes in family and
child care, in health and nutrition, and in gardening,

sewing, tie-dying, weaving, and other income-generating
skills. Since the good health of the family has been
identified as a prerequisite and a tool for development,
health and nutrition are stressed in all of the programs to a lesser or greater extent.

Teaching methods include discussions and demonstrations with health and other extension personnel. There
are vegetable gardens for demonstration purposes under
the supervision of the Department of Agriculture extension
staff. Philosophically, the concepts of self-help,
self-reliance, and the use of appropriate technology are
married to our national slogan of Te-sito (to tighten
one's belt). The use of available resources is always
encouraged and almost all educational demonstrations
stress the use of locally available materials. For instance, talks deal with the preservation of food, including perishable fruits (mangoes, oranges, paw-paws,
tomatoes), and women are taught how to make jams, juices,
or purees with them. In tie-dying, local natural dyes
from the bark of mango trees or from onion peels are
used with local chemicals like alum. Educational visits
are also organized so that local women leaders may meet
women from other areas to discuss their mutual problems.
This type of educational tour may also expose rural women
to programs and new ideas that they can then apply to
their own locale.

Cooperatives in the Gambia date back to the early
1950s, when the first farmers' cooperatives were formed
and later registered. Since then, involvement has grown
strongly and the total membership now stands at over
70,000. The two-layer pyramid-like structure of the
Gambia's cooperative movement consists of primary
societies and a secondary apex organization, the Gambia
Cooperative Union Ltd. (Co-Union). The Co-Union is the
largest licensed buying agent of the Gambia Produce
Marketing Board (GPMB). The marketing of members'
produce, mainly groundnuts, is undertaken by primary
farmers' cooperatives, which presently handle over 55
percent of the national crop, valued at over D25 million
(about $12.5 million). In addition to marketing, soci-
eties are involved in the distribution of production
credit (seed, fertilizer, and farming implements) and
cash credit to their members.[1]

The need to mobilize the potential of both rural
and urban women cannot be overemphasized. Petty traders,
artisans, rice growers, gardeners, and other women involved in productive activities have been encouraged
to form cooperative thrift and credit societies. This
type of cooperative, composed mainly of women, is one
of the best established institutions for rural women
in the Gambia. Although there is much more to be done

by way of encouraging more women to be involved in cooperatives, there are presently forty cooperative thrift and credit societies registered or proposed, 90 percent of whose membership is made up of women.  On a small scale, the societies help their members improve their economic and social condition by encouraging savings and thereby creating funds to be loaned to members of the society for productive or other necessary purposes.

These societies, which generally average forty members, are found throughout the countryside and in the city of Banjul.  Towns and villages with cooperatives are shown in Table 14.1.  In addition, there are a number of proposed societies that are not yet registered.

TABLE 14.1
Locations of Cooperative Thrift and Credit Societies, The Gambia

| AREA (TOWNS/VILLAGES) | REGISTERED SOCIETIES |
|---|---|
| Banjul | 17 |
| Western Division | |
|     Brikama | 1 |
|     Gunjur | 3 |
|     Sukuta | 5 |
|     Serrekunda | 3 |
| North Bank Division | |
|     Barra | 1 |
|     Ker Gallo | 1 |
| McCarthy Island Division | |
|     Georgetown | 3 |
|     Kaur | 1 |
|     Bansang | 1 |
| Upper River Division | |
|     Basse | 1 |

In all the thrift and credit societies, members agree on the price of a share and an amount of periodic savings.  Savings average D5.00 ($2.50) per month, the

savings level of urban women being higher than that in
the rural areas, presumably because of the lack of surplus income in rural areas.   After a period of regular
savings, members apply for credit from their society.
Applications are processed and financing is sought from
the Co-Union.   Most societies are members of the Co-
Union, which was established primarily to facilitate the
operations of its member societies; the latter maintain
accounts with the Co-Union.   If a loan application is
approved by the Co-Union, each member approved by her/
his society is given a credit of twice her/his total
assets in the society (shares and savings). This is then
repaid in a period of six to nine months with a minimum
amount of interest added.   Interest paid on loans is
used to meet the cost of administrative staff and office
equipment of the Co-Union.   One hundred percent repayment by all members is a prerequisite for fresh loans
from the Co-Union.

The RDP of the Gambia emphasizes the development of
cooperatives.   Production credit is presently channeled
through farmers' cooperatives and women are issued rice
seeds and fertilizers.   Women have been organized into
precooperative groups and members are saving until such
time that the societies are registered.   Activities go
beyond the strictly financial.   There are plans for organizing cooperative literacy classes for women involved
in the Lower River Division.

The workings of the thrift and credit societies and
the problems that they face can best be seen with specific examples.   I'll discuss briefly three societies, the
Cooperative Rice Growers' Society, the Gardening Society,
and the Handicraft Producers Cooperative Thrift and
Credit Society.

The Cooperative Rice Growers' Society of Macarthy
Island Division was one of the first cooperatives to
be started in the Gambia.   It is a marketing cooperative
whose members are mainly men.   Women do not join the same
cooperative societies as the men, but form their own.
They are highly disadvantaged, however, in the current
working of the cooperative structure.

Women do most of the rice growing in the Gambia.
However, the marketing of the rice is done in the name
of their husbands, and husbands are given the total proceeds for the sale of the crop.   Thus, for example, in a
compound or household with ten women producers who
jointly operate a rice farm, the entire crop would be
sold in the name of the male household head.   He in turn
would normally return the proceeds to the women. Women
typically use part of their profits to purchase goods
for the family--clothing, cooking utensils, and household supplies, for example.   The rest is given to the

husband for "safe-keeping." Men may and do use their
wives' money for their own ends, for their own social
satisfaction.

A man, for example, may use his wives' "safe-keeping" funds to marry an additional wife. In previous
times, women were content with that; a woman could feel
proud that through her labor an additional wife arrived
to share chores and to be answerable to her. Today,
however, women are beginning to join cooperative thrift
and credit societies. These differ from the marketing
cooperatives in that they are mainly for savings and
loans. Women still give part of their earnings to their
husbands, but more and more, they are beginning to save
a portion for their own use.

The selling of rice through the men creates additional problems. Men who sell rice through the market
societies become eligible for farm loans, but their
wives do not. Yet, women need loans for farming inputs
at the beginning of the growing season. Moreover, cooperative societies must have a 100 percent loan repayment
rate from their members. Thus, a producer may be unable
to obtain loans for agricultural inputs. At the same
time, a man may have little incentive to repay a loan
from a cooperative. To solve this problem, women's
marketing cooperatives are being formed alongside the
men's marketing societies. Facilities have been given
over to the women to allow them their own marketing
section. Much of their produce is now beginning to be
sold under their own names in this  separate marketing
system.

The Gardening Society was formed to encourage demonstration crops and to raise vegetables for sale.
Health is a major concern in the Gambia. In an effort
to reduce the frequency of preventable nutrition-related
diseases, the Gardening Society encourages the growing
of vegetables. The society falls under the category of
thrift and credit marketing societies. Thus, the garden
produce theoretically is meant to be sold. But in order
to improve the Gambian diet, we encourage members to
consume only. In keeping with the objectives of the
women's programs, the demonstration work is based on
produce indigenous to the Gambia. The activities of the
Gardening Society, too, are integrated into the work
of the extension services of various ministries, including those of Agriculture and Health.

Women's cooperative societies also play a very important role in the tourist industry. The Tourist Market
Cooperative Thrift and Credit Society, now registered as
the Handicraft Producers Cooperative, maintains one of
the largest markets that sells crafts to tourists. All
locally produced goods in the Gambia can be found in
their market. Though the members are not only women,

the majority are female, and the market was first
established by the women.  Currently, unfortunately, men
are threatening the women's control of the society, for
they have seen how well the women are doing financially.

A major problem for the Handicraft Producers Cooperative Thrift and Credit Society is that the market
is seasonal. When the tourist season ends, producers
must find a way to store their goods until the next
year or find some other place to market them.  Thus,
the government is seeking facilities for the external
marketing of handicrafts.  One possible outlet will be
through GAMCO (Gambia Artisans Marketing Cooperative).
With funding by the World Bank, GAMCO buys up the best
quality in tie-dyed fabrics, beads, baskets, and other
handicrafts and resells them in the next tourist season.

Recently, GAMCO was involved in an innovative project to assist women in other countries to learn craft
skills.  A group of twelve Malian women, sponsored in
part by the Women and Development Program of the American Friends Service Committee, spent one week in Banjul
learning to tie and dye.[2]  The project was so successful
that many others wished to visit the Gambia to be
trained.  Our cooperative members, however, refused to
allow additional women to come; understandably, they
were concerned that increased competition could hurt
the sale of their own products.

The attitude of the handicrafts women is reflected
among other women in the Gambia. Rural people are in-
telligent and understand very well their own problems.
They try to do things on their own with little assistance from the government. These days, they will put a
stop to any programs that the government proposes that
they feel are not in their interests.  Rural women are
illiterate in a technical sense but highly literate in
the sense that they are aware of what happens in the
Gambia and are very adept at thinking for themselves.
With a little more of the training and assistance that
they request, members of the Gambian cooperative thrift
and credit societies will make their organizations some
of the best in Africa.


NOTES

1. I wish to acknowledge the assistance of the
Assistant Registrar for Training Cooperative Staff, who
provided the historical information included here.

2. For a detailed report on the project, see Susan
L. Caughman, "New Skills for Rural Women," unpublished
paper, American Friends Service Committee, Philadelphia,
Pa. 1977.

# Notes on Contributors

EDNA G. BAY is an Africanist historian who received her PhD from Boston University in 1977. She has done field research on women in Benin and has written on women's political activities in precolonial West Africa, particularly in the kingdom of Dahomey. She is currently Assistant Director of the Graduate Institute of the Liberal Arts at Emory University.

CLAUDIA CAMPBELL is studying for a PhD in economics at Washington University. After residing in Latin America from 1969-74, she earned an MA in economics at Vanderbilt University (1977), examining as her thesis the impact of industrialization on female employment in Ghana.

COUMBA CEESAY-MARENAH received her secondary education in the Gambia and worked for the Gambia Cooperative Movement for five years. She earned a diploma in community and social development at the Pan African Institute of Development (Cameroon) and a certificate in a course on rural women and technology sponsored by the British Council. She is Head of the Women's Programme Unit of the Department of Community Development in the Gambia.

ELEANOR R. FAPOHUNDA is Senior Lecturer in the Department of Economics of the University of Lagos. As a specialist in labor economics and industrial relations, she has been particularly interested in the practical problems of African women in the urban labor market including child care, job discrimination, and family financial management. Her writings also treat the theoretical aspects of the supply of women's labor.

LOUISE FORTMANN is a rural sociologist who is Senior Research Fellow at the Center for International Studies, Cornell University. She has been seconded to the Ministry of Agriculture, Republic of Botswana, to undertake research in the communal areas. She serves on the International Committee on Women and Development and has written on women's involvement in agriculture in Tanzania and in Botswana.

GRACE S. HEMMINGS-GAPIHAN received her PhD in anthropology from Yale University in 1981. She has done thirty months field research on women and development in Upper Volta and has evaluated a women's component for a project in Shaba province of Zaire. She is presently doing research on Peuhl women in Senegal.

BARBARA LEWIS is Associate Professor of Political Science at Rutgers University. Her earlier research focused on group cohesion and collective action among both truckers and market women in the Ivory Coast. Her 1974 survey of urban women's fertility, employment and social attributes is the basis of several publications including her contribution to this volume. Recently she has written on food policy in West Africa and on the impact of development planning on women.

CAROL P. MACCORMACK is a Lecturer in Social Sciences at the Ross Institute of the London School of Hygiene and Tropical Medicine. She has published widely on the Sherbro and Mende ethnic areas of Sierra Leone where she has carried out intermittent field work since 1969. Her recent publications include the edited volumes, Nature, Culture and Gender (with Marilyn Strathern) and Ethnography of Fertility and Birth.

MAUD SHIMWAAYI MUNTEMBA is Senior Lecturer in History at the University of Zambia, currently on secondment to the Institute of African Studies where she is conducting research on women in agriculture in the railway region of Zambia. She has been researching rural political and socioeconomic change since 1968 with an emphasis over the last three years on peasant women.

ENID SCHILDKROUT, who earned her PhD in social anthropology at Cambridge University, is Associate Curator in the Department of Anthropology of the American Museum of Natural History. She has done research on migration

and ethnicity in Ghana and Nigeria, including two years
research in Kano, northern Nigeria, the site of her
article in this volume. In 1978 she published People of
the Zongo. She is currently researching women and
children in Northern Nigeria.


ILSA SCHUSTER is Lecturer in Anthropology at the Universities of Haifa and Tel Aviv. Author of The New Women of
Lusaka, which is based on several years of fieldwork in
Zambia, she received her PhD from the University of Sus-
sex in 1976. Her interest in African women and work grew
from her enthusiasm at the new opportunities open to
women in the first decade of Zambia's independence.


KATHLEEN A. STAUDT received her PhD in political science
from the University of Wisconsin in 1976. She has published in a variety of journals that include Development and Change, Journal of Developing Areas, and Comparative Politics. She recently completed a monograph
on women and participation in rural development for the
Cornell University Rural Development series. In 1979,
she took a leave from the University of Texas at El
Paso, where she teaches political science and coordinates the liberal arts honors program, to work as a
social science analyst for the Office of Women in Development, USAID.


WILLIAM F. STEEL's research has focused on Africa  since
his 1970 PhD dissertation at M.I.T. on industrialization
in Ghana. His teaching and research interests in economic development and discrimination have stimulated
concern for the role of women in development. His work
on employment and small-scale enterprises while teaching
at the University of Ghana led to subsequent investi-
gation of the employment status of women in the Ghanaian
economy. He recently left Vanderbilt University to work
on research studies for the African Development Bank in
Abidjan, Ivory Coast.


E. FRANCES WHITE, Assistant Professor of Black Studies
at Hampshire College, earned her PhD at Boston University. Her interests in African women and work stem
from a desire to combine feminists' concerns with non-
elitist history and to explore her own roots as an Afro-
American woman. She has published in the International
Journal of African Historical Studies and the Journal of
the Historical Society of Sierra Leone.

FRANCILLE RUSAN WILSON is an historian with a special interest in the labor history of Africans and Afro-Americans. The fieldwork for her contribution to this volume was completed in 1976 as part of a research project on African women and work sponsored by a May Elvira Stevens Traveling Fellowship from Wellesley College. She is presently at the Institute of Labor and Industrial Relations of the University of Michigan.

BARBARA A. YATES is Associate Professor of Comparative Education at the University of Illinois at Urbana-Champaign and director of the Office of Women and International Development at the University. She is Vice-President (President-elect) of the Comparative and International Education Society.

# Index

This book is based on the 1979
Spring Symposium of the African
Studies Program at the
University of Illinois at
Urbana-Champaign. A complete
list of Symposia follows:


1974 -- Technology in African Development

1975 -  Education and Politics in Africa*

1976 -- Farming and Food Production in African Economies

1977 -- Cultivator and State in Precolonial Africa**

1978 -- Language and Politics in African Education

1979 -- Women and Work in Africa

1980 -- Literature, Film and Society in Africa

1981 -- Food Problems in Africa


*Published as: V.C. Uchendu (ed.), Education and Politics in Tropical
   Africa, Conch, 1979.
**Published as: D.E. Crummey and C.C. Stewart, Cultivator and State in
   Precolonial Africa, Sage, 1980.

african studies

university of illinois at urbana-champaign
1208 w california · room 101
urbana, illinois 61801
(217) 333-6335

CPSIA information can be obtained at www.ICGtesting.com
Printed in the USA
LVOW04s1739190315

431247LV00014BA/847/P